Rio Pl

Rio Plus Ten

Politics, Poverty and Environment

Neil Middleton and Phil O'Keefe

Pluto Press
LONDON • STERLING, VIRGINIA

First published 2003 by Pluto Press
345 Archway Road, London N6 5AA
and 22883 Quicksilver Drive, Sterling, VA 20166-2012, USA

www.plutobooks.com

The right of Neil Middleton and Phil O'Keefe to be
identified as the authors of this work has been asserted
by them in accordance with the Copyright, Designs
and Patents Act 1988.

British Library Cataloguing in Publication Data
A catalogue record for this book is available from
the British Library

ISBN 0 7453 1955 6 hardback
ISBN 0 7453 1954 8 paperback

Library of Congress Cataloging in Publication Data
Middleton, Neil, 1931–
   Rio plus ten : politics, poverty and the environment / Neil
Middleton and Phil O'Keefe.
      p. cm.
Includes bibliographical references and index.
   ISBN 0–7453–1955–6 (hardback) — ISBN 0–7453–1954–8 (pbk)
  1. World Summit on Sustainable Development
(2002 : Johannesburg, South Africa) 2. Sustainable development.
3. Environmental policy—Political aspects. 4. Poverty—
Environmental aspects. I. O'Keefe, Philip. II.
Title.
   HD75.6 .M534 2003
   338.9'27—dc21
                                                    2003005372

10 9 8 7 6 5 4 3 2 1

Designed and produced for Pluto Press by
Chase Publishing Services, Fortescue, Sidmouth, EX10 9QG, England
Typeset from disk by Stanford DTP Services, Towcester, England
Printed and bound in the European Union by
Antony Rowe Ltd, Chippenham and Eastbourne, England

Contents

List of Boxes and Tables

ETC

This book is an ETC project. Founded in The Netherlands and now established in India, Sri Lanka, Kenya, Britain and Ireland, ETC exists to encourage and support local initiatives towards sustainable development. It is organised under the umbrella of ETC International, which is located in The Netherlands. It recognises that local knowledge and experience are the building blocks for any developmental activity and that those communities for whom aid projects of any kind are constructed must have substantial influence on their design. Employing people from many and varied backgrounds, ETC can offer expertise in sustainable agriculture, agroforestry, energy, water supplies, humanitarian assistance, institutional development and extension courses. For further information write to ETC UK, 117 Norfolk Street, North Shields, Tyne and Wear, NE30 1NQ.

Abbreviations and Acronyms

ACEM	adaptive and collaborative environmental management
AGTHM	Association Générale des Hygiènistes et Techniciens
ATC	Agreement on Textiles and Clothes
AWG	Anglian Water
CBD	Convention on Biological Diversity
CFC	chlorofluorocarbons
CSCE	Commission on Security and Cooperation in Europe (see OSCE)
ECOSOC	Economic and Social Council of the United Nations
FAO	Food and Agricultural Organisation of the UN
FDI	foreign direct investment
GATS	General Agreement on Trade in Services
GATT	General Agreement on Tariffs and Trade
GDP	gross domestic product
GEF	Global Environmental Facility
GEO	*Global Environment Outlook*
GMO	genetically modified organism
GW	giga-watts
HCFC	hydrochlorofluorocarbons
HFC	hydrofluorocarbons
HIV/AIDS	human immunodeficiency virus/acquired immune deficiency syndrome
IACSD	Inter-Agency Committee on Sustainable Development
ICC	International Criminal Court
IFCS	Intergovernmental Forum on Chemical Safety
IMF	International Monetary Fund
INGO	international non-governmental organisation
IPCC	Intergovernmental Panel on Climate Change
IUCN	International Union for the Conservation of Nature
LA21	Local Agenda 21
MDGs	Millennium Development Goals
MFA	Multi-Fibre Arrangement
NAFTA	North American Free Trade Association
NAS	National Academy of Sciences (USA)
NEPAD	the New Partnership for Africa's Development
NGO	non-governmental organisation

OAU	Organisation of African Unity
ODA	overseas development aid
OECD	Organisation for Economic Cooperation and Development
OSCE	Organisation for Security and Cooperation in Europe (formerly CSCE, Permanent Conference on Security and Cooperation in Europe)
ppp	parity purchasing power (as in pppUS$)
Prepcoms	Preparatory Committees (for the WSSD)
SAGEP	Société Anonymes de Gestion des Eaux de Paris
SEDIF	Syndicat des Eaux d'Ile de France
SEI	Stockholm Environment Institute
SIAAP	Syndicat Interdépartmental pour l'Assainissement de l'Aglomération Parisienne
SIDS	small island developing states
TNC	transnational corporation
TRIPS	trade-related aspects of intellectual property rights
UNCED	United Nations Conference on Environment and Development
UNCTAD	United Nations Conference on Trade and Development
UNDP	United Nations Development Programme
UNEP	United Nations Environment Programme
UNFCCC	United Nations Framework Convention on Climate Change
WCED	World Commission on Environment and Development
WEC	World Energy Council
WEHAB	water and sanitation, energy, health, agriculture, biodiversity
WSSD	World Summit on Sustainable Development
WTO	World Trade Organisation
WWF	World Wildlife Fund

Introduction

'May you live in interesting times', a commination variously attributed to, among others, the ancient Chinese and John F. Kennedy, would seem to have been visited upon us. The stuff of nightmares lies, apparently disordered, all about us: US unilateralism and its reckless and bloody interference in West Asia, of which its support for Israel's onslaught on the Palestinians is a part; global warming leading to unpredictable, but certainly catastrophic change for most of the world's population; the global predations of financial markets rendering the exclusion of the poor more absolute than ever before; environmental destruction and pollution on an unprecedented scale; all of these elements and very many more are leading to increased social instability, the weakening of such democracy as may be found in the world and to what Gilbert Achcar has described, in his book of that title, as the 'clash of barbarisms'.[1] By that he means the barbaric attacks, both military and economic, by the capitalist hegemonies of the developed world on weaker nations, to which those in desperate circumstances can only respond with puny, but also barbaric, acts of terrorism. The argument is familiar, but what Achcar offers is a brilliant analysis of the dynamic of 'the new world order' and of the forces of resistance to it. The origins of contemporary troubles are complex and multiform so, too, are many of the responses to them, but, as we have argued elsewhere and argue again in this book, they are patently linked.[2] Above all, they have been brought together by the US's latest and most preposterous imperial adventure and George W. Bush's unconscionable hijacking of the atrocity of 11 September 2001 in its justification. All wars are waged against civilian populations and the US suggestion, limply backed by its UK supporters, that surgical strikes will limit the numbers killed is as absurd as it is monstrous: 'cruise missiles ... are to surgery what chain saws are to scalpels'.[3]

As in every major misfortune, it is the poor who will suffer most, the rich and powerful will largely be able to buy their way out. The victory of the capitalist world in the Cold War led by the US will cost us all dear, but it is important to recognise that the entirely reasonable gloom now enveloping us is not unremitting – sane voices can be heard. Protest over Iraq, both against the iniquities of Saddam and

1

at the bombing of innocent Iraqis to get rid of him, is worldwide and cannot, without violent repression, finally be ignored, but there are voices elsewhere and many of them have long pre-dated the present crisis. Some of them may even be heard, no matter how inadequate they may be, among the bureaucrats and politicians in power in both the developed and the 'developing' world. This book is devoted to a discussion of these voices and what they have and have not achieved.

Despite a widespread failure to act effectively, poverty and environmental degradation have been high on national and international agendas and we trace the battles to get them there. Part of that battle has been about priorities – should the environment or poverty take precedence in our concerns? We argue that the two are inseparable, but that purely, or even mainly, environmental agendas frequently ignore the needs and rights of poor people; the intimate relationship between the two issues must always be the point of departure. In support of this position we trace the story of the international commissions, conferences and summits that led to what might reasonably be called the two most significant public events in that progress: the United Nations Conference on Environment and Development (UNCED), held in Rio de Janeiro in 1992 and, ten years later, the UN's World Summit on Sustainable Development (WSSD), which took place in Johannesburg in 2002. It is our position that by ignoring the political and economic situation, the almost universal condemnation of the latter by international non-governmental organisations (INGOs) seriously missed the point. This failure arises from the acceptance by the INGOs of the fundamental policies of market-led economies – they talk of targets, of regulating markets and tariffs, of transferring technologies and managerial skills, in short they are demanding mechanisms for incorporating the poor into the world of global finance. Since our argument is that the inexorable demands of finance capital are directly responsible for the creation and maintenance of poverty, the proposition is oxymoronic.

Our purpose is to discuss what actually happened at Johannesburg, its importance and its place in contemporary events. There are no obvious and immediate solutions to worldwide poverty and exclusion, nor to environmental degradation; predictions made about either in such a fragmented stage in history belong to the readers of tea-leaves, but it is our view that unless we are clear about the politics of those problems, solutions will never be found. The principal areas of concern to the WSSD were the Millennium Development Goals

(MDGs) established several years ago and which promised massive reductions in poverty by the year 2015 and the principal means by which they might be achieved. Two issues became particularly important – the provision of clean water and safe sanitation for those who lack them and the provision of the energy needed for any serious development. The plan of this book is simple: it begins with a review of the origins of the Summit and some of the issues surrounding it and the second chapter examines the principal documents emerging from it: the *Johannesburg Declaration on Sustainable Development* and the *World Summit on Sustainable Development Plan of Implementation*. Chapter 3 deals with water and sanitation and Chapter 4 discusses energy. The fifth chapter discusses the other and, for the Summit at least, less central issues that emerged and the last is our theoretical analysis of the problems we face.

Note: This book was completed shortly before the United States–British invasion of Iraq.

1 Origins

The World Summit on Sustainable Development, held at the end of August 2002 in Johannesburg, is the most recent irruption in a lengthy chain of events. These events emerged from a complex history following the Second World War and the establishment of what became known as the 'Keynesian compromise' between industry, government and people; they were extensively conditioned by the subsequent Cold War waged by the US and its allies against the now vanished Soviet Union. For our purposes we may take the publication, in 1962, of Rachel Carson's *The Silent Spring* as a starting point – it was the first book to bring to the notice of a general public the alarming extent of environmental degradation. Pollution had been seen as an unfortunate, but inevitable, by-product of necessary economic development, particularly in a post-bellum world. Carson drew attention to the worldwide scale of it and to its dangers and she advocated a system of environmental monitoring and protection. Subsequent public awareness of those issues and the consequent political pressure on governments to take some action owe much to her work.

The roots of the other, and later, consciousness – that of unequal development – are even more tangled. They include the final collapse of the British Empire and the ability of many of the newly independent political leaders to publicise their causes, the emergence of welfare-ism, the growing influence of non-governmental organisations (NGOs), the rise of neo-colonialism (especially on the part of the US) and, particularly in Britain, the recruitment of selected populations, from what became known as the Third World, as cheap labour to fill unpopular jobs. Few voices, in the decade or so following the Second World War, were raised in making the now relatively commonplace connection between environmental degradation and poverty. Nonetheless, the growing consciousness in the developed world that, on the one hand, relations between the older and richer states and the new, mostly poor nations were increasingly unjust and, on the other, that all was not well environmentally, finally led to international action.

In 1972, the United Nations Conference on the Human Environment was held in Stockholm and was expected to address the issue of the degradation of the environment and the deterioration of living conditions in the developing world; it ended with a declaration of twenty-six common principles. The first of these endorsed the universal right to freedom, equality and adequate conditions for life, but the main weight of that endorsement rested on the parallel 'solemn responsibility' for the protection of the environment. The remaining twenty-five were unequivocally environmental. At the time, few people recognised the extent to which this was an important shift in priorities. Concern for the environment and the effects of its destruction on human lives and not, directly, concern for the manifold causes of poverty, now headed the agenda. This order of business has affected all subsequent debate about development and has produced a peculiarly environmentalist approach to what are, essentially, human and humanly created difficulties. Since the Stockholm Conference (as it is more generally known) most effort has been devoted to fixing a damaged environment, rather than attacking the causes of the damage, many of which are also the causes of poverty.

Three years later, in 1975, a Conference on Security and Cooperation in Europe (CSCE) was held in Helsinki and produced a declaration (known as the Helsinki Declaration) in which, among other things, the thirty-five nations present (including the USSR) agreed to cooperate on matters to do with the environment.[1] Geopolitics prevented much in the way of follow-up and a suspicious Soviet Union refused to cooperate; fifteen years passed before the Conference became an organisation of importance, and security seemed to have ousted the environment as a matter in which it was concerned. In 1977, the Independent Commission on International Development Issues was created; chaired by Willy Brandt, a former Chancellor of the then Federal Republic of Germany, it is better known as the Brandt Commission. Its purpose was to examine the issues involved in the rapidly increasing inequalities between rich and poor countries and to suggest ways of overcoming them – it was probably the last major attempt at asking the right questions. Entitled *North–South: a Programme for Survival*, its report was published in 1980: aid to the least developed countries should be increased by a minimum of US$4 billion per annum over a period of about twenty years; it should made easier for developing countries to get to the funds available from the global financial institutions and these funds should be provided on preferential terms. The report also called for expenditure on agricultural development to be increased by US$8 billion over the same period; it proposed that protectionist barriers, erected by the states of the 'North' against agricultural products from the 'South', should be removed. In matters of trade, the Commission again called for the ending of the North's protectionist regulations. Long-term financing for the development of energy supplies in developing countries was also suggested. The report and its proposals received widespread publicity and acclaim, but was resolutely ignored by the governments and institutions of the North. Prior to its disbandment in 1983, the Commission published another report entitled *Common Crisis* which the governments of the wealthy world neglected as enthusiastically as they had neglected *North–South*, though both reports played a part in other events taking place in the UN.

The issues would not go away. Disparities between rich and poor nations increased, inevitably accompanied by greater international instability. Both sides in the Cold War supported client governments throughout the developing world and turned a blind eye to, when not actually encouraging, predatory oligarchies and dictatorships which not only sequestered vast sums of international 'aid', but also preyed on their own people. The price of this bounty was permission for international corporations to help themselves to the resources and assets in the countries of these vassal governments – countries in which the welfare of workers and care for the environment were not serious considerations and where the further impoverishment of the already poor could be ignored. That tale is well-known and for the most infamous examples we have only to remember Union Carbide's activity in India or Shell's performance in Ogoniland in Nigeria, but there are countless others. Continued impoverishment and massive environmental destruction were the price paid by the poor for the Cold War and for the growth of the 'free' market. The need to address these problems became apparent to the wealthier governments and to the UN, partly because they added to international instability and partly because public clamour became increasingly insistent.

In the same year that the Brandt Commission published *Common Crisis*, the UN General Assembly set up the World Commission on Environment and Development (WCED), chaired by Gro Harlem Brundtland who was then Prime Minister of Norway. Its brief was to examine environmental and developmental crises and to make proposals for 'a global agenda of change'.[2] *Our Common Future*, its report (commonly referred to as the Brundtland Report), was published in 1987 and caused a not inconsiderable stir. In her foreword, Brundtland set out what it was that the General Assembly had asked for:

- to propose long-term environmental strategies for achieving sustainable development by the year 2000 and beyond;
- to recommend ways concern for the environment may be translated into greater cooperation among developing countries ... that take account of the interrelationships between people, resources, environment and development;
- to consider ways and means by which the international community can deal more effectively with environment concerns;
- to help define shared perceptions of long-term environmental issues and the appropriate efforts needed to deal successfully with the problems of protecting and enhancing the environment.[3]

Commentaries on the Brundtland Report are legion, including one by the present authors, so it is unnecessary to cover the ground again, the point here is to recognise that the phrasing of the call by the General Assembly conformed to the priorities first laid out in Stockholm.[4]

Both Stockholm and Brundtland were the progenitors of the United Nations Conference on Environment and Development, held in Rio de Janeiro in June 1992 (referred to, variously, as the UNCED, the Earth Summit or Rio: see Dodds and Middleton, 2001). Klaus Töpfer, formerly a minister of the environment in Germany and now Executive Director of the United Nations Environment Programme (UNEP), has remarked on its huge importance. To an extent previously undreamt of, it thrust the environment into the centre of politics. It was an extraordinary achievement and one with which many of the world's most powerful governments are still struggling to come to terms. Neither Rio nor its outcome were ever a direct challenge to the objectives of what has been called the 'overdeveloped world', but the Conference was a political phenomenon and, to use Bismarck's cliché, politics is the art of the possible.[5]

Rio produced some remarkable, if largely aspirational, documents. Principles were enunciated in the Rio Declaration based on the Stockholm Declaration. It is important to note that both declarations, and subsequent modifications of them, are glosses on the Universal Declaration of Human Rights and the European

Convention for the Protection of Human Rights and Fundamental Freedoms, a point to which we shall return. Agenda 21 was the framework, constructed by UNCED, for an ambitious programme for sustainable development: both a guideline for governments, INGOs and multilateral agencies, and a basic document for local initiatives, particularly among municipal authorities.[6] It has led to the foundation of over 2,000 groups throughout the world known as 'LA21s' (Local Agenda 21).[7] The Agenda is totally committed to the proposition that: 'Economic conditions ... that encourage free trade and access to markets will help make economic growth and environmental protection mutually supportive for all countries, particularly for developing countries and countries undergoing the process of transition to market economies.'[8] Another less than world-shaking document produced by the Rio Summit was the cumbersomely entitled 'Non-legally Binding Authoritative Statement of Principles for a Global Consensus on the Management, Conservation and Sustainable Development of All Types of Forests'; this was the nearest that the Conference could get to an agreement on forests in the face of the intransigence of the overdeveloped nations' determination to continue to see them as an essential resource for their own industries. It was a depressing document, if only because the needs, livelihoods, rights and the societies of the arboreal and peri-arboreal dwellers were resolutely ignored.

Two agreements were reached: the Framework Convention on Climate Change (UNFCCC) and the Convention on Biological Diversity (CBD). 'Framework' conventions are skeletons, given flesh by a series of subsequent protocols – in the case of the UNFCCC, the only protocol, so far, is that made at Kyoto in December, 1997, but there is a case for seeing the Montreal Protocol as an agreement affecting the Convention. The CBD was a sorry affair since it was agreed in the face of powerful and well-established transnational corporations (TNCs) busily exploiting the profitability of, on the one hand, the biological attributes of the natural world and, on the other, the extension of monoculture and genetically modified organisms (GMOs). Powerful states closed ranks with the TNCs and refused to countenance much more than an admonitory role for the Convention. Nonetheless, in their different ways, both conventions have prompted some movement, no matter how minimal, in those wealthy states least in thrall to their lumpen right. They have also become points of departure for that contemporary phenomenon of widespread, single issue political protest.[9]

Two other influential bodies came into being as a consequence of what was achieved at Rio: the UN Commission on Sustainable Development and the Inter-Agency Committee on Sustainable Development (IACSD). The former was created, under the wing of the Economic and Social Council of the United Nations (ECOSOC), to oversee the implementation of Agenda 21, but, among many other tasks, it also set up the International Panel on Forests and the International Forum on Forests. Towards the end of the century, it was instrumental in creating a mechanism through which the UN General Assembly could discuss oceans. Another of its achievements was to bring the threats to the environment posed by tourism into official discussion by forming the International Work Programme on Sustainable Tourism. The IACSD is essentially a management structure designed to ensure the coordination of the various bodies overseeing the implementation of Agenda 21, but it has two other important organisations responsible to it: the committees on Oceans and Coastal Areas and on Water Resources. Both are areas of increasing international political concern.

This abbreviated account of some of the products of UNCED is to reinforce our point that the Conference did succeed in politicising environmental issues.[10] We cannot be surprised that its politics were a supine surrender to the agendas of neo-liberal capital and that, by concentrating on the problems of the environment rather than of people within the environment, it enabled venal world leaders to evade many of the issues. The most publicised of the agreements, the UNFCCC, was given some content by the Kyoto Protocol. It is widely recognised that the success of the Protocol lay not in any serious effect it might have on the environment, that could only be minimal, but on the fact that it was reached at all. Its principal consequence has been the creation of a profitable new international market in trading emission permits which has been led by Richard Sandor working with, among others, BP, DuPont and Ford – a cynic might see in this the only hope of rescuing that tattered agreement from the rejectionist position taken by the far right, particularly in the US and Australia.[11]

Apart from politicising environmental concerns, UNCED also prompted substantial developments in thinking about the relationship between poverty and the environment – not the least because it put the equivocal, but invaluable, concept of sustainability, at the centre of the debate. It is equivocal since a consensus about its meaning is assumed to a point where its user seems to invoke a moral authority in its use, yet exactly what is to be sustained and by what means are rarely carefully defined and, with very few exceptions, the word is used in portmanteau fashion to carry quite specific political and economic programmes. In any discussion of poverty and development, we may discount ludicrous extremes like the argument that sustainable development is possible only through the complete liberation of the market, but we should bear in mind some of the baggage of apparently more benign proposals. The encouragement of artisanal livelihoods in places where the overall economic situation inhibits them (as in areas where migration to industrial centres offers greater returns) is an instance and seems to have emerged from a view of how things ought to be, rather than how they are. Another may be seen in the clumsy and largely ineffectual apparatus of much of the targeting of aid. In the case of environmental issues, the once fashionable debt for nature swaps, which were, in effect, forms of colonisation, provide an instance of the triumph of a particular ideology in the understanding of sustainability.

In recent years the intimate connections between poverty and the environment have become central to any discussion of sustainable development and this shift has made the criticism of past practice possible. More importantly it provides space for the analysis of the baggage contained in any use of the term 'sustainability'. Analysis itself cannot be entirely neutral since it must derive from a set of assumptions and its outcome will be conditioned by the expectations of the analysts; indeed, where the process leads to prescription, it would be deficient if it lacked ideological drive. What matters is the recognition and consequent judgement of the nature of the ideology, itself an ideological process. Ideology is at issue in the most central question of all: what is sustainable development? If it is the achievement of some equilibrium between human action and ecological possibility, how is that to be measured, if it is ever achieved, and what would be its effect on human inequity and inequality? In practice, since we may be faced with humanly induced ecological disruption or even catastrophe, the question of what it might mean is put aside in favour of argument about how best to keep identifiable and present dangers at bay.

That brief excursion into the obvious is the preface to a discussion of two major tendencies in that debate – best exemplified by *The Living Planet Report, 2002*, published by the World Wildlife Fund (WWF), on the one hand and the Global Scenario Group of the Stockholm Environment Institute (SEI) on the other. WWF is essentially a conservation INGO, but is also an international pressure group which gives it a directly political agenda.[12] Its Report summarises the parlous state of the planet as a consequence of human pollution and is largely based on work by the International Union for the Conservation of Nature (IUCN) – it was specifically intended to influence the WSSD.[13] Its central metaphor is the 'human ecological footprint' and, in his preface, the Director General of WWF, Dr Claude Martin, describes it as 'compar[ing] countries' consumption of natural resources with the Earth's biological capacity to regenerate them' which, for the sake of brevity, the Report refers to as 'bio-capacity'. The Report ends with 'The Living Planet Index', a useful tabulated quantification of the world's biocapacity covering arable farming, grazing, forests and fishing, divided into regions and the countries within them. Throughout the document, the principal unit of measurement is the 'global hectare' defined as '1 hectare of average biological productivity'. It can come as no surprise that this statistical analysis leads WWF to an alarming conclusion:

> The global ecological footprint covered 13.7 billion hectares in 1999, or 2.3 global hectares per person ... About 11.4 billion hectares, slightly less than a quarter of the Earth's surface, are biologically productive ... The productive quarter of the biosphere corresponded to an average 11.9 global hectares per person in 1999. Therefore human consumption of natural resources that year over shot the Earth's biological capacity by about 20 percent.

Based on UN and the Intergovernmental Panel on Climate Change (IPCC) projections, the Report goes on to consider the probable situation in the year 2050. It begins with the UN's suggestion that the world's population will have increased almost to 9 billion. The Report offers two projections, both assuming that growth will be rapid, new technologies will appear, that economic globalisation will be yet greater than at present and that regional inequities will decline; in the first projection it assumes that the world will derive the necessary energy from an equal mix of fossil and non-fossil fuels; in the second, it assumes that protecting the environment will be of equal concern to the production of energy. Further projections to do with CO_2 emissions, relatively benign technological development and less nakedly acquisitive corporate structures are all proposed. Nonetheless, the most optimistic estimate of CO_2 emissions offered by the Report is an increase from the present annual rate of about 7 billion tonnes to 11.7 billion tonnes by 2050, the most pessimistic assessment suggests an increase to 16 billion tonnes. In the same period, cereal consumption is expected to rise by 66 per cent, consumption of forest products will increase by 120 per cent, and meat and fish consumption will grow by 100 per cent.

If, over the next forty to fifty years, such massive increases were to occur, then the human ecological footprint would expand such that its demands would be between 80 per cent and 120 per cent greater than the world's biocapacity. The Report goes on to remark that '9 billion people would require between 1.8 and 2.2 Earth-sized planets in order to sustain their consumption of crops, meat, fish, and wood, and to hold CO_2 levels constant in the atmosphere'. This is clearly an absurdity and is designed to underline WWF's principal message that consumption must not exceed the limits of the world's biological capacity. The current rate of consumption, the argument runs, ends in mining, and thus progressively reducing, that capacity. The Report proposes a series of ameliorative and, ultimately, curative measures. These, in summary, are to improve systems of production, to change patterns of consumption and to control population. Such measures would, in the view of the authors of the Report, lead to a reduction of the human ecological footprint and eliminate what they call 'the ecological deficit'.

Although it would be foolish to deny all the premises of WWF's argument, the present authors have a number of difficulties with it. One of these is the fundamental structure of measurement used by both WWF and the IUCN to establish the 'human ecological footprint'. They have divided the productive area of the world's surface by the number of people living from it to arrive at a figure for population pressure. Although they refer to the need for better 'production systems', by which they must mean technological development, they have not used it as a factor in their equation. Had they done so, the result would have been to make the ecological footprint at least uncertain.

Uncertainty is unnerving for those attempting to influence such a political event as the WSSD, but it is of the first importance if we are to evade the dangerously Malthusian economics to which WWF's formula would lead us. For an example of uncertainty we may consider the rate of human reproduction – that is, the number of children per family – which has, since 1960, declined, although the number of people continues to rise, even if more slowly than in the recent past, because approximately half of the world's population is below the age of twenty-five.[14] However, rates of deceleration or acceleration remain unpredictable and predicting a geometric rise is as rash as supposing that there will be no significant increase. Thomas Malthus famously wrote: 'Population, when unchecked, increases in a geometrical ratio. Subsistence increases only in an arithmetical ratio.'[15] He elaborated this claim by supposing that the population doubles in size every twenty-five years, a supposition based on censuses taken in the US in 1790 and 1800.[16] In passing, it is worth noting that both censuses were fairly meaningless since they were taken before the emancipation of slaves, who, of course, were not counted, and without reference to patterns of immigration. Malthus was opposed to relief for the poor, except in the form of workhouse labour, largely on the grounds that enabling poor people to purchase their basic needs without making them economically productive would simply increase prices and hence make no difference.[17] The need to think of controlling the world's population as a condition for establishing a sustainable human ecological footprint is remarkably close to that Malthusian patrician pessimism which has long been at the heart of capitalist economics.

But even if the vatic alarmism of WWF's Report fails to convince, there are clearly grounds for concern. These are examined with far greater care in the work of the Global Scenario Group and in UNEP's *Global Environment Outlook 3* (usually known as *GEO*).[18] The Global Scenario Group has published three significant studies, *Branch Points: Global Scenarios and Human Choice*, *Bending the Curve: Toward Global Sustainability* and *Great Transition: the Promise and Allure of the Times Ahead*. The first remarks that the 'concept of sustainability implies the reconciliation of long-term development and environmental goals' and goes on to offer a 'taxonomy of scenarios' for the ways 'in which future events could unfold'; the second is devoted to an examination of 'what it would take to steer human development onto a more sustainable pathway during the 21st century'.[19] The latter is essentially an expansion of the first (four of its five authors were responsible for the first report). The third is an attempt at a programme for future action and a brief socio-historical prediction. Both UNEP and the Global Scenario Group offer a variety of scenarios, but each divides them differently.

UNEP sets out the scale of environmental change and damage within specific categories (land, forests, biodiversity, freshwater, coastal and marine areas, atmosphere, urban areas and disasters), and considers the outlook in general and its implications for the regions of the world (Africa, Asia and the Pacific, Europe, Latin America and the Caribbean, North America, West Asia and the two Poles). Scenarios for each region are set out as the consequences of four differing choices:

- allowing the globalised market to continue to 'dominate social and political agendas';
- attempting to deal with environmental crises and poverty by legislation and governmental pro-environment and anti-poverty policies;
- creating 'islands of advantage', by wealthy states, from which the poor and their conflicts are excluded and which offer some security and economic benefit to 'dependant communities, but ... exclude the disadvantaged mass of outsiders';
- allowing a 'new environment and development paradigm [to emerge] ... in response to the challenge of sustainability, supported by new, more equitable values and institutions.'[20]

This list forms a hierarchy, four curves plotting an outcome are shown in each graph, the worst case follows the first of these choices and the best is a consequence of the fourth. The obvious weakness in this method lies in treating at least the first three as mutually exclusive. Nonetheless, *GEO 3* provides an invaluable and comprehensive environmental analysis which can usefully be put alongside, for example, the United Nations Development Programme's (UNDP) Human Development Index (UNDP, 2002).

In *Branch Points*, the Global Scenario Group makes its projections in the light of three generalised futures, but, before doing so it observes that a sustainable world would be one in which:

- absolute poverty, malnutrition and famine are eradicated, and access to basic health care and education are universal;
- quality of life is improving, with satisfactory material conditions and expanding opportunities for fulfilment for all;
- inequity between rich and poor is diminished;
- environmental quality is increasing, with critical biological resources recovering, pollution under control, and climate stability in sight;
- violence and armed conflict are infrequent;

- human solidarity is stronger at family, community and global levels;
- global population growth ceases.[21]

One might consider these proposals modest and unexceptionable, even statements of the obvious, but their importance lies in a simple change in the nature of the discourse: by moving from argument about environmental damage and economic policy to listing perfectly common human aspirations, which are undeniably and universally apposite, the Group has reopened the way to rational socio-political discussion and action.

Predictive scenarios are commonly based on variable assumptions, frequently quantitative; the authors of *Branch Points* suggest that such an approach is inadequate and that the overall and varying socio-political and economic circumstances in which assumptions are made are conditioning factors. In a fashion similar to that used in *GEO 3* (some of the authors of *Branch Points*, together with the SEI, were also involved in UNEP's report), they 'classify scenarios within a two-tier hierarchy: *classes* based on fundamentally different social visions, and *variants* reflecting a range of possible outcomes within each class'.[22] The three classes suggested, rather than the four used in *GEO 3*, are labelled, respectively, 'Conventional Worlds', 'Barbarisation' and 'Great Transition'; each is a macrocosm, but each is also immediately recognisable from other discourses. The first assumes a world going on much as it is now, reacting to problems as they arise, but not fundamentally changing its neo-liberal progress. Barbarisation is the process in which the older liberal values of democratic societies are abandoned and fortress societies, more thoroughgoing than those at present being constructed in North America, Australia and Europe, will become the norm. '*Great Transitions* explore visionary solutions to the sustainability challenge, including new socio-economic arrangements and fundamental changes in values.'[23] The major difference between the positions adopted by *Branch Points* and those by the later *GEO 3* is that the former does not need to be quite so politically circumspect. Indeed, it suggests that substantial popular opposition to the prevailing market oriented economies will be called for.[24] In 1998, the Global Scenario Group produced *Bending the Curve*, in which it elaborated the theses of the earlier report and proposed strategies for the achievement of sustainability. Its authors use the Conventional Worlds classification, where we are now, as the reference point from which 'to examine emerging problems' and they offer the customary indicators (see Table 1.1). Their reason for starting from that point is that 'the center of the policy discussion today lives in the *Conventional Worlds* niche of the landscape of future visions'.[25] They entitle the analysis based on this starting point the 'Reference' scenario – whatever ambition we may entertain for the future shape of affairs, it is necessary to start from where we are now. We shall return subsequently to the third study, *Great Transition*.

In 1995, the UN held a summit conference in Copenhagen called the World Summit for Social Development. The second of its commitments was: 'To eradicate poverty in the world through decisive national actions and international cooperation, as an ethical, social, political and economic imperative of humankind.'[26] In the following year, the World Food Summit proposed the target of cutting the number of the world's undernourished poor by half – this was to be achieved by the year 2015.[27] Yet another summit, the UN Millennium Summit held in September 2000, adopted this target as part of what it christened the 'Millennium Development Goals'. Subsequently, an elaborate set of guidelines for creating a policy framework for such an ambition was prepared for member states of the Organisation for Economic Cooperation and Development (OECD) – at the time of writing over a third of the period between the two summits' proposals and the target date has elapsed with little or no sign of the promised reduction.[28] The authors of *Bending the Curve*, also in fairly optimistic mood, have proposed somewhat more probable targets. In the case of food, which may stand for them all, they suggest that 'halving undernourishment by 2025 and halving it again by 2050' is achievable.[29]

The Global Scenario Group point to an immediate problem in establishing a 'proper balance between the goals of sustainability in the long term and development in the near term' – for the poor countries of this world, it may be necessary to add to environmental damage in order to achieve some minimum standards for their people (we return to this point in Chapter 4).[30] It has frequently been observed, not the least by the Brundtland Report, that sustainable development is that which is designed to meet current needs without compromising resources for future generations. An obvious political difficulty arises which is in urgent need of resolution: that precept is one which is most popular in the developed world and which is not unreasonably seen by the poor as part of the armoury of the wealthy in their determination not just to have what they hold, but to increase it. Even so, if only a few elements of WWF's eschatological predictions come to be, life will, at best, be very uncomfortable for everyone, but it is well-known that those who suffer most and first from adverse environmental conditions are those too poor to buy their way out of whatever predicament they face. With something of this sort in mind, the Group has set out indicators and targets for environmental improvement (see Table 1.2).

Table 1.1   Selected Indicators by Region in 1995

Region	Hunger (%)	Unsafe water (%)	Illiteracy (%)	Life expectancy (years)	GDP/Cap ($)	Poorest 20% divided by richest 20%
Africa	34	49	45	55	1,620	0.13
China	16	20	18	69	2,890	0.14
Latin America	14	17	14	69	6,000	0.07
Middle East	16	27	38	65	5,260	0.10
S & SE Asia	19	35	40	63	2,580	0.18
Eastern Europe	1	7	0	71	5,950	0.23
FSU	4	8	0	67	4,110	0.22
North America	2	0	0	77	26,950	0.11
Pacific OECD	1	0	0	79	21,100	0.16
Western Europe	1	1	4	76	15,730	0.19

Source: Global Scenario Group, 1998, 10.

The modesty and common sense of these targets stand in some contrast to the over-heated air of the OECD's declaration of intent, but it is necessary to remind ourselves of the difficulties in the way of their achievement. For example, the OECD states, and the EU in particular, reached a patchy and indifferently enforced agreement to reduce over-fishing. It was an agreement which met with some success, but chiefly in seas, like the North Sea, where stocks had collapsed to the point that no catch was possible; the response of the industry was, on the one hand, to raid the stocks of poorer states, particularly in littoral Africa, which were less able to regulate, and on the other, to begin to fish for species living at greater depths. The latter of these two practices will probably cause even greater ecological damage, since deep-water stocks reproduce far more slowly than the fish which live in more accessible waters and little is known about their place in the food chain. Reservations of this kind apart, *Bending*

Table 1.2 Environmental Indicators and Targets

Indicator	1995	2025	2050
Climate			
World			
CO$_2$ concentration	360 ppmv		stabilise at <450 ppmv by 2100
Warming rate			average 0.1%/decade, 1990–2100
CO$_2$ emissions			<700 GtC cumulative, 1990–2100
OECD			
CO$_2$ emissions rate	various and rising	<65% of 1990 (<90% of 1990 by 2010)	<35% of 1990
non-OECD			
CO$_2$ emissions rates	various and rising	increases slowing energy efficiency rising	reach OECD per capita rates by 2075
Resource use			
OECD			
Eco-efficiency	$100 GDP/300 kg	4-fold increase ($100 GDP/75 kg)	10-fold increase ($100 GDP/30 kg)
Materials use/per capita	80 tonnes	<60 tonnes	<30 tonnes
non-OECD			
Eco-efficiency	various but low	converge toward OECD practices	converge toward OECD practices
Materials use/per capita	various but low	converge toward OECD per capita values	converge toward OECD per capita values
Toxics			
OECD			
Releases of persistent organic pollutants and heavy metals	various but high	<50% of 1995	<10% of 1995
non-OECD			
Releases of persistent organic pollutants and heavy metals	various and rising	increases slowing	converge toward OECD per capita values

Freshwater			
World			
Use-to-resource ratio	various and rising	reaches peak values	0.2–0.4 maximum (in countries > 0.4 in 1995, less than 1995 values)
Population in water stress	1.9 billion (34%)	less than 3 billion (<40%)	less than 3.5 billion, begins decreasing (40%)
Ecosystem pressure			
World			
Deforestation	various but high	no further deforestation	net reforestation
Land degradation	various but high	no further degradation	net restoration
Marine over-fishing	fish stocks declining	over-fishing stopped	healthy fish stocks

Source: Global Scenario Group, 1998, 16.

the Curve, intentionally or otherwise, provided a workable agenda for achieving sustainability beginning from where we are at present.

The Group has its own reservations. It considers what would be needed to achieve the targets within the Reference scenario and, in the section on climate, asks whether the relatively modest goals for the climate could be met. Its cautious answer is that if governments adopt coherent policies for regulating carbon emissions then it is possible, but buried in the careful account of the means is the remark: 'the global carbon emission budget is allocated to regions (and ultimately countries) on the basis of economic, technological and equity considerations, and *political feasibility* [emphasis added]'.[31] In the light of the increasing adoption, by the wealthy states, of the policy of Barbarisation, described in the Group's earlier report, even the Reference scenario begins to look astonishingly optimistic. Yet the two reports, synthesised and developed in *Great Transition*, bring together the complex of humanistic thought that formed the better part of the history we have briefly described. They also effectively spelt out what the greater part of the world hoped for from the WSSD.[32]

Hope is a fine thing, but it commonly bumps up against *realpolitik*; it is well to remind ourselves of the circumstances in which the Summit was held. It has been observed, to the point of tedium, that the world was changed by the events in the US, of 11 September 2001, but, like many such observations, it exaggerates. That particular atrocity became the catalyst bringing together elements already present within the structure of the world's economy, or economies. The US, the most powerful of the world's economies, has for long been determined to advance what it sees as its own best interests, at all costs and without much reference to multilateral treaties. Bush's purchase, largely with energy industry funds, of the Presidency and his appointment of oil industry executives to many of the senior posts about him allowed the far right of the US administration to pursue these unilateralist aims quite openly, virtually without visible national opposition and without much reference to international responses.[33] His administration has abandoned 'the Anti-Ballistic Missile Treaty, the Kyoto Protocol (largely at the bidding of his oil industry cabal), the Rome Statute of the International Criminal Court, a convention on the sale of small arms and a protocol to the Biological Weapons Convention'; more recently it has rejected the agreement to allow cheaper drugs to be made available to poor countries.[34]

Not satisfied with crippling the UN by withholding or delaying its subscriptions, the administration has also begun to muzzle those parts of the organisation with which it feels uncomfortable. Marshalling a welter of completely unsubstantiated charges of poor management style and suspect financial control, the US government has successfully ousted the independent and relatively progressive Director-General of the Organisation for the Prohibition of Chemical Weapons, José Bustani.[35] These charges were repeated in the UK House of Lords, still without a shred of evidence, by a place-person of Blair's government. The real objection to Bustani was his under-mining of the claims made in support of the US–UK excuses for war on Iraq.[36] It has also effectively censored intergovernmental debate on climate change by forcing the dismissal, early in 2002, of the chair of the IPCC, Robert Watson and the employment of R.K. Pachauri, thought to be more sympathetic to the US view. That particular manoeuvre was made at the bidding of the US oil giant, ExxonMobil.[37] The most recent victim of this process has been the ejection of the independent and relatively outspoken High Commissioner for Human Rights and former President of Ireland, Mary Robinson – not the least because she criticised the treatment of detainees in the US gulag at Guantanamo Bay in Cuba. She has been replaced by a far more inoffensive UN career diplomat, Sergio Vieira da Mello.[38] At the time of writing, the Bush administration is blackmailing the UN by threatening it with 'irrelevance' if it fails to endorse its war on Iraq.

The horrifying events of 11 September 2001 have, with unseemly rapidity, been commandeered by Bush and his allies in support of their expansionist agenda. Their collaboration with the tyrannies and petty war-lords of Central Asia, in the course of forming their ill-defined and plainly propagandist alliance against terrorism, has shown their absolute contempt for the concept of human rights. 'Terrorism' is used to describe the unquestionably abhorrent, but usually small scale, attacks on hegemony by poorly equipped guerrillas, while the US bombing on a massive scale in, for example, Afghanistan and Iraq, is offered as a fine instance of a moral defence against it. We prefer to recognise such actions simply as other incidents in a long history of state terror since the Second World War, of which South East Asia is the most memorable instance.[39] Coercive action by the United States, including its military and political support for Israel's determination to destroy the Palestinian hope for a viable and independent state, is directed either towards securing its control over the world's oil supplies or towards securing its commercial advantage *vis-à-vis* other powerful economies.

Both the opposition to the behaviour of the US, its allies and their corporations and the supporters of that triad invoke 'human rights'. This is possible because the concept of social justice has become hopelessly confused with human rights with the consequence that most of the opposition begins with analyses of particular situations in which rights have been compromised or denied. Rights to food, housing, health, education, freedom, gender equality and a host of other things are seen as rights vested in individuals – each and every person, or family has them. It is customary to insist that all policies designed, for example, to alleviate poverty should be rights based – we have already referred to Stockholm and Rio. Human rights must, indeed, be defended, but using them in this fashion is to ignore the essentially *social* dimension of human existence. Just as individuals can only be understood as such in relation to others – as social beings – any account of rights must be a social account. They are vested simultaneously in society and in the individuals who form that society. Where rights are denied it is because the society has become dysfunctional; the restoration of rights can only be achieved by a societal transition. Not to recognise this is, ultimately, to accept that fragmentation of social consciousness, of social space, which lies at the core of capital's ideology. This principle must be borne in mind in any examination of the outcome of the WSSD.

Every generation is alarmed by the social and natural dangers by which it feels encompassed and ours is no exception. Nonetheless, what is facing us at present does seem exceptionally disturbing; apart from the United States' open-ended war on almost everything that troubles the sleep of President Bush, other examples include: appalling levels of poverty, the contemporary plague of HIV/AIDS, global warming which will, quite possibly, lead to dramatic and catastrophic changes in climate and, most recently, the suggestion that Earth's magnetic field is about to 'flip' with consequences no one can imagine.[40] All these phenomena, and many more besides, are ineluctably linked to a global political volatility in which the old, liberal certainties of democracy are increasingly undermined and disregarded. They also form the socio-political circumstances in which the WSSD was held. It is from this dispiriting situation that we must now consider what that Summit achieved and what the consequences might be.

2   What Did They Agree?

Two documents were finally agreed at the Johannesburg Summit – the *Declaration on Sustainable Development* and the *Plan of Implementation* – and both, since they were compromises, leave much to be desired.[1] So far, most critics of any persuasion seem to have missed the point that it is astonishing that agreement on either document was possible. There were four intergovernmental and five regional Preparatory Committees (Prepcoms); of the latter, the last two failed to arrive at a chairperson's statement, a lack which led to some speculation, particularly among INGOs, about a possible cancellation of the Summit.[2] Chairperson's statements were intended to provide a framework for the Summit debates and the failure by two Prepcoms to produce them was a measure of US intransigence, largely in the matter of energy.

Public pressure, worldwide economic and political instability and past commitments had brought this Summit about, but it is essential to recognise the kind of battle being fought at it. Globalisation and an unfettered market had opened the way for the most economically and militarily powerful state, the US, to pursue unilaterally what it saw as its best interests. It is notorious that public interest in foreign affairs in that state is a minority pursuit and that internal opposition is fairly weak. Because international finance capital is simultaneously intertwined and mutually competitive, other economically powerful states, whose governments were more constrained by their electorates, were at once ambivalent about US policies and profoundly interested in not endangering financial alliances. The Summit was not isolated from this ambivalence and to illustrate it we may turn to Bush's attack on Iraq.

Bush and his camp followers have, to a considerable degree, substituted the destruction of Saddam Hussein for the more generalised war on terrorism and, in particular, for the pursuit of Osama bin Laden. Few people, even in the US administration, are bothering to deny that its war is in the interests of securing control of Iraq's oil reserves, the second largest in the world – a control that certain elements in the US, particularly the energy industry, consider essential for satisfying a Gargantuan appetite for fossil fuels and in the light of increasing turmoil in the Middle East. Control of such vast reserves will also allow the US to dictate world oil prices. European responses have been confused and, although not much remarked upon, the reasons are fairly obvious. Most of the strongest states in the EU are led by right-wing or centre-right governments and, in the ordinary course of events, would have little difficulty in supporting the belligerence of a fellow and powerful member of the OECD. But they have become increasingly disconcerted by Bush's unilateralism which is further undermining a chronically labile system of world trade. Added to this is the other underlying reason for Bush's demand for the destruction of Saddam's regime, not just the seizure of the oil, but the ending of the contracts that regime made with European states and their oil interests. Both Russia and France have made huge investments in the Iraqi oil industry and, since Bush has made a deal with the dubious opposition parties from Iraq in which he will support their power if they will declare null and void the oil contracts made during Saddam's reign, they face gigantic losses. Other states have similar, though smaller, contracts and the total investment that Bush hopes to appropriate is thought to exceed US$1 trillion.[3] The governments of Russia, France and some smaller investors are making a fundamental mistake in supposing that in dealing with the US, they are dealing with a conventional democratic state in which policies can change or be modified to suit electoral shifts. In practice they are dealing with the place-people of the oil TNCs; once control of Iraqi oil is a *fait accompli*, subsequent US administrations will not find it possible, nor feel it necessary, to relinquish their position.

The present authors do not suggest that, had the Summit been convened in more genial times, it would necessarily have arrived at completely satisfactory conclusions, but US unilateralism and war-mongering, its disregard for external criticism (the latter exemplified by its recent dumping of otherwise unsaleable genetically modified maize on African states, describing it as 'aid' for the starving) and its patent contempt for the UN, all made constructive agreement among the nations participating in the WSSD singularly difficult. In the light of this we feel that the prompt dismissal of the Summit's outcome by so many INGOs, on the ground that it consisted only of vague aspirations and lacked binding undertakings and targets, somewhat misses the point. It does so in two ways: on the one hand, it underestimates the value of a framework of objectives to forthcoming campaigns and, on the other, it fails effectively to criticise some of the less well-publicised elements in both the process and its outcome.

It would be pointless to deny that the *Declaration on Sustainable Development* is, in many ways, little more than a homily, but in listing 'The Challenges We Face' it once more reaffirms the importance of eradicating poverty (by which it means reducing the numbers in acute poverty), the management of resources and the removal of: 'The deep fault line that divides human society between the rich and the poor and the ever-increasing gap between the developed and developing worlds [which] pose a major threat to global prosperity and stability.' It sees globalisation and the 'rapid integration of markets, mobility of capital and significant increases in investment flows' as opening 'new challenges and opportunities for the pursuit of sustainable development', but it does go on to remark that many people are not benefiting from this afflatus; its somewhat magniloquent use of 1 Corinthians 13.1 at this point is interestingly ambiguous.[4] Equity is about the universal right to what Sen called a 'bundle of entitlements' adequate to the maintenance of a reasonable human life and is bound up with what the *Declaration* has to say about poverty.[5] But it also makes a plea for equality, that is the knowledge of, and recognition of, other 'civilisations ... peoples, irrespective of race, disabilities, religion, language, culture and tradition'.[6] At this point, the document gathers pace and gives a lengthy list of matters to be dealt with in the 'focus on the indivisibility of human dignity': water, sanitation, shelter, energy, health care, food security, protection of biodiversity, access to financial resources, the opening of markets, capacity building, the transfer of technology, human resource development, education and training. '[T]hreats to the sustainable development of our people' must be dealt with and they, too, are listed: 'chronic hunger; malnutrition; foreign occupation; armed conflicts; illicit drug problems; organised crime; corruption; natural disasters; illicit arms trafficking; trafficking in persons; terrorism; intolerance and incitement to racial, ethnic, religious and other hatreds; xenophobia; and endemic, communicable and chronic diseases, in particular HIV/AIDS, malaria and tuberculosis.' Its final programmatic determination is 'to ensure that women's empowerment and emancipation, and gender equality are integrated in all activities encompassed within Agenda 21, the Millennium Development Goals and the Johannesburg *Plan of Implementation*'.[7]

It is all a bit breathless, possibly even clichéd, but no matter how inadequately backed up, it is a declaration of intent which demonstrates that whatever battles for implementation may be ahead, at least the principles have been accepted. The present authors have only two immediate reservations about this listing of priorities: the first is that questions of women's emancipation and of gender appear almost as an afterthought. This is the case in so many international policy documents and may be a consequence of committee writing dominated by men: they know that gender issues are important, but they do not really understand them, so they add them to texts wherever they seem to fit. A good example of this syndrome may be found in the OECD's *DAC Guidelines: Poverty Reduction* on which the present authors have commented elsewhere.[8] The second reservation lies in the endorsement without qualification of Agenda 21, which, as we have already observed, is unequivocally based on a policy of market globalisation.

The major weakness of the *Declaration* appears, variously, in paragraphs 18, 20, 22 and 36 where the authors make it contingent on the *Plan of Implementation*. In many ways, the latter uses more cautious turns of phrase than the former and, in some instances, substantially modifies the *Declaration*'s commitments. Nonetheless, both documents were agreed by the Summit and both are now incorporated into UN policy, even if, at moments, they seem to be saying slightly different things. We must now turn to the *Plan of Implementation*, a document of some 27,000 words which reaffirms the MDGs and, to some degree, extends them. Like all such instruments, it is written relentlessly in the passive mood and that, combined with its length, underlines both its aspirational form and its not infrequent vacuity. Mercifully, the UN has also published a summary, entitled *Key Outcomes of the Summit*, which is adequate for those who need only the gist of the *Plan* and which serves as a structured guide for the rest of us (see the UN's summaries of outcomes and commitments, Box 2.1 and 2.2).[9] It also lists ten categories of goals, differing slightly in order from that of the *Plan*:

- poverty eradication,
- water and sanitation,
- sustainable production and consumption,
- energy,
- chemicals,
- management of the natural resource base,
- corporate responsibility,
- health,
- sustainable development of small island states,
- sustainable development for Africa.

Plainly, several of these overlap and are intertwined, particularly in the cases of the first two, the fourth and the eighth, all of which are dealt with in the initial long section on eradicating poverty.

Box 2.1 Key Outcomes of the Summit

- The Summit reaffirmed sustainable development as a central element of the international agenda and gave new impetus to global action to fight poverty and protect the environment.

- The understanding of sustainable development was broadened and strengthened as a result of the Summit, particularly the important linkages between poverty, the environment and the use of natural resources.

- Governments agreed to and reaffirmed a wide range of concrete commitments and targets for action to achieve more effective implementation of sustainable development objectives.

- Energy and sanitation issues were critical elements of the negotiations and outcomes to a greater degree than in previous international meetings on sustainable development.

- Support for the establishment of a world solidarity fund for the eradication of poverty was a positive step forward.

- Africa and the New Partnership for Africa's Development (NEPAD) were identified for special attention and support by the international community to better focus efforts to address the development needs of Africa.

- The views of civil society were given prominence at the Summit in recognition of the key role of civil society in implementing the outcomes and in promoting partnership initiatives. Over 8,000 civil society participants attended the Summit, reinforced by parallel events which included major groups, such as, NGOs, women, indigenous people, youth, farmers, trade unions, business leaders, the scientific and technological community and local authorities as well as Chief Justices from various countries.

- The concept of partnerships between governments, business and civil society was given a large boost by the Summit and the *Plan of Implementation*. Over 220 partnerships (with $235 million in resources) were identified in advance of the Summit and around sixty partnerships were announced during the Summit by a variety of countries.

Source: www.johannesburgsummit.org, 2002

Following a brief preamble (part I), part II of the *Plan* is entitled 'Poverty Eradication' and starts with paragraph 6; 6a repeats the kernel of the MDGs: 'Halve, by the year 2015, the proportion of the world's people whose income is less than $1 a day and the proportion of people who suffer from hunger and, by the same date, to halve the proportion of people without access to safe drinking water.' The remaining sub-sections of paragraph 6 point to what has to be done

Box 2.2   Key Commitments Agreed in the Implementation Plan

Water and Sanitation

- Commitment to halve the proportion of people without access to sanitation by 2015; this matches the goal of halving the proportion of people without access to safe drinking water by 2015.

- The United States announced $970 million in investments over the next three years on water and sanitation projects.

- The European Union announced the 'Water for Life' initiative that seeks to engage partners to meet goals for water and sanitation, primarily in Africa and Central Asia. The Asia Development Bank provided a $5 million grant to UN Habitat and $500 million in fast-track credit for the Water for Asian Cities Programme.

- The UN has received twenty-one other water and sanitation initiatives with at least $20 million in extra resources.

Energy

- Commitment to increase access to modern energy services, to increase energy efficiency and to increase the use of renewable energy.

- To phase out, where appropriate, energy subsidies.

- To support the NEPAD objective of ensuring access to energy for at least 35 per cent of the African population within twenty years.

- The nine major electricity companies of the E7 signed a range of agreements with the UN to facilitate technical cooperation for sustainable energy projects in developing countries.

- The European Union announced a $700 million partnership initiative on energy and the United States announced that it would invest up to $43 million in 2003.

- The South African energy utility Eskom announced a partnership to extend modern energy services to neighbouring countries.

- The UN has received thirty-two partnership submissions for energy projects with at least $26 million in resources.

Health Commitments

- Commitment that by 2020, chemicals should be used and produced in ways that do not harm human health and the environment.

- To enhance cooperation to reduce air pollution.

- To improve developing countries' access to environmentally sound alternatives to ozone depleting chemicals by 2010.

Initiatives

- United States announced commitment to spend $2.3 billion through 2003 on health, some of which was earmarked earlier for the Global Fund.

- The UN has received sixteen partnership submissions for health projects with $3 million in resources.

Agriculture *Commitments*

- The Global Environment Facility (GEF) will consider inclusion of the Convention to Combat Desertification as a focal area for funding.
- In Africa, development of food security strategies by 2005.

Initiatives

- The United States will invest $90 million in 2003 for sustainable agriculture programmes.
- The UN has received seventeen partnership submissions with at least $2 million in additional resources.

Biodiversity and Ecosystem Management *Commitments*

- Commitment to reduce biodiversity loss by 2010.
- Commitment to reverse the current trend in natural resource degradation.
- Commitment to restore fisheries to their maximum sustainable yields by 2015.
- Commitment to establish a representative network of marine protected areas by 2012.
- Commitment to improve developing countries' access to environmentally sound alternatives to ozone depleting chemicals by 2010.
- Undertake initiatives by 2004 to implement the Global Programme of Action for the Protection of the Marine Environment from Land Based Sources of Pollution.

Initiatives

- The UN has received thirty-two partnership initiatives with $100 million in resources.
- The United States has announced $53 million for forests in 2002–5.

Cross-cutting Issues *Commitments*

- Recognition that opening up access to markets is a key to development for many countries.
- Support the phase-out of all forms of export subsidies.
- Commitment to establish a ten-year framework of programmes on sustainable consumption and production.
- Commitment to actively promote corporate responsibility and accountability.
- Commitments to develop and strengthen a range of activities to improve natural disaster preparedness and response.

Initiative

- Agreement to the replenishment of the GEF – $2.9 billion.

Source: www.johannesburgsummit.org, 2002.

to achieve the goal: a voluntary 'world solidarity fund' is to be created, which must not duplicate any 'existing United Nations Funds' and is to be raised, at least in part (for here the language is opaque), from the 'private sector and individual citizens' (6.b). National programmes for sustainable development and the allevia-tion of poverty are to be developed and, as contemporary jargon has it, 'owned' by those countries where the poor are to be found (6.c). Women are to have equality in 'decision-making ... economic oppor-tunity, land, credit, education and health-care services' and violence against them is to be eliminated (6.d). Indigenous people are to be accorded the same rights and are to have their cultures and forms of production respected (6.e). Basic health services are to be made available for everyone and, where necessary, medical technology and training must be offered to developing countries (6.f). Primary education must be provided for all boys and girls and everyone must have equal access to all other levels of education (6.g). Agricultural resources, 'sustainable agricultural techniques', techniques for natural resource management, including fisheries, and basic rural infrastruc-ture must be made available to, or provided for, 'people living in poverty, especially women and indigenous communities' (6.h, i, j). Food must be available, affordable and equitably and efficiently dis-tributed (6.k). Desertification and land and water degradation must be eliminated (6.l). Clean water and proper sanitation must be provided as part of a strategy to improve health and reduce mortality among infants and children (6.m and paragraph 7). Paragraph 7 elaborates the issue of clean water and sanitation, paragraph 8 covers energy and paragraph 9 the need for industrial development. Paragraph 10 proposes that 'a significant improvement in the lives of at least 100 million slum dwellers' should be achieved and reminds the world that this commitment was made in the UN's 'Cities Without Slums' initiative and takes from that document another target – the year 2020.

We remarked, in Chapter 1, that a third of the period in which these goals are to be achieved has elapsed already and that, so far, there is little sign of change. We may take what comfort we can from the fact that they were reaffirmed by representatives of the world's governments at this Summit in 2002, but we must also bear in mind the faint indications of the means by which they might be achieved. The 'world solidarity fund to eradicate poverty' is to be raised, if at all, by 'encouraging the role of the private sector and individual citizens relative to Governments' (6.b). In the clause calling for the building of 'basic rural infrastructure', there is a recommendation that the poor should be given 'access to markets [and] market information' (6.i); nothing is said about the meaning of the word 'market', but it is safe to assume that it includes, for example, that curiously exploitative system usually known as contract farming.[10] Agricultural technology and 'knowledge', including techniques for natural resource management, are to be 'transferred' and this is to be accomplished with the aid of 'multi-stakeholder approaches and public–private partnerships' (6.j). In these passages we hear distinct echoes of the World Trade Organisation's (WTO) agenda; those echoes get louder as the *Plan* turns towards two of the most crucial elements in any alleviation of poverty – water and energy.

Part III of the *Plan* is headed 'Changing Unsustainable Patterns of Consumption and Production' and, like part II, it is paved with good intentions. It opens with an interesting gloss on principle 7 of the *Rio Declaration on Environment and Development*, which we should revisit:

> States shall cooperate in a spirit of global partnership to conserve, protect and restore the health and integrity of the Earth's ecosystem. In view of the different contributions to global environmental degradation, States have common but differentiated responsibilities. The developed countries acknowledge the responsibility that they bear in the international pursuit of sustainable development in view of the pressures their societies place on the global environment and of the technologies and financial resources they command.[11]

The UN Secretary General's comment on 'differentiated responsibilities' makes clear that they refer, primarily, to the responsibilities of the states of the 'industrialized and developing countries in dealing with environmental issues' and that they are conditioned by the extent to which each state creates environmental problems: 'States whose societies impose a disproportionate pressure on the global environment and which command high levels of technological and financial resources bear a proportionally higher degree of responsibility in the international pursuit of sustainable development.'

The *Plan* seems to abandon the premise that some particularly powerful industrialised states have a larger debt to settle than smaller and poorer states. Part III of the *Plan* begins by invoking principle 7, but the 'differentiated responsibilities' become a matter of 'Governments, relevant international organizations, *the private sector* and all major groups ... [playing] an active role in changing unsustainable consumption and production patterns' (paragraph 13, emphasis added). Unsustainable consumption and production are the obvious causes of environmental difficulties, but, despite 'governments' opening the list of those who must change the pattern, in using this formula the *Plan* has moved away from attributing responsibility to states. Nonetheless, paragraph 14 provides a relatively unexceptionable list of desirable activities: common systems of measuring and analysing progress; measures to promote sustainable consumption and production – bearing in mind the degree of suitability of some such measures for poorer countries; improving 'products and services ... while reducing environmental and health impacts'; developing awareness; developing a voluntary, 'effective, transparent, verifiable, non-misleading and non-discriminatory' system of information; increasing eco-efficiency, supporting capacity building and transferring and exchanging technology, particularly to developing and transitional countries. Few would quarrel with such a list, but the incorporation of the private sector into the equation moves the issue even further from the values advanced by principle 7. The *Plan*, to a far greater degree than the *Rio Declaration*, thus inevitably fudges the issue of the private sector's motivation, which is rarely disinterested.

Paragraph 15 begins by calling for more investment in cleaner production throughout the world and for incentives to help enterprises, particularly in developing countries, to improve their environmental records. The incentives suggested, a little cautiously, are 'state financed loans, venture capital, technical assistance and training programmes for small and medium-sized companies', but the final clause of the sentence attaches the crippling condition that 'trade distorting measures inconsistent with WTO rules' must be avoided. Since these rules are little more than protectionist devices for large, particularly US, corporations and their investors, little movement on this front is likely. The issue is pursued a little further in paragraph 17, which proposes that states should: 'Enhance corporate environmental and social responsibility and accountability.' That enhancement should take the form of encouraging industry to do all sorts of worthwhile things (see sub-clauses a, b and c), like improving 'social and environmental performance through voluntary initiatives' which should include 'environmental management systems, codes of conduct, certification and public reporting on environmental and social issues', all this in the light of principle 11 of the *Rio Declaration*. Once again, that light has been dimmed in the process, since principle 11 begins by saying: 'States shall enact effective environment [*sic*] legislation. Environmental standards, management objectives and priorities should reflect the environmental and developmental context to which they apply.' Legislation normally imposes statutory obligations, it does not ask for volunteers.

Encouragement continues to be called for in paragraph 18, in this case it is for 'relevant authorities', by which the drafters seem to mean public bodies. Once again, there is a list of what these authorities should be encouraged to do: 'support ... the development of sustainable development strategies and programmes, including in decision-making on investment in infrastructure and business development' (18.a); 'promote the internalization of environmental costs and the use of economic instruments, taking into account the approach that the polluter should ... bear the costs of pollution' (18.b); 'promote public procurement policies that encourage development and diffusion of environmentally sound goods and services' (18.c). But there is a proviso: these things should be encouraged 'without distorting international trade and investment' (18.b), a caveat absent from the *Rio Declaration*. It is a lethal caveat, for an example we have only to think of the US's determination to overthrow, by means of WTO rules, the European ban on that wonder of chemical science and environmental disaster that the US calls 'beef'. In another direction, the provisions of the General Agreement on Trade in Services (GATS) will further severely limit the room for manoeuvre available either to governments or to appropriate authorities.

Paragraph 19 is concerned with policies for energy and, once more, we have the familiar litany: 'financial resources, technology transfer, capacity-building and the diffusion of environmentally sound technologies' (19.a); industrialised countries are urged to make greater use of renewable sources of energy and to help underdeveloped countries to do the same. At the same time, developing countries should be helped, with the assistance of the private sector, to 'reduce [the] flaring and venting of gas associated with crude oil production' (19.f). Energy efficiency, the technology for it and need to transfer that technology is also mentioned throughout the paragraph, as is the importance of cleaner forms of production. One of the more important sub-clauses recommends:

[T]hat international financial institutions and other agencies' policies support developing countries, as well as countries with economies in transition, in their own efforts to establish policy

and regulatory frameworks which create a level playing field
between the following: renewable energy, energy efficiency,
advanced energy technologies, including advanced and cleaner
fossil fuel technologies, and centralized, distributed and decentralized energy systems. (19.j)

Despite the uncertain punctuation, the meaning is clear, but it is just
a recommendation and unlikely to move many hearts in, for
example, the multiple boardrooms of ExxonMobil. At present the
world's energy industry is dominated by corporations using fossil
fuels in ways that pollute at almost every stage of production and
which are protected by a multitude of preferential deals, turnings of
blind eyes and the surrender of governmental authority (not the least
by the US administration), yet they are not included, in this sub-
paragraph, as possible players on a level field – no doubt this was
just a drafting oversight.

Most of the remainder of this paragraph is given over to counsels
of perfection: programmes, policies and frameworks for energy
efficiency are proposed; the development of clean technologies is to
be accelerated; renewable sources of energy are to be further explored
and developed; financial resources are to be made available to
developing countries, particularly to the least developed and to small
island states, such that they can meet their needs for 'reliable,
affordable, economically viable, socially acceptable and environmentally sound energy' (19.n); energy markets are to be made transparent,
stable and predictable and distortions in them reduced. What more
could be desired? This list is conditional only on not disturbing the
sensibilities of the WTO and the global financial institutions – a
condition attached to almost every recommendation in this
document and made explicit in 19.q: 'Take action, where appropriate, to phase out subsidies ... that inhibit sustainable development,
taking fully into account the ... different levels of development ...
and considering their adverse effect, particularly on developing
countries.' That final admonition must be understood in the light
of recent history which is littered with examples of pressure on
developing countries, designed to force *them* to abandon subsidies
and other protective measures originally put in place to combat the
worst ravages of poverty. Another, but unspoken and hugely
important condition attached to the *Plan*'s list is, of course, that the
oil industry should not take umbrage.

In paragraph 20 we find an anodyne set of proposals for transport which really add up to little more than a suggestion that it should be improved, particularly in developing countries. It is one of the few paragraphs not to insist that all progress must involve private capital, but, since it is short (it has only two sub-sections), little may be deduced from this absence. An even shorter paragraph follows (paragraph 21), dealing with waste, recycling and environmentally friendly materials. Apart from urging the promotion of 'waste prevention and minimization by encouraging production of reusable consumer goods and biodegradable products and developing the infrastructure required' (21.b), we need not be surprised that there is no mention of the inexorable and universal rise of ever more elaborate packaging.

These two brief paragraphs are followed by a significant passage dealing with the management of chemicals (paragraph 22). It relies heavily on a number of international instruments, the Rotterdam and Stockholm Conventions, the *Bahia Declaration* and the commitment advanced by Agenda 21. The *Rotterdam Convention on Prior Informed Consent Procedures for Certain Hazardous Chemicals and Pesticides in International Trade* (PIC) was held in 1998 and its purpose is explained in its first article:

> The objective of this Convention is to promote shared responsibility and cooperative efforts among Parties in the international trade of certain hazardous chemicals in order to protect human health and the environment from potential harm and to contribute to their environmentally sound use, by facilitating information exchange about their characteristics, by providing for a national decision-making process on their import and export and by disseminating these decisions to Parties.

It might be supposed that following the huge scandals of the toxic materials dump at Koko in Nigeria and the subsequent *Karin B* and *Deepsea Carrier* story, industry in the developed world would be more circumspect in the largely illegal and totally immoral dumping of such waste, but evidence suggests otherwise.[12] Early in the 1990s a Swiss company called Achair Partners together with an Italian partner called Progresso made a contract with an official of Ali Mahdi Muhammad's government which would have allowed them to build a facility in Somalia capable of storing 10 million tonnes of hazardous waste. UNEP discovered the arrangement and succeeded in preventing the contract from proceeding. Subsequently, it became clear that the Swiss and Italian enterprises were shadow companies acting as proxies for a number of larger corporations. Benin has a dismal record: between 1984 and 1986, the Soviet Union dumped significant quantities of radioactive waste in that country and, in 1988, Benin made an agreement with France in which it would accept French radioactive waste in return for economic assistance over the following thirty years. In the event only one shipment was made before public protest in France forced the cancellation of the agreement. Mexico was less fortunate: in 1981 a major US recycling company, called the RSR Corporation, engaged the services of a Californian company, Alco Pacific, to extract lead from old car batteries – the latter's plant for the purpose was in the Mexican *maqiladora*. The process not only retrieves the lead, but also creates an extremely hazardous waste in the form of lead sulphate: 'The 80,000 tons of lead sulfate produced at the facility were mounded in open fields near a local dairy. In addition, discarded battery acid was dumped on the plant grounds, causing an underground fire.'[13] Eventually, the RSR Corporation was heavily fined, in the US, for these activities, but the waste is still in Mexico. Eastern European countries, all of them desperately in need of foreign exchange, have also been the recipients of the industrialised world's hazardous detritus; toxic waste has been deposited in, among other countries, Romania, Bulgaria, Poland, the Baltics and Ukraine.

In the light of this cheerless history we should consider the enthusiasm shown by the industrialised world for the two conventions and the *Bahia Declaration*. The Rotterdam Convention was signed at the time by seventy-three states, but some others have signed subsequently. Article 26 of the Convention allows it to come into force only after fifty countries have ratified it; the figure so far is thirty-three. Below is a list of the countries which have ratified, together with a list of the countries in the industrialised world which, so far, have failed to move (Table 2.1).

The Stockholm Convention was signed by a total of 155 states including some who signed after the Convention had been agreed. It contains a provision that permits countries voluntarily to bring it into force for themselves, but for it to become an internationally binding instrument it, too, needs fifty ratifications. So far only twenty-seven states have ratified, but since the agreement was first reached in 2001, it is a little early to discover whether the target of fifty is achievable in a reasonable time. Again the list is divided into all ratifications and the industrialised defaulters (Table 2.2).

Table 2.1 Ratification of the Rotterdam Convention

Ratification: all states	Non-ratification: industrialised states only
Austria, Bulgaria, Cameroon, Canada, Czech Republic, El Salvador, Gambia, Germany, Guinea, Hungary, Italy, Jamaica, Jordan, Kyrgyzstan, Libya, Luxembourg, Malaysia, Mongolia, Netherlands, Nigeria, Norway, Oman, Panama, Samoa, Saudi Arabia, Senegal, Slovenia, South Africa, Suriname, Switzerland, Thailand, United Arab Emirates, Tanzania	Australia, Belgium, China, Denmark, European Union, European Community, Finland, France, Greece, Israel, Japan, New Zealand, Republic of Korea, Spain, Sweden, United Kingdom, United States of America

Source: list of signatures and ratifications, www.pic.int

Table 2.2 Ratification of the Stockholm Convention

Ratification: all states	Non-ratification: industrialised states only
Austria, Bulgaria, Canada, Czech Republic, Fiji, Finland, Germany, Guinea, Hungary, Iceland, Japan, Jordan, Kyrgyzstan, Lesotho, Liberia, Nauru, Netherlands, Norway, Rwanda, Samoa, Santa Lucia, Saudi Arabia, Slovakia, South Africa, Sweden, United Arab Emirates, Vietnam	Australia, Belgium, China, Denmark, European Union, France, Ireland, Israel, Italy, Luxembourg, Mexico, New Zealand, Republic of Korea, Russian Federation, Switzerland, United Kingdom, United States of America

Source: list of signatures and ratifications, www.pops.int

It can be seen from these comparative tables that few of the most powerful industrialised states have ratified either convention, which effectively reduces them to little more than admonitions.

The *Bahia Declaration* (2000) was made by the participants in the Intergovernmental Forum on Chemical Safety (IFCS), and is essentially a list of the steps necessary to secure the 'sound management of chemicals in sustainable development and the protection of human health and the environment'. International acceptance of these steps, as opposed to any regulation by individual states, depends on the coming into force of the Rotterdam and Stockholm Conventions; in the case of the former, the IFCS expected it to be in force in 2003, and the latter in 2004. In the light of the rate of ratification and, even more importantly, of US unilateralism, these are heroic expectations. We may get some clue to the leanings of the US's attitude from the position adopted by the American Enterprise Institute for Public Policy Research. This unlovely and right-wing organisation, treated by the Bush administration as a favoured think-tank, is largely the public policy finger of the corporate world. Its trustees include senior officials from, among several others, ExxonMobil, Geneva Steel Holdings, the Dow Chemical Company and Motorola. It has recently published a series of attacks on virtually all forms of environmental protection, including protection from some dangerous chemicals, and its environmental publications are of the school that approves of regulation so long as it does not interfere with the operations of the market. It need not surprise us that Bjørn Lomborg is its favourite 'environmentalist'.[14]

Part IV of the *Plan* deals with '[p]rotecting and managing the natural resource base of economic and social development' and gives a list of actions necessary for that protection and management. Most of them are obvious enough and are usually general in scope. The first deals with the issue of safe water and adds a specific demand, derived from the MDGs, that the proportion of people without safe water should be halved by 2015. This is followed by the unquestionably correct, but nonetheless familiar list: technology to be transferred and capacity building supported; information to be available to all; water pollution prevention to be intensified and the sustainable use of water to be promoted (paragraph 24). Paragraph 25 proposes the development of 'integrated water resources management and water efficiency plans by 2005' which would include 'national/regional strategies, plans and programmes with regard to integrated river basin, watershed and groundwater management' (25.a). The final sub-clause to this paragraph brings us back to the unremittingly market-oriented ideology of the governments of the industrialised states:

Facilitate the establishment of public–private partnerships and other forms of partnership that give priority to the needs of the poor, within stable and transparent national regulatory frameworks provided by Governments, while respecting local conditions, involving all concerned stakeholders, and monitoring the performance and improving accountability of public institutions and private companies.

Paragraphs 26 and 27 deal with assessments of the quality and quantity of water available to developing countries and with the management and 'scientific understanding' of it. The final paragraph concerned with freshwater calls for international and intergovernmental bodies to work with the UN on the question (paragraph 28).

Part IV of the *Plan* then turns to '[o]ceans, seas, islands and coastal areas'; the opening paragraph 29 makes the usual plea for coordinated and integrated resource management and suggests that the 'ecosystem approach' (this refers to the Declaration made, in the autumn of 2001, by the Reykjavik Conference on Responsible Fisheries in the Marine Ecosystem) should be applied by the year 2010. This is followed, in the next paragraph, by a far more contentious question – that of the attempt to 'achieve sustainable fisheries' (paragraph 30). Its first three sub-clauses deal with stock levels and management agreements, but 30.d is the point at which matters become more contentious, since it demands the implementation of two Food and Agricultural Organisation of the UN (FAO) plans of action. The first calls for the international management of fishing capacity, the *Plan* sets 2005 for its operation; the second, to be in place by 2004, is to 'prevent, deter and eliminate illegal, unreported and unregulated fishing'. These two demands are followed by another, for the establishment of 'effective monitoring, reporting and enforcement, and control of fishing vessels, including by flag states ... to prevent, deter and eliminate illegal, unreported and unregulated fishing'. The remainder of the paragraph deals with the means by which these demands might be met. This is one of the few occasions in which the *Plan* directly challenges an industry and proposes action by governments and by intergovernmental bodies, rather than by some dubious mix of state and corporations. Nonetheless, it is compelled to make a forlorn plea for the implementation of the Jakarta Mandate on the Conservation and Sustainable Use of Marine and Coastal Biological Diversity – a mandate designed to move towards action on the CBD which, in turn, was agreed in Rio de Janeiro in December of 1993. Its final sub-clause is a plea for the implementation of yet another neglected international instrument, the Ramsar Convention on Wetlands of International Importance which was agreed as long ago as 1971 (31.e).

The *Plan* next turns its attention, in paragraphs 32 and 33, to marine environmental protection. These are cheerless paragraphs, since they are devoted to unimplemented UN measures: the Global Programme of Action for the Protection of the Marine Environment from Land-Based Activities (Washington, 1995) and the attempt, through the Montreal Declaration, to push governments into implementation (Montreal, 2001). The International Marine Organisation's failure to finalise its International Convention on the Control and Management of Ship's Ballast Water and Sediments is also mentioned. Many of the apparently dead letters referred to in all six marine paragraphs (paragraph 34 is to do with scientific understanding, technology, reporting and capacity) were accepted as international legal instruments, often with official enthusiasm, by the majority of the world's governments. Given the extent of the fishing industry's objections to careful management of marine resources, we are at least left with the suspicion that such instruments tend not to survive interventions by the private sector.

Paragraph 35 is a perfunctory programme for dealing with natural hazards, but, since towards the end it brings in the need for predicting 'extreme weather events, especially El Niño/La Niña', it leads into the section on climate change caused by global warming (paragraphs 36–7). It amounts simply to a mild reaffirmation of the importance of the UNFCCC and of the Kyoto Protocol as means of achieving the 'ultimate objective of stabilization of greenhouse gas concentrations in the atmosphere at a level that would prevent dangerous anthropogenic interference with the climate system'. That the Protocol is inadequate is rarely disputed, but it is the only agreement we have. By October 2002 ninety-six countries had either ratified or acceded to it; the laggards in the industrialised world are Australia, Canada, Israel, New Zealand, Republic of Korea, Russian Federation, Switzerland and the US – the last of which has, notoriously, retracted its signature. Apart from urging the acceptance of the 'commitments and obligations' imposed by the UNFCCC, it simply calls for 'systematic observation' and monitoring – the section has nothing else to say about what is at least an issue of grave international public concern.

Paragraph 37 is a brief excursion into the problems of air pollution and precedes a slightly more substantive paragraph 38 on agriculture. The objective of halving the number of people suffering from hunger by 2015 appears once more, and once more we must consider whether, or not, it is simply a mantra. Much of the remainder of the paragraph is sound common sense: integrated land management, the sustainable use of water, support for productive indigenous forms of farming, the prevention of environmental degradation whether from silting or increased salinity, and the construction of policies and introduction of laws that will guarantee rights in land occupancy and the use of water (38.a–i). The point at which the paragraph is in danger of becoming oxymoronic comes in sub-clauses 38.j–k: the first of these urges the reversal of the decline in public-sector investment in sustainable agriculture, but the second comes close to arguing for the opposite. Sub-clause 38.l calls for the use of 'market-based incentives for agricultural enterprises and farmers to monitor and manage water use and quality'; but from, for example, the agri-culturally destructive practices that marked the beginning of the green revolution to the adoption of intensive oasis farming and the rise of contract farming, the world is littered with the catastrophic effects of using 'market-based incentives'. The last of these three sub-clauses calls for greater access to markets, and the creation of new markets for the makers of 'value-added agricultural products'. Yet again, the world's plenipotentiaries have made what sounds like a sensible case only to destroy it by leaving a lethal ambiguity about one of its main terms – in this case 'market' which, in its differing uses, remains totally undefined. There are further sub-clauses (38.m–r), of which the only one of note is 38.q. It '[i]nvite[s] countries that have not done so to ratify the International Treaty on Plant Genetic Resources for Food and Agriculture'; the Treaty was agreed in November of 2001 and at the time of writing only eight countries had ratified it. Given the leisurely way in which most states approach UN agreements, this is, perhaps, hardly surprising, but it may be worth noting that of the eight ratifying countries only Canada is obviously among the wealthy industrialised states.[15]

Desertification and mountain ecosystems occupy paragraphs 39 and 40 and are uncontentious; so, too, is paragraph 41 which deals with sustainable tourism. But paragraph 42, one of the longest in the *Plan*, is another matter, since it deals with biodiversity. The CBD was agreed in June 1992 and, as we remarked in Chapter 1, is a heavily compromised instrument, but, even so, the US has refused to ratify it. We might note that the US is in impressive company, of the 168 states which signed the Convention only six have not ratified, apart from the US the others are: Andorra, Brunei, The Holy

See (Vatican), Iraq and Thailand. Early in 2000, in the course of two meetings, one in Cartagena, Bolivia and the other in Montreal, a protocol to the CBD was agreed. Known as the Cartagena Protocol, its purpose is to provide safeguards in matters to do with GMOs. So far 103 states have signed, but only thirty-six have ratified it. Paragraph 42 invokes the Bonn Guidelines to the CBD drawn up by an *ad hoc* committee established by the parties to the Convention which met in Bonn in October 2001.

The problems have frequently been rehearsed: biodiversity is rapidly being reduced by unsustainable development, logging, tourism and a host of other onslaughts. Destruction is likely to have unpredictable effects on a multitude of ecosystems and, in its own way, is as threatening as global warming caused by anthropogenic greenhouse gasses, which, in turn, will have a profound effect on ecosystems. It has also long been recognised that biologically diverse ecosystems are sources of organisms of untold value to medicine, science and industry. The issues raised by this recognition are also well-aired – the sustainable use to which they are put by indigenous people who live in, and are indeed part of, the richest ecosystems, is under attack not just from incidental destruction, but also from the depredations of TNCs anxious to control these valuable resources. Attempts to patent organisms are frequent. GMOs, often made possible by research into natural elements, may themselves be a further threat, not only to human health, but also to the continued existence of many unmodified organisms. Despite these dangers, there is nothing inherently wrong with the exploration and use of biological diversity, all that is necessary is the regulation of the explorers and users such that they not only do not kill the goose, but also that they do not steal the golden egg – particularly from its indigenous owners. Nevertheless, in the interests of the operation of a completely free market, that regulation has been stoutly resisted, particularly by the international drug companies. Paragraph 42 does not seriously engage with these matters and confines itself to a weak plea for equity.

Forests and trees are dealt with even less convincingly in paragraph 43, which begins by pointing out what trees do for the world's ecosystems, including humanity, and goes on to urge a number of steps for the protection and the sustainable exploitation of forests and trees (the distinction matters since, for example, commercially planted and harvested trees are included). All the proposals are fatally weakened by the common problem: they depend on the cooperation of the private sector. The policy document of the Collaborative

Partnership on Forests refers to the need to co-opt it; the UN Forum of Forests has among the major groups participating in it one described as 'Business and Industry'; the Intergovernmental Panel on Forests relies on Chapter 11 of Agenda 21 (on forests) which refers constantly to the need to recruit the private sector – all three bodies are central to the proposals in paragraph 43.[16] No one doubts that the wholesale destruction of forests can only be stopped if the private sector collaborates, but, at present, inviting it to join the international policy-making bodies is like inviting the fox into the chicken-coop. Logging is, quite possibly, not the greatest destroyer of forests – that accolade goes to agricultural expansion – but it is probably the most brutal.[17] For an example of a combination of the two, we have only to think of the private sector's activities in Borneo where some of the world's largest tropical forests are to be found. Loggers and the rubber and palm oil planters have combined to destroy not only huge areas of those forests (12 per cent in the 1980s alone), but, with the collaboration of the Indonesian army, have killed many thousands of the indigenous people and displaced and marginalised very many more.[18] No attempt seems to have been made by the WSSD to address this kind fundamental difficulty in engaging with the private sector.

The final paragraph in part IV of the *Plan* is devoted to mining and makes a few anodyne suggestions about its 'environmental, economic, health and social impacts' (44.a) and the 'participation of stakeholders, including local and indigenous communities and women, to play an active role in ... mining development' (44.b), but does not address any of the major problems. Quite aside from the appalling conditions under which so many miners must continue to work, no mention is made of the conflicts surrounding the extraction of resources. Diamond wars in Sierra Leone, the Democratic Republic of Congo and Angola are well-known, but there are many others that do not attract media attention. Among them is the combined operation of Freeport-McMoRan Copper and Gold Inc. and the Indonesian army, which seized the land of the Amungme and Kamoro people to create the world's largest open-cast gold mine.[19] Working conditions are appalling and the exploitation of the environment as, among other things, a dump for heavily polluting tailings, is on a massive scale. Most importantly, the Indonesian military, with substantial financial assistance from the mining company, has waged an intermittent war on the opposition to these depredations, killing thousands in the process. This might, we suppose, be an example of the public–private partnerships from which the drafters of the *Plan* are expecting salvation.

Part V of the *Plan* is headed 'Sustainable Development in a Globalizing World' and is refreshingly free of content. It begins by announcing that globalisation offers 'opportunities and challenges for sustainable development' (paragraph 45); into the first of these categories it puts an impressive list of abstractions: 'new opportunities ... [for] trade, investment and capital flows and advances in technology, including information technology, for the growth of the world economy, development and the improvement of living standards'. As to the last, it does not say for whom. Among the challenges it includes 'serious financial crises, insecurity, poverty, exclusion and inequality within and among societies'. Since we are living with these 'challenges', we might have hoped that the *Plan* would tell us how globalisers intend to meet them, but that is plainly regarded as work for another day. Instead it suggests promoting multilateral trading and financial systems that will benefit all those states in pursuit of sustainable development (on the face of it, the last condition would seem severely to limit such systems – 45.a). For reasons not always apparent, the drafters lapsed, from time to time, into Latin numbering: paragraph 45.*quinquies* makes obvious the difficulties in the way of multilateral trading as an aid to development.

> Urgent action at all levels [is needed] to ... [s]trengthen regional trade and cooperation agreements, consistent with the multilateral trading system, among developed and developing countries and countries with economies in transition, as well as among [sic] developing countries, with the support of international finance institutions and regional development banks, as appropriate, with a view to achieving the objectives of sustainable development.

But the existing regional agreements are improbable aids to development, not the least since they were made under, or modified by, the Marrakesh Agreement of 1994 which set up the WTO. The North American Free Trade Association's (NAFTA) disastrous effects, not only in the creation of the *maqiladora* industries and the destruction of the border environment, but also in forcing millions of small farmers off the land, is a case in point.[20] We may see another in the continuing history of the Multi-Fibre Arrangement (MFA) and its associated Agreement on Textiles and Clothes (ATC). The former permitted the industrialised countries temporarily to erect tariff barriers to protect their own clothing and textile industries. These were supposed to be reduced gradually as the MFA drew to an end in 2005, but these reductions have been minimal. Bangladesh, although subject to several restrictions, was the only developing country to be given some special exemptions from tariff barriers by the MFA. During the Uruguay Round of GATT (General Agreement on Tariffs and Trade) negotiations the ATC was reached, which allowed industrialised states actually to increase trade barriers and successfully defeated even the miserly exemptions given to Bangladesh. The ATC is also to end in 2005 when the World Trade Agreement comes into force, but there is no reason to suppose that the industrialised countries will not produce a new version of it.[21]

Part VI follows and it incorporates another of the MDGs, the reduction, 'by the year 2015, [of] mortality rates for infants and children under five by two thirds, and maternal mortality rates by three quarters, of the prevailing rate in 2000' (47.f). We must observe, yet again, that progress in this matter is indiscernible, though that could be partly because figures since 2000 are not yet available. We should also bear in mind that since, in the cases of infant and under-five mortality in the least developed countries, it took thirty years, from 1970 to 2000, to reduce the rates by approximately one third, we cannot afford to be too be optimistic.[22] Most of the sub-clauses in this section (paragraphs 46–50), like those in the other sections, are sound common sense and urge action with which few would quarrel, but nowhere in it is there any reference to the interests and influence of the drug corporations. Despite the recent battles over drugs for poor people afflicted by HIV/AIDS, the only direct references to private finance are in 47.l, 48.d and 49.a. The first of these calls for action on safe water, sanitation and waste disposal 'through public–private multisector partnerships'; the second suggests that 'private financial resources for research and development on diseases of the poor' should be encouraged; the third asks for 'regional and national programmes' to be strengthened 'including through public–private partnerships.' It is difficult to see how a *Plan* could avoid any consideration of one of the most central issues, health care, particularly for the poor, in quite such a cavalier fashion.

Small island developing states, known as SIDS, are recognised by the UN as 'a special case both for environment and development'. The Alliance of Small Island States has, at present, forty-three members, though it is steadily recruiting more.[23] It may be due to its influence that '[s]ustainable development of small island developing states' is the subject of part VII (paragraphs 52–5). They are especially affected by the actions of far larger states and, therefore, need specific help in 'managing in a sustainable manner their coastal areas and exclusive economic zones and the continental shelf' (52.c). Most of the proposals for development are in line with those offered throughout the *Plan*, but one of them seems curiously understated: 52.j proposes that SIDS be assisted 'in mobilizing adequate resources and partnerships for their adaptation needs relating to the adverse effects of climate change, sea level rise and climate variability'. Since, if seas continue to rise, Tuvalu and large parts of Vanuatu are likely to disappear altogether, their chances of adapting seem slender, but many more, not only in the Pacific, will suffer coastal erosion to an extent that will seriously undermine their economic survival.

Parts VIII and VIII.*bis* deal with sustainable development by region; VIII is devoted to Africa; VIII.*bis* covers Latin America and the Caribbean, Asia and the Pacific, West Asia and the Economic Commission for Europe. The first begins with a generalised list of the problems facing African states, but without distinguishing them, or setting them in any historical or political context. It goes on to welcome the creation of NEPAD which, to use its own description, 'is a programme of the African Union designed to meet its development objectives. The highest authority in the NEPAD implementation process is the Heads of State and Government Summit of the recently launched African Union, formerly known as the OAU [Organisation of African Unity].'[24] Following that welcome comes the usual list of measures and conditions understood to be necessary for development: economic growth; the development of technology; providing education for all without gender distinction; increased productivity in industry; financial and technical support; assistance in the development and distribution of energy in line with NEPAD's objectives; help with the effects of climate change; assistance with reforestation and the problems of desertification; establishing health services for everyone and, in particular, dealing with HIV/AIDS, malaria and tuberculosis and the control of ebola; dealing with the displacement of people following conflict and natural hazards; integrating water resources and ensuring potable water, education in hygiene and better sanitation; improving water management; increasing agricultural and livestock production; making land tenure more equitable; managing chemicals; bridging the 'digital divide'; promoting eco-tourism and conserving African biodiversity (paragraphs 56–65).

The means by which this elaborate programme is to be realised are found in paragraph 61:

> (c) Improve market access for goods, including goods originating from African countries, in particular least developed countries, within the framework of the Doha Ministerial Declaration, without prejudging the outcome of the WTO negotiations and also within the framework of preferential agreements;
> (d) Provide support for African countries to improve regional trade and economic integration between African countries. Attract and increase investment in regional market infrastructure.

It may be otiose to remark that these means have not been entirely free of guilt in causing many of the problems now besetting that continent and that foreign direct investment (FDI) in Africa is astonishingly low (Table 2.3). Since, for example, the European cattle industry and the US cereal producers regard Sub-Saharan Africa as a convenient dumping ground for their heavily subsidised produce and since a host of other corporations see the region as a useful source of cheap minerals, including fossil fuels, this situation is unlikely to change very quickly.

Table 2.3   Distribution of FDI – 1998 (world total US$619,258 million)

National income category	Total US$	Proportions* (%)
Low income	10,674	1.7
Middle income	160,267	26.0
High income	448,316	72.5
Region	*Total*	*Proportions*
East Asia and Pacific	64,162	10.4
Europe and Central Asia	24,350	3.9
Latin America and Caribbean	69,323	11.2
Middle East and North Africa	5,054	0.8
South Asia	3,659	0.6
Sub-Saharan Africa	4,364	0.7

* Discrepancies due to rounding.

Source: World Bank, 2000/2001, Development Indicators (table 21).

The three other regions are dealt with, very briskly, in part VIII.*bis*, paragraphs 67–74, which are all quite short and contain very little more than the usual clichés. We turn instead to the final part of the

Plan entitled 'Means of implementation'. In many ways this section is a summary of everything that has gone before; but while it identifies the institutions and processes necessary for the reduction of poverty, the protection of the environment, the worldwide extension of education, health care, the banishment of discrimination of all kinds, but particularly the subjugation of women, it does no more than exhort states and their institutions to start on this immense programme. Concern for the truth should have prompted the drafters to replace the word 'means' with some more accurate word like 'instruments', since 'means' must have to do with persuading wealthy states to implement the agreements into which they have already entered. It is significant that the *Plan*, twenty years after the target was first set, is still calling for the developed countries to increase their overseas development aid (ODA) budgets to 0.7 per cent of GNP (79.a), yet commitment to the social objectives of the WSSD would probably call for an even greater proportion.

Paragraphs 75–9 summarise preceding commitments: Agenda 21, the Millennium Declaration, the Third United Nations Conference on the Least Developed Countries (Brussels, May 2001) and the Global Conference on the Sustainable Development of Small Island Developing States (Barbados, April 1994), the International Conference on Financing for Development (Monterrey, March 2002) and the Fourth WTO Ministerial Conference (Qatar, November 2001). The next major issue appears in paragraph 83 which deals with 'unsustainable debt burden[s]'; it offers nothing new and cites paragraphs 47–51 of the outcome of the Monterrey Conference, known as the Monterrey Consensus. Among other things, this passage asserts that responsibility for debt and its management is divided more or less evenly between creditors, debtors and ODA donors, a proposition which, given the history of the phenomenon, the present authors find surprising. Apart from urging the implementation of the Heavily Indebted Poor Countries initiative and calling for further conferences, it suggests that some progress might be made by adopting measures like the neo-colonialist 'debt-for-sustainable-development swaps' (83.e).

The *Plan* next deals with trade; it recommends the dismantling of the various impediments which prevent poorer countries from exporting to the developed world, but modifies that reasonable request by urging the active pursuit of 'the WTO work programme to address the trade-related issues ... affecting the fuller integration of small, vulnerable economies into the multilateral trading system' (paragraph 88). It refers to 'the benefits for developing countries' to be got from 'public–private partnerships' and urges that they should be helped to develop the technology necessary to becoming modern trading nations (paragraphs 89–93). This passage is followed by a number of worthy recommendations about the transfer of technology and the building of scientific capacity, much of it through the inevitable public–private partnerships (paragraphs 94–108.*bis*). Paragraphs 84–98 are the closest we get to what the Summit means by 'development'. It will surprise no one that it consists of creating the circumstances in which every state has liberalised its economy and is competitively engaged in the free market. The present authors will comment more fully on this proposition in the final chapter of this book.

Education comes next, but adds nothing to what is said in the main body of the text (paragraphs 109–17). Capacity building, environmental information, indicators and observation are all called for in paragraphs 119.*ter*–119.*octies*; so, too, is an increase in 'efforts to prevent and mitigate the impacts of natural disasters' (119.*noviens*).

Part X, the final section, deals with the institutions necessary for sustainable development, but has little to say about them. It covers the roles of the General Assembly, the Economic and Social Council, the Commission on Sustainable Development and international institutions. The latter are the relevant UN institutions (UNEP, UN-Habitat, UNDP, United Nations Conference on Trade and Development) and the Bretton Woods group (principally the World Bank, the IMF and the WTO).

In the final part of their summary document, *Key Outcomes of the Summit*, under the cross-heading of 'Key Initiatives and Announcements from the Johannesburg Summit', the drafters list five main arenas for action: water, energy, health, agriculture, and biodiversity and ecosystem management. All five were adopted prior to the WSSD as the basis for its agenda; Kofi Annan, the Secretary General, set up a body, known as the WEHAB (water and sanitation, energy, health, agriculture, biodiversity) group, whose job was to propose frameworks for each of these sectors which would serve as discussion papers. Since the final *Plan* had only the sketchiest resemblance to any of these frameworks, we have used them only in one sector, health, where we make rough comparisons between the framework and the outcome. Of the five sectors, the first two, water and energy, are the most important in any assessment of future development and we shall devote the following two chapters to them.

3   Cold Water

In the September–October 2001 issue of the US journal *Foreign Policy*, Sandra Postel and Aaron Wolf published an article entitled 'Dehydrating Conflict', in which they estimated that fifty-one states situated on seventeen river basins are at risk of major conflict over water – of these states eight are in Africa and six in Asia. One obvious case is the dispute between Israel and Syria, since the former's continued occupation of the Golan Heights has more to do with its control of the River Jordan than with any fear of Syria's capacity to wage war. Postel and Wolf also point out that 'since 1950, the renewable supply per person has fallen 58 percent as world population has swelled from 2.5 billion to 6 billion'. 'Water stress' has become a commonplace expression as well as a widespread phenomenon, of which the lack of clean water, addressed by the WSSD, is a substantial part. It is defined as a situation in which people are consuming more than 10 per cent of renewable freshwater resources.[1]

Most of our planet is covered in water (an estimated 1,386,000,000 km^3): 96.54 per cent of it is found in oceans and seas, and almost another 1 per cent is either saline or brackish groundwater or is in saltwater lakes. About 2.5 per cent is freshwater, most of which, almost 70 per cent, lies in glaciers, permanent snow or permafrost. We depend on a massive global circulatory system for survival. An enormous quantity of water evaporates from the seas together with a smaller amount from land surfaces; most of it, when it is precipitated, falls again on the seas, but about 20 per cent, or 119,000 km^3, falls on the land.[2] That it does so selectively is obvious and, within the ambit of recorded human history, has always done so. Three things have changed: the world's population has increased dramatically; a third of it lives in areas suffering from water stress; climate change, whether or not as a result of human activity, has brought alarmingly increased drought to many arid or semi-arid regions.[3] Paradoxically, it has also produced periodic large-scale floods in the same regions which have wreaked even more havoc in an environment seriously undermined by drought. Sudan is an example. Since that third of the world's people consuming water unsustainably encompasses a substantial number of those to whom the WSSD has promised clean water and improved sanitation, it is clear that, in addition to massive investment, water policies and management are of the first importance.

West Asia, the region with the smallest population consuming water in excess of renewable resources, is also the region under the greatest stress, but it will serve as an example for all.[4] Like much of the rest of the world, the region's need for more water is partly generated by substantial increases in population – from 37.3 million in 1972 to 97.7 million in 2000. Many of the states in the region have adopted policies of agricultural self-sufficiency, some are exporters of fruit and vegetables to the supermarkets of the developed world – for both purposes agriculture uses 82 per cent of the available water. Domestic water demand accounts for only 10 per cent of consumption and industry the rest. Not only is irrigation for agriculture frequently inefficient, it also pollutes substantial reserves of water in its careless use of agrochemicals – industrial effluents also cause extensive damage. Because the overuse of water leads to the mining of groundwater reserves, salination is an increasing problem. The consequences, particularly for the poor, are considerable: the quality of water declines, waterborne diseases increase and, in several states, water is rationed by means of cutting off supplies in towns and cities, either for several days in the week or for several hours in the day.[5]

Water supplies and management are a major problem for West Asia, but the region is by no means unique. Throughout the world, a total of approximately 2.4 billion people live in areas with severe water stress (Table 3.1). Living with water stress is clearly not synonymous with poverty; for example, many people, though not all, who live in parts of Europe and North America which have severe water shortages do have at least a moderately reasonable standard of living, access to clean drinking water and adequate sanitation despite water shortages. But even if the numbers from those two regions are deducted from the total, over 2 billion people living with water stress, again not all of them poor, live in regions in which most countries have large impoverished populations; it is probable, therefore, that a very high proportion of them becomes the object of the Millennium Development Goal. There are, of course, many regions where there is no particular shortage of water, even if it is poorly managed, but which also suffer from intense poverty and are objects of those goals – large parts of West Africa and Latin America are instances.

These circumstances matter because they highlight that confusion in much of the thinking about poverty evinced in setting the MDGs

Table 3.1   Population Figures for Regions Suffering from Severe Water Stress

Region	Millions
Asia and the Pacific	1,693
Europe	239
Africa	172
North America	124
Latin America and Caribbean	112
West Asia	74
Total	2,414

Source: constructed from figures in UNEP, 2002.

and to which we have already referred. One goal is to halve the number of those living in poverty by 2015; poverty, in this proposition, is defined as living on less than pppU\$1.00 per day. The number of the acutely poor is somewhere between 1.2 billion, a figure emanating from the World Bank, and 1.7 billion suggested by the UNDP.[6] But living on less than pppUS\$1.00 per day is usually a measure not simply of poverty, but of absolute destitution. 'Usually', because even the destitute sometimes have at least minimal networks of support, though these rarely survive for long.[7] There are other measures: many countries, but not all, have their own national poverty lines which, even in the highly developed world, are rarely generous. Statistics are available for only 59 of the 112 countries listed by UNDP as 'developing', but between them they account for somewhat over a further 1 billion people living below levels that their own states would regard as adequate.[8] Any sane account of poverty must include them. The goal of halving the number of those living in poverty refers only to the completely destitute and whatever figure is put on the size of that population, it is plainly smaller than the figure indicated by our brief account of water difficulties. Since it is probable that those without access to clean water and adequate sanitation constitute a larger population than the absolutely poor and that they are geographically even more widely dispersed, the target of reducing their number by half (that arbitrary, but somehow thaumaturgic, proportion) becomes an even more heroic proposition.

In *Bending the Curve*, the Global Scenario Group offers a bleaker prospect: if the world proceeds on its present course, that is the refusal, in the interests of a free market ideology, to address environmental problems seriously, then, by 2050, the proportion of the world's population living 'in areas experiencing some form of water stress' will rise to 50 per cent.[9] The process has already become a vicious circle in which the consumption of non-renewable water reserves and exploration for new reserves causes yet greater environmental damage which, in turn, affects water reserves and supply. We have already seen that the greatest demands on supplies are made by agriculture, yet agricultural development is one of the motors offered for development. Development in the sector is largely interpreted, by the industrialised world, as a greater movement towards intensive farming which, despite genetic modification to produce more drought resistant crops, is a massive user of water, but, by definition, it is unable to make use of the ancient, community-oriented techniques of water conservation.

So long as the current market model for development holds sway, or remains unmodified, there is an irresoluble contradiction between the two MDGs under discussion, at least in those countries suffering from water stress. Yet circumstance, in the form of massive humanitarian crises and the consequent instability, may compel that modification and some policies, which do not upset market priorities, may be adopted. In such a case the Global Scenario Group points to ways in which the contradiction might be resolved. The Group's contention is that if the goals set out in Table 1.2 are achieved, then water demand and supply can be balanced, but the route to this will be through policies established, and measures taken, by each individual country. Policies and measures will vary slightly from country to country, depending on each situation and the degree of severity of the problem. They take two forms: technological solutions and substantial reforms in current practice.

The main technological solutions are desalination and the treatment and recovery of waste water, but, as the Group points out, these are expensive processes and of limited use; for example, at present West Asian states get only 1 per cent of their supplies by these means. They are also of more use to littoral states; Kuwait meets 50 per cent of its needs by using this technology. Nonetheless, the Group suggests that, for the whole region, this could rise to a more substantial proportion (6 per cent) by 2050. Reforms in current agricultural practice are relatively simple, depending on the geology of the terrain, while systems of irrigation can be changed such that they dramatically lower water demand; examples offered in *Bending the Curve* are changing from spray to 'trickle and drip' methods, or covering open canals to reduce evaporation and sub-irrigation.[10]

Domestic consumption could painlessly be reduced by making more efficient appliances available, but it is probable that these would only be accessible to the more affluent. It is possible to set standards for water conservation in industry, combining them with substantial increases in the prices for supply – Israel, despite its determination also to sequester as much of the renewable resources of the region as it can, is offered as an example of success in using these instruments.

It is, perhaps, worth pointing out that although Israel has reduced the use of water in industry, its massive use of water in fulfilling its ambition to 'make the desert bloom' has led to serious problems. In the *Jordan Times*, Dr Ahmad Y. Majdoubeh of the University of Jordan quoted a remark made to Reuters by Yossi Bar-On, deputy director of infrastructure for Israel's Environment Ministry: 'All three of Israel's main water resources – the Sea of Galilee, a coastal aquifer and a West Bank mountain aquifer shared with the Palestinians – are dangerously depleted.'[11] That word 'shared' should be treated with caution since Israel's share amounts to 83 per cent of what is extracted; a similar situation exists in Gaza where 'Israel controls 35 per cent of the water supply' and the effect of drilling deep wells to support Israeli settlements in the region has been to salinate Palestinian wells.[12]

Israel's water difficulties and the solutions it is adopting depend not only on technological and policy reforms, but also on military conquest – a route which, fortunately, is open only to a minority of the other states undergoing water stress. Israel is also a European–US implant in the region and is a powerful mixed economy; its robust state institutions are capable of the sort of regulation necessary for dealing with a problem as fundamental as severely limited renewable supplies of water. The same cannot be said of many of the states whose inhabitants are without clean water and safe sanitation, particularly the nascent state of Palestine; the history of developing countries since decolonisation is littered with instances of new governments with excellent intentions falling into a mire of corruption and oligarchy – frequently a consequence of meddling by the industrialised world. There are many examples of change, but new, reforming governments have inherited fatally weakened economies, huge debt burdens and inadequate skills for governance. In the light of that generally dismal picture we must look a little more carefully at what the *Plan of Implementation* suggests for reducing the huge numbers without good water and sanitation.

Before we do so, we should turn briefly to another text, which was superseded by the *Plan*. It was produced by the WEHAB working party and makes the following observation:

> Water is not only the most basic of needs but also at the center of sustainable development and essential for poverty eradication. Water is intimately linked to health, agriculture, energy and bio-diversity. Without progress on water, reaching other MDGs will be difficult if not impossible. Despite this, there is a low priority assigned to water by countries as evidenced by the decrease of ODA for this sector, by the reduction of investments by International Financial Institutions, by the low priority in national budgets, and by the absence of water as a central feature in major regional programmes.[13]

This should be kept in mind, since, in the *Plan*, the last sentence was considerably softened to: 'Provide access to potable domestic water, hygiene education and improved sanitation and waste management at the household level through initiatives to encourage public and private investment in water supply and sanitation that give priority to the needs of the poor.' Whose susceptibilities were ruffled sufficiently for the criticism to be removed, is not clear to the present authors.

Poverty eradication is the first item in the *Plan*'s agenda and it links the reduction by half of those living on less than pppUS$1.00 a day with the reduction, by the same proportion, of those without access to safe drinking water; these are the two gauges by which poverty is measured (part II, paragraph 6.a). At the beginning of the paragraph there is a sentence which includes the premise that 'each country has the primary responsibility for its own sustainable development and poverty eradication'; later in the paragraph it does say that at least some of the cost of poverty-eradicating development should be met by 'the provision of adequate and predictable financial resources (6.l)', but does not add by whom. A vague plan of action is offered in part II, paragraph 7; its headings are:

(a) Develop and implement efficient household sanitation systems;
(b) Improve sanitation in public institutions, especially schools;
(c) Promote safe hygiene practices;
(d) Promote education and outreach focused on children, as agents of behavioural change;

(e) Promote affordable and socially and culturally acceptable technologies and practices;

(f) Develop innovative financing and partnership mechanisms;

(g) Integrate sanitation into water resources management strategies.

This list is given a little more content in paragraphs 24 and 25, but a number of difficult issues are left simply as demands or statements. For example, 25.a calls for the development and implementation of 'strategies, plans and programmes' to integrate the management of groundwater, watersheds and river basins, but at no point adverts to the degree of dispute already surrounding the last of these: we have mentioned Israel and Syria, but there is also considerable tension surrounding Turkey's developments on the Euphrates; there are still difficulties between China and Burma over the river Salween; and the struggle between India and Pakistan includes, among very many other issues, disagreement over the rivers Indus and Sutlei – there are many more. There can be no question about the importance of the sustainable management of river basins, just as there can be no serious question about the need to reduce greenhouse gas emissions, but the implementation of the WSSD's proposals for alleviating poverty, let alone for development, are fantasies unless these matters are addressed.

The longest and most detailed passage on water and sanitation in the *Plan of Implementation* is to be found in part IV. It is headed 'Protecting and managing the natural resource base of economic and social development' (paragraphs 23–8). In the first of these it refers to the need 'to implement strategies ... to protect ecosystems and to achieve integrated management of land, water and living resources' – the demand for integration, once made, is then resolutely ignored in the course of the *Plan*'s prescriptions. It goes on to make the obvious demands for the mobilisation of financial resources, the transfer of technology, greater access for everyone to information, the reduction and monitoring of water pollution and the introduction of measures to promote the sustainable use of water. In 25.b it slips in one of the most important and debatable proposals:

> Employ the full range of policy instruments, including regulation, monitoring, voluntary measures, market and information-based tools, land-use management and *cost recovery* of water services, without cost recovery objectives becoming a barrier to access to safe water by poor people. (emphasis added)

This passage is clarified by another in 25.g:

> Facilitate the establishment of public–private partnerships and
> other forms of partnership that give priority to the needs of the
> poor, within stable and transparent national regulatory frameworks
> provided by Governments, while respecting local conditions,
> involving all concerned stakeholders, and monitoring the per-
> formance and improving accountability of public institutions and
> private companies.

This position is supported in part VIII, entitled 'Sustainable
Development for Africa':

> Promote integrated water resources development and optimize the
> upstream and downstream benefits therefrom, the development
> and effective management of water resources across all uses and the
> protection of water quality and aquatic ecosystems, including
> through initiatives at all levels, to:
>
> (a) Provide access to potable domestic water, hygiene education
>   and improved sanitation and waste management at the
>   household level through initiatives to encourage *public and
>   private investment* in water supply and sanitation that give
>   priority to the needs of the poor, within stable and transpar-
>   ent national regulatory frameworks provided by Governments,
>   while respecting local conditions involving all concerned
>   stakeholders and monitoring the performance and improving
>   the accountability of public institutions and private
>   companies; and develop critical water supply, reticulation and
>   treatment infrastructure, and build capacity to maintain and
>   manage systems to deliver water and sanitation services, in
>   both rural and urban areas. (paragraph 60, emphasis added)

In the months succeeding the conference, the way in which implementation is to be achieved became clearer; 'partnerships' are being
formed between public and private bodies and INGOs, which will
attack each sector in need of attention. At the time of writing, over
200 of them had been established to deal with energy, freshwater,
oceans (including coastal areas and fisheries), early warning
(including disaster preparedness), desertification, climate change
(including air pollution), agriculture (including food security and

rural development), mountains, biodiversity, forests, minerals and mining.[14] Prior to the Summit, a set of guidelines, 'Guiding Principles for Partnerships for Sustainable Development', was drawn up; among other things it proposed that all partnerships should prosecute the aims of WSSD and be

> of a voluntary, 'self-organizing' nature ... based on mutual respect and shared responsibility of the partners involved ... They can be arranged among any combination of partners, including governments, regional groups, local authorities, non-governmental actors, international institutions and private sector partners. All partners should be involved in the development of a partnership from an early stage, so that it is genuinely participatory in approach.[15]

Given these guidelines, it is instructive to look at some of the partnerships formed, both during and following the Summit, to increase the availability of clean water and sanitation. The French partnership includes: the French government, NGOs (Water Aid, Protos, IRC International Water and Sanitation Centre, Solidarité Eau Europe, Programme Solidarité Eau and others), French local governments and twinning committees (Association des Maires de France), water agencies (Cercle Français de l'eau, Agence Eau Seine Normandie – AESN), professionals (Syndicats des Eaux: SEDIF, SAGEP, SIAAP, AGTHM) and private sector corporations (Vivendi Environnement, Ondeo, SAUR).[16] The three corporations are all major transnationals with very wide interests; for example, English readers will undoubtedly recognise Vivendi as the owner of, among many other enterprises, the Connex rail company. Organisations listed as 'water agencies' and 'professionals' are a mix of corporations (for example, SAGEP) and semi-public bodies. The partnership is led by Programme Solidarité Eau, a large NGO concentrating, as its name suggests, on water and sanitation.

Whether or not we accept that slightly obscene distinction, created by the comfortably placed, between destitution and just poverty, it is important to recognise that it is not just the concern of developing, or 'least-developed', states. South Africa, not usually described as a developing country, has a substantial population living in extreme poverty and without access to clean water and good sanitation. Because of its enormously variable patterns of rainfall, it also suffers from water stress, though possibly not on the scale of the countries we have so far discussd. Its major partner (a word unemployable without a certain sense of irony) in water services is Suez, a French corporation which describes itself as providing global water services and which includes, among other large companies, the Ondeo group. The division between those with adequate access to water and those without runs, more or less, along apartheid lines and the Suez corporation has been resolute in observing it. That division has been pithily summarised: 'Around 12% of South Africa's water is consumed by households, but of that amount more than half goes into (white people's) gardens and swimming pools, and less than a tenth is consumed by all black South African households.'[17] Patrick Bond, in *Unsustainable South Africa*, describes a typical example in Stutterheim in the Eastern Cape where Suez and its associate company, Water and Sanitation South Africa, failed 'to serve any of the 80% of the region's township residents' and pushed municipalities into the mass cutting of supplies, leaving the predominantly black population with no option but to use the 'bucket system' of sanitation. The corporation silenced protest by employing the principal civic leader.[18]

The United Kingdom's water partnership also includes the government of South Africa, as well as Nigeria and Uganda, and is even more heavily weighted towards the private sector. So far it has not included any intergovernmental financial organisations, but it 'may involve working with organisations such as the World Bank'.[19] Its steering group consists of Anglian Water, the Babtie Group, the Chartered Institution of Water and Environmental Management, the Institution of Civil Engineers, Northumbrian Water – Ondeo Services, the Parkman Group, Severn Trent Water, Tearfund, Thames Water, WaterAid and WWF. The Babtie Group is a large technical and management consultancy; the Parkman Group PLC is an expanding corporation specialising in transport, property and its management, water, construction, environmental matters and social housing – both must make a profit, but the Parkman Group is quoted on the stock exchange which means that it must also satisfy the expectations of market traders. The four water companies in the partnership are all large. Anglian Water, known as AWG, has interests in, among other places, Prague, Santiago and Bangkok; Northumbrian Water is part of Ondeo, the multinational included in the French partnership as part of the Suez group; Severn Trent Water is part of Severn Trent International operating in Belgium, Portugal, Germany, Italy, Eastern Europe and Africa; Thames Water, despite its name, has interests throughout the UK and, internationally, in the US, Egypt, West Asia, Turkey and South East Asia. It would not be too rash to see this partnership as heavily influenced by New Labour's ideological commitment to market solutions for all developmental problems. It would be idle to speculate about corporate motives for joining such partnerships, but it may be worth noting that both South Africa and Nigeria are potentially wealthy states whose infrastructure and industrial organisation are open to profitable development. Investment in Uganda seems more problematic since its principal export has been wood from indiscriminate logging in its eastern forests; it will be interesting to see how much effort this partnership will devote to that country.

Few, if any, water companies can make sufficient profit from the provision of water, even if they add to it the construction of urban sewerage systems. AWG will serve as an example: in the year 2000, the company moved into the construction industry, not the least because it was facing major difficulties in deriving profits from its provision of water in East Anglia. During the acute water shortages that occurred in several parts of England in the 1990s, it discovered, along with several other water companies, that it could not economically justify the repair of pipes through which substantial losses of water were occurring. That is to say, profits and consequently share prices would be seriously affected if the public good of saving water were to take precedence over them. Largely because water, treated as a commodity rather than as a service, could not generate sufficient profit, the company extended its activities from water and sewerage to all the utilities. In the course of 2001, it went further: because it found water too capital intensive, too big a 'drag' on corporate profits and with too high a ratio of customer debt, it separated that activity from the rest of its enterprises. The new company, H2go, almost disappeared in mid-2002 when its operating profit was severely reduced.[20]

Since it is more economic to supply almost anything to places where the greatest number of people are to be found, and since the UK Partnership Programme suggests that the 'focus ... should be on secondary towns and peri-urban areas in Africa', it is reasonable to assume that the main effort in achieving the goal of providing clean water for half of those at present without it will be made in rapidly growing urban areas. For those outside them, often in very remote communities, simpler technologies will have to be employed and are readily available. But in either case investment sufficient to meet the goal would be immense and an even greater drag on company profits than that experienced by AWG in eastern England. Two explanations for the willingness of corporations to become involved in such capital-intensive ventures offer themselves: the scope for treating water as a commodity, particularly for sale to nascent but developing industries, is far greater in weak economies than in strong; the second explanation is that water is simply a gateway to other, very profitable, activities. Neither explanation bodes well for the 'customers'.

Hanging over this is that provision in paragraph 25.b in the *Plan of Implementation* and on which we have already remarked, which suggests the use of 'policy instruments, including ... cost recovery of water services, without cost recovery objectives becoming a barrier to access to safe water by poor people'. We are obliged to ask how the people and their communities surviving in the direst poverty, the greatest part of the objective of this particular MDG, can find the price. It is improbable in the extreme that water can be supplied to them as a by-product of supplying the better off and industry; it is even more improbable that the infrastructure necessary for delivery could be paid for in this way. Yet the corporations at issue must make a return on their capital investments in the customary short term allowed by the need to preserve shareholders' equity and to pay regular dividends. The caution shown by the authors of *Bending the Curve*, in selecting a later date for any significant reduction in poverty, seems more than justified and what we may see in this partnership, as in others, is the degree of unreality produced precisely by the segmentation of the objectives – in this case the treatment of water in isolation from all the other issues of development (a problem that occurs in all sectors). Even more important is the failure to admit that corporations are not charities; their function is to make money for the investors that own them, not to alleviate poverty.

Waters are muddied by the persistent use of the phrase 'private sector', but there is no such beast as private capital. Perhaps the most dramatic change effected in the course of the twentieth century was that of the site of power within the bourgeois democracies. Hobsbawm has described the emergence of the '*grande bourgeoisie*' as a ruling class, made possible by the revolutions of 1830 and, although he does not say so, of 1848.[21] This bourgeoisie consisted of 'bankers, big industrialists and sometimes top civil servants, accepted by an aristocracy which effaced itself or agreed to promote primarily bourgeois policies'.[22] Arriving on the crest of the Industrial Revolution, the new rulers set about a revolution of their own which, despite itself, as Karl Marx never tired of pointing out, brought about progressive change. The rise of capitalism and its dependence on an urbanised workforce created a proletariat which, combined with economic change, compelled the modification of bourgeois power; a movement which accompanied revolution in agrarian Europe. Chartism, trades unions, universal suffrage and the rise of left-wing politics were all part of that change, the first of these providing much of the impetus for all the others. Even if we accept the argument that the economic and industrial needs of the ruling bourgeoisie, rather than proletarian protest and action, forced those changes, the result is much the same. In those states in which the bourgeoisie did not actually rule, their economic power and activities effectively created a hegemony. It was a system that gave rise to liberalism and a separation of powers, both within state machinery and, to a limited degree, in social structures.

The First and Second World Wars, frequently seen as one war, particularly by Hobsbawm, ended the hegemony of industrial capital and created the conditions for the rise of financial capitalism which, although it is built on foundations laid by industrial capital, is an entirely different beast.[23] Neo-liberalism has succeeded liberalism and such gentilities as the latter evinced, political and cultural, have been smashed by their successors. Perry Anderson, in an extended review of Hobsbawm's great tetralogy remarked that: 'Never since the Gilded Age have financial buccaneers and industrial magnates stalked the earth with such giant strides, trampling over labour and swaggering through culture, from heights of wealth and power Gould or Morgan could scarcely have imagined.'[24] He added to this outraged and ringing comment the point that national governments, rendered irrelevant to much of what 'financial buccaneers' actually do are simultaneously increasingly unable to govern, but also unable to ignore their citizens: 'The result of this impasse is inevitably a politics of official evasion, obfuscation or plebiscitary manipulation. In much of the West, contemporary elections have become little more than "contests in fiscal perjury".' The point, of course, is that financial capital, its controllers and its international instruments of governance (for example, the WTO, the World Bank, several military alliances, international stock exchange rules and so on) have, with their hegemonic control, to a substantial degree replaced rule by bourgeois national governments. It is because of the extent of this phenomenon that it makes decreasing sense to think in terms of private capital. States continue to be important as organisational bases for corporations and the principal purpose of their governments is to facilitate corporate activity by regulation and legislation. At the time of writing the US government, for example, is preparing to launch a brutal war on a West Asian dictatorship, not in the name of freedom, but to secure supplies for the oil industry and to enhance its campaign to secure the resources of the whole of Central Asia. We live in a world in which private capital has become public as it increasingly establishes hegemonic rule – in all such hegemonies, capitalists keep the instruments of public control in their own hands.

Partnerships, of the kind we have mentioned in this chapter, must be seen in the context of the new hegemony. We have already remarked that corporations exist to make money for their shareholders, but what makes them curiously unfitted for social programmes of the sort envisaged by the WSSD is the astonishingly short time in which investors look for profitable return, even in the economies of the industrialised world. In the case of investment in the Third World, that period becomes even shorter because the risk is thought to be greater.[25] Nonetheless, the modalities of finance capital's operations have dictated the forms which the Summit and, come to that, most Western governments and their NGOs have chosen for the achievement of the MDGs and the beginning of sustainable development. Such modalities also account for the structural segmentation of developmental objectives which the present authors see as self-defeating. There is little concrete in the Summit's call for the provision of clean water and adequate sanitation and, as it is outlined in the *Plan of Implementation*, we detect an air of total unreality.

4   Hot Air

No development, sustainable or otherwise, can take place without adequate supplies of energy. Unless those countries that are home to the greatest numbers of the world's poor are allowed to industrialise, in whatever contemporary form, and allowed to trade with the rest of the world without impediment from the rich world's protective barriers, then the MDGs are little more than propaganda, principally designed to stifle protest within the liberal democracies. Paragraph 8 of the *Plan of Implementation*, which falls into the section dealing with 'Poverty eradication', acknowledges this when it agrees to:

> Take joint actions and improve efforts to work together at all levels to improve access to reliable and affordable energy services for sustainable development sufficient to facilitate the achievement of the millennium development goals, including the goal of halving the proportion of people in poverty by 2015, and as a means to generate other important services that mitigate poverty, bearing in mind that access to energy facilitates the eradication of poverty.

We have noted earlier that the *Plan* equates the eradication of poverty with achieving the MDGs – an equation which, had it not emerged from such exalted sources, we might be justified in considering a little disingenuous. Even if the MDGs are reached by 2015, the number of those living on pppUS$1.00 per day will still be substantially in excess of half a billion and disabling poverty, not measured by such an absurd indicator, will, as we pointed out in Chapter 3, remain the norm for a large proportion of the world's population.

Energy, or rather its lack, is of course directly related to poverty. Over 2 billion people have no access to electric light and so are unable to escape that greatest tyranny of nature – darkness. The promotion by the European Commission of electricity from renewables, consolidated in the Johannesburg meeting, at first sight seems remarkably liberal in intent. The reality is entirely the reverse, for renewables are the most expensive way of providing electricity and recommending them for the poor simply prices lighting out of their reach. In both rural and urban areas, the dominant source of energy is fuelwood, chiefly consumed as charcoal. It is increasingly scarce and its price is rising, but it remains the principal fuel of choice, even for the rich. In poor countries there is no automatic movement up the energy ladder – from wood through charcoal, kerosene and gas to electricity – because each of these resources is vulnerable to the disruption of supplies. But the rich have access to all five, while the poor only have wood. In passing it should be noticed that wood consumption as energy is not the major cause of deforestation – that triumph goes to the colonisation of land for agriculture.

The rate of electricity production is, nonetheless, an invaluable guide to the scale of both economic and environmental problems (see Table 4.1) and it is instructive to note that Europe and North America produce and consume over 60 per cent of the world's energy, but constitute only 19 per cent of the world's population.

Table 4.1   Comparative Electricity Production

Region	1999 (gigawatt-hours)	% of world production*	% of world population*
Africa	413171	2.79	13.11
Asia/Pacific	4248168	28.65	58.13
Europe	4433215	29.94	13.50
Latin American/Caribbean	922118	6.23	8.57
North America	4517341	30.59	5.18
West Asia	281089	1.90	1.63

* Discrepancies caused by rounding.

Source: UNEP/DEWA/GRID and *GEO 3*.

But if the development of energy production, other than by renewables, is a major element in the escape from poverty in the Third World, then the issue of climate change as a consequence of global warming becomes even more pressing. As the present authors, among many others, have observed, the tune is called by the oil lobby. The most obvious but by no means the only example may be seen in the rejection by the US of the Kyoto Protocol. Bush did his utmost to discredit the findings of the IPCC when he asked the US National Academy of Sciences (NAS) to review them with the object of finding discrepancies between their summary conclusions and the evidence in front of the panel. The NAS, not known for its radical political stances, not only failed to find these discrepancies, but added its own voice in support of the panel's findings and even suggested that they were too cautious. Bush promptly changed the ground of his attack on Kyoto by saying that it would damage the US's economy and was unfair because it did not include some developing countries, particularly China and India, which were discharging greenhouse gasses at rates comparable with the industrialised world.[1] Despite a reference to 'lay-offs', what Bush means by the US economy is the fortunes of the large corporations, particularly oil, but in the second of his objections, he is simply cooking the books. We give comparative figures in Table 4.2.

Table 4.2   Comparative CO_2 Emissions

Country	Metric Tonnes (millions)	Population (millions)	Tonnes of Emissions (per person)
Total G7 nations	9,061	688	13.2
USA	5,302	273	19.4
Canada	409	31	13.2
Germany	861	82	10.5
UK	557	59	9.4
Japan	1,168	126	9.3
Italy	403	58	6.9
France	362	59	6.1
Rest of the World	13,629	5,209	2.6
World Total	22,690	5,897	3.8

Source: based on Foster, 2002. Figures from World Bank, 2000/2001.

In 1992, the World Bank predicted the ratios of energy consumption between developing and OECD countries. The prediction was cautious and the Bank assumed that social and technological changes would result in a gradual decline in consumption in the OECD states. Nonetheless, the ratios, calculated as barrels of oil equivalent per capita, are telling: in the year 2000 – 5:51, 2010 – 7.5:39, 2020 – 9:35, 2030 – 12:35. Neither India nor China are members of the OECD. In 1996, India's population was 1 billion, its per capita emissions were 1.1 tonnes amounting to 4 per cent of the world's total; China's population was 1.25 billion, its per capita emissions were 2.8 tonnes amounting to 14.8 per cent of the world's total; the US's population was 273 million, its per capita emissions were 5.6 tonnes amounting to 23.3 per cent of the world's total – a percentage considerably greater than India's and China's put together.[2]

We have rehearsed the facts behind Bush's rejection of the Kyoto Protocol because it overshadowed the Summit's deliberations about energy. Faced with the NAS's confirmation of the IPCC's account of global warming and climate change Bush, rather than searching for ways to reduce those emissions and to stabilise matters, has chosen to attempt technological solutions to the problem. He has commissioned extensive research into ways in which carbon emissions can be countered or absorbed so that the rapid increase in US emissions can continue unabated. John Bellamy Foster gives a hilarious, if appalling, account of some of them.[3] Absurd and far-fetched as many of these measures seem, they have captured the enthusiasm of some sections of the US business world. A curious but influential group called the United States Council for International Business has endorsed Bush's rejection of Kyoto. Its President, Thomas M.T. Niles, in writing to President Bush remarked that '[w]e share your concern over the risks of climate change. The US should move quickly to chart a path forward that will avoid the Kyoto Protocol's unrealistic targets, timetables and lack of developing country participation', but in their own report of this letter, the Council set out its own claims. If any of Bush's hare-brained schemes for sequestering carbon should bear fruit, the Council wants business to have its share. Following a proposal that each country should 'choose the most appropriate means to reduce emissions', it suggests 'market incentives to facilitate least-cost options for improvement' but, at the same time, 'it endorses measures to support the development, commercialisation and dissemination of new technologies to reduce emissions world-wide'.[4]

Once again, we have to remind ourselves of what corporations are prepared to accept as 'options for improvement'. Under long sustained pressure from a variety of social groups, the US government, in the course of the 1960s and 1970s, introduced legislation designed to protect the environment, in particular, the National Environmental Policy Act of 1969 and the National Forestry Management Act of 1976.[5] Legislation of this kind was widely regarded by corporate interests in much the same way as Mr Niles sees the Kyoto Protocol – an unwarrantable interference with the natural and necessary process of business. Late in 2002, the Bush administration proposed to allow logging in the US's protected national forests and to devolve the management of them to local officials who would decide what was in the best interests of everyone concerned. The White House functionary who introduced this measure is Mark Rey; he is responsible for the nation's forests, was formerly vice-president of the American and Forest Paper Association and also coordinated substantial industrial support for Bush's capture of the White House.[6] His new regulation would effectively scrap the 1976 Act and severely damage the Environmental Policy Act, but it would have the effect of pleasing the giant logging industry. A fig leaf would be offered in the form of a replanting programme.[7] The administration is also attempting to modify the Appeals Reform Act, which enables public participation in the management of state land.

Another indicator of corporate attitudes may be seen in the history of spills from oil tankers. These are more or less constant, but only a few actually make the news headlines; among the earliest of these is the disaster which took place on Pollard's Rock between the Scilly Isles and Land's End, in March 1967. A ship, the *Torrey Canyon*, carrying approximately 103,800 tonnes of oil, struck the rock, broke up and spilled its cargo, causing massive ecological damage. Subsequent enquiry produced a mixture of reasons for the accident, but also made the point that a series of minor human errors, all normal in the operation of any large ship, did not help, but were not, ultimately, responsible. The major factors were the delay in notifying the ship's master of its destination, the absence of the necessary charts and the pressure put on the master to make up time. Lateness of notification is a practice that continues; the owners of the cargo leave the destinations until the last moment in order to capitalise on the best available prices in the regions in which the ships are sailing. In the case of the *Torrey Canyon*, the notification of its destination came at a point in its journey where the safe manoeuvring of the ship, a super-tanker, was very difficult. This difficulty was compounded by the failure of the oil companies and the ship owners to ensure that all the charts necessary for any destination in the ship's region were on board. Speed of delivery was also important to the oil company, since shipping time adds to costs. In short, safety was sacrificed in the interest of reducing costs and so increasing profits. Similar stories may be told of other major disasters: the *Amoco Cadiz* which sank off the Brittany coast in 1979 (spillage, 230,000 tonnes); in March 1989, the *Exxon Valdez* sank in Prince William Sound (spillage, 36,181 tonnes); the most recent disaster, in November 2002, was caused by the sinking of the elderly and obsolete oil tanker, the *Prestige*, off the Galician coast (spillage, at the time of writing, 6,700 tonnes, but more is expected).

Corner cutting by the oil industry is common to all these disasters and many more – dealing with the results is a problem for others.

But even public consciousness of those results is undermined. An astonishing web page, addressed to children, has been created by the US National Oceanic and Atmospheric Administration, expressly to minimise the importance of the *Exxon Valdez* oil spill. It begins by pointing out that the US uses 700 million gallons of oil each day, that the entire world's consumption is 3 billion gallons per day and that the 11 million gallons spilled in this event was under 2 per cent of the US's daily use. This is followed by a simple chart enabling children to understand the volume at issue: the spill would fill '9 gyms', or '108 houses', or '430 classrooms', or '797 living rooms'. These are cosy images and, given the geographical scale of the US, successfully convey the impression that much fuss has been made about very little. The company itself claims that the clean-up was successful and that long-term damage was slight.[8]

This digression is necessary since all solutions to the issue of energy in the developing world, proposed by the WSSD, involve public–private partnerships:

> Countries are urged to develop and implement actions within the framework of the ninth session of the Commission on Sustainable Development, including through public–private partnerships, taking into account the different circumstances of countries, based on lessons learned by Governments, international institutions and stakeholders and including business and industry, in the field of access to energy, including renewable energy and energy-efficiency and advanced energy technologies, including advanced and cleaner fossil fuel technologies.[9]

The Summit's view, backed by many commentators, that developing countries are well placed to supply much of their energy through renewable resources would, in a perfect world, be true. But the imperfections of this world include the determination of the fossil fuel industries to keep control of the raw materials of energy production, and the general failure of the governments of the industrialised world to invest adequately in the research and development of renewable sources of energy.

Renewable sources of energy, principally hydroelectric, wind, wave and solar systems of generation are repeatedly advanced by, among others, the present authors, as solutions to many environmental problems. Hydroelectricity now accounts for 19 per cent of the world's supply, but its development can be as great a disaster as any it might mitigate. Arundhati Roy has written brilliantly about the destruction of lives and culture involved in the construction of India's Narmada dam and the full story of the human devastation caused by building China's Three Gorges dams has yet to be told.[10] It is possible to build environmentally sustainable hydroelectric generators, but they must be small and politically unimpressive. They would, of course, be of little help to those nations suffering acutely from water stress. It is also possible to build wind farms that are neither ecologically dangerous nor aesthetically unacceptable and, in the long run, they could provide a substantial proportion of the world's energy – the World Energy Council (WEC) suggests that, by 2010, they could be producing 140 giga-watts (GW) and, at some unspecified point in the future, up to 20 per cent of the world's power; but, as the Council also points out, this is subject to 'political support, both nationally and internationally, and further improvements in performance and costs'. It is also necessary to remember that, like hydroelectric power, wind power depends on the existence of a suitable wind regime, but there are many parts of the developing world where this does not exist. Wave energy is at an early stage of development, but it is thought possible that future development would allow it to provide up to 10 per cent of world requirements. Solar energy is, potentially, the most important of all the renewable sources and the Council suggests that, by 2050, it could provide as much as 50 per cent of the world's requirements. However, not only would this call for far more intensive research into solar generated power than takes place at present, but the structure of the energy industry and the means of distribution would have to be changed radically, the cost of building solar panels is also enormous.[11] Renewable sources of energy could undoubtedly play a major part in its worldwide production, but the constant suggestion that it is a route to development available now to poor countries is cynically to palter with the truth.

At the very least there is a conflict of interest evident in any attempt to involve 'business and industry' in making 'advanced technologies, including ... cleaner fossil fuel technologies' available to developing countries. 'Business' is unlikely to act in this way unless it can derive profit from the process and, since the oil industry is the most significant energy provider, the price is likely to be beyond the purses of the poor. We have touched briefly on its record in the transport of oil, but that is only one area among many in which safety, environmental questions and public interest have been subjugated to return on investment. We have only to think of the unhappy cost-cutting which played a large part in the 1979 Ixtoc 1 oil platform explosion in Mexico's Bay of Campeche, or, in a different context, the dubious role played by oil companies in the long civil war in Angola, or the extent of irresponsible oil flaring.[12]

In its recommendations for the development of sustainable energy, not just for developing countries but for the world as a whole, the *Plan of Implementation* sets out the framework of what has to be done; its prescriptions for the developing world follow the formula repeated in all the other major sectors examined by the Summit. Action is called for to 'improve access to modern biomass technologies' and to sources of biomass fuels; to 'support the transition to the cleaner use of liquid and gaseous fossil fuels'; to 'develop energy policies and regulatory frameworks' to allow for the development of 'sound energy services for sustainable development and poverty eradication'; to 'enhance regional and national cooperation'; to 'assist and facilitate ... the financial and technical assistance ... [from] developed countries, including through public–private partnerships'; to 'strengthen the contribution of industrial development to poverty eradication and sustainable resource management' (paragraphs 8–10).

The Global Scenario Group, in *Bending the Curve*, had already pointed to the technical demands that the establishment of any programme, such as that proposed by the WSSD, would entail.[13] It begins by making the point that the 'modest' development of renewable sources of energy in which the industrialised world has engaged, even combined with the contemporary interest in energy conservation, will not be enough to 'meet sustainability goals'. In 1995, the world's demand for energy amounted to 384 EJ.[14] Unusual weather patterns, at present experienced throughout the world, may already be the result of the cheap but primitive way in which this enormous amount of energy is produced. If matters continue as they are, then by 2050 the demand will reach 929 EJ and even if some progress is achieved in producing energy in a cleaner way, the effects on climate will become completely unpredictable.

Modesty in the matter is obviously inadequate and the Global Scenario Group proposes what it calls 'aggressive action', that is the formulation of tough international policies designed, in the first instance, to reduce the rate of consumption. The first of these should be the adoption of very efficient uses of energy: in buildings, domestic and industrial, this means the installation of better systems for heating, cooling and lighting and improvements in insulation and glazing; in industrial production, recycling basic materials, ensuring that motors are efficient and using 'combined heat and power technologies'. In energy generation, the Group advocates the use of 'combined thermal and integrated coal and biomass gasification'. Its most important suggestion is that demands for energy should be met by the greater use of natural gas until renewable resources and the technologies for their use have been sufficiently developed. It is also a contentious suggestion because it puts the basis of development in the hands of the oil industry.

If all these measures are adopted, then the Group estimates that demand, although it will increase by 2050, will do so at a slower rate and will reach 599 EJ, substantially lower than the prediction for a world in which the policies we have at present do not change. It has assumed that the OECD states will lead in the adoption of these methods and that, by 2050, their collective use of energy will decline by 40 per cent. Until about 2030, developing countries will increase their consumption of energy quite rapidly, but that too will then decline, more swiftly, but from a higher base. From 2050, that decline will continue at a steady rate and energy will be produced by far less polluting technologies. But the Group also lists the kinds of policy necessary to achieve such a goal: a variety of fiscal measures can be adopted, including taxes on emissions, systems of trading emission permits, the greater reduction of taxes on renewable sources relative to those on fossil fuels and the removal of fossil fuel subsidies. Tougher standards for the efficient use of energy can be imposed and greater financial support can be given to the development of renewable resources. The Group also suggests that the technological improvements that would emerge from the adoption of such policies could be transferred to 'developing economies'.

In 1989, a number of powerful business interests, principally from the oil companies, formed a lobbying organisation called the Global Climate Coalition. It came together because its members, alarmed by the direction taken by the WCED, decided that its interests were threatened by international reactions to environmental damage and, in particular, to possible climate change. It was a major presence at UNCED and was successful in its campaign to water down the UNFCCC. Internationally, on the domestic front in the US and even locally, it fought first against the presuppositions that led to the Kyoto Protocol, challenging the validity of scientific findings, and then against the US ratification of the Protocol. It is depressing to read the Coalition's little cry of triumph, dated 3 December 2002:

The Global Climate Coalition has been deactivated. The industry voice on climate change has served its purpose by contributing to a new national approach to global warming.

The Bush administration will soon announce a climate policy that is expected to rely on the development of new technologies to reduce greenhouse emissions, a concept strongly supported by the GCC.

The coalition also opposed Senate ratification of the Kyoto Protocol that would assign such stringent targets for lowering greenhouse gas emissions that economic growth in the U. S. would be severely hampered and energy prices for consumers would skyrocket. The GCC also opposed the treaty because it does not require the largest developing countries to make cuts in their emissions.[15]

Deactivated it may be, but clearly only within limits. It continues to post quotations and articles on its web site which challenge both scientific findings and the need to take special steps to counter the problems in climate change. Its object is to ensure that nothing will impede the activities of those corporations involved in the production of energy or in the extraction of fossil fuels and we have already seen Bush's response to the exceedingly modest demands made in the Kyoto Protocol.

Three things are at immediate issue: climate change, modest proposals for its abatement and the development of energy production in the Third World. We have to remind ourselves that the continuing arguments about whether or not the effects of industrial production are already apparent both in the unarguable increase in the world's mean temperature and in virtually unprecedented climatic events are irrelevant. It is enough that both the IPCC and the NAS are agreed that the discharges of greenhouse gasses are affecting the climate and will continue to do so, possibly in catastrophic ways. It is a judgement that renders futile any discussion of, for example, whether particular and unexpected El Niño or La Niña activities are consequences of global warming or are simply random incidents in a relatively uncharted history. If they are caused by the greenhouse effect, they are, at one crucial level, simply phenomena which make the point; if they are not, the problem of the ultimate effects of climate change are still there to be solved. Among the simplifications that the IPCC and others have employed to bring home the probable effects has been the generalisation that hot, dry places will get hotter and more arid and that wet places will get wetter. Since a large proportion of the world's poorest lives in hot dry places, the effects of climate change also have to be taken into account if the WSSD's determination to meet the MDGs is to bear fruit.

But, of course, arguments about climate change are not to do with what is actually happening, but with politics and economics. The authors of *Bending the Curve* have made their proposals and they are reinforced by *GEO 3*. Both volumes preface their recommendations with a survey of future carbon dioxide emissions calculated on the basis of four broad directions which the industrialised world might take. *GEO 3* lists them as putting 'markets first', 'security first', 'policy first' or 'sustainability first'; plainly the adoption of the last of these would be the most desirable outcome, but to expect it would call for heroic optimism. If the industrialised world pursues its present course in which markets are preeminent and understood as the best mechanism for reaching agreement about this and most other difficulties, then *GEO 3* predicts that, by 2030, carbon emissions will have increased from their present level of about 8 billion tonnes per annum to about 16 billion tonnes. Putting security first by creating economic fortresses like, for example, fortress Europe, or fortress America, will increase emissions in the same period to 14 billion tonnes per annum. If the kinds of policy advocated by the Global Scenario Group were to be adopted by the major polluters, emissions could be reduced to below 12 billion tonnes and a gentle decline would continue. In the improbable event of sustainability becoming the accepted way forward, emissions would first increase slowly to about 9 billion tonnes and then decline, bringing the 2030 figure down to around 7 billion tonnes, but in an accelerating rate of diminution.

Climate change and the means by which it may be stabilised both bear on our third issue, the reduction of worldwide poverty by encouraging the development of what we piously hope will be sustainable livelihoods. One minor conceptual difficulty is the association of the word 'livelihood' with an artisanal form of production – we may see its mirror image in Bush's reductionist, if not infantilising, use of the word 'folk'. Both words are capable of concealing dubious agendas. The route to reducing poverty on any meaningful scale will involve some politically difficult achievements. Throughout the *Plan of Implementation* the demand is made that international markets should be opened to the poorer states, barriers to their full participation should be lowered and that they should be allowed to process their own products for sale to the rest of the world. Parts of this demand have already been met and we may see this in the developments in agriculture which have enabled Third World growers to produce fruit, vegetables and other comestibles for Western markets. But we have already commented on the ecological damage wreaked by this trade and have written elsewhere about the peonage it frequently involves.[16] Real development can only mean autonomous control of all resources, including the agricultural kind; in a world created by capital, one in which urbanisation is increasing at astonishing rates, industrial development, in addition to small-scale artisanal production, is the other part of the solution to poverty. We remarked, at the beginning of this chapter, that sources of energy must be developed in and by the states which are at present acutely poor.

In a different way, the authors of *Bending the Curve* make the same point in their projections for the worldwide growth of GDP. They use 1995 as a base line and make two sets of projections: the first is based on the assumption that the future holds out hope for little more than tinkering with present policies; the second assumption is founded on the introduction of modest policies designed to moderate the destructive effects of rampant competition. We reproduce below their projections for the developing world and, on the assumption that growth is not entirely appropriated by the wealthy, even the modest proposals would take the world a long way towards the elimination of widespread destitution (see Table 4.3). This point is underlined by the Group's parallel projections for world hunger. If matters continue much as they are, then by 2025 Africa's population will have reached 1.5 billion (719 million in 1995) and 25 per cent of it will still be in hunger. Should reasonable policy changes be introduced, then in 2025 the population will be slightly smaller (1.4 billion), but the proportion in hunger will be reduced to 12 per cent. By 2050, if things go unchanged, the continent's population will be a little over 2 billion, of whom 20 per cent will be malnourished; with the adoption of modest policies, the population will reach 1.9 billion, of whom 5 per cent will be malnourished.[17]

Perhaps among the most modest of policies might have been the general acceptance of the Kyoto Protocol. Even though its modesty was such as to make very little difference, its symbolic importance is clear, particularly since its rejection by the oil lobby. In the nineteenth edition of the *Survey of Energy Resources* (2001), the WEC estimated that at the end of 1999 the world's total stock of recoverable oil amounted to 142.5 billion tonnes.[18] New discoveries continue to be made, but the rate at which this happens has declined.

More importantly, some of these discoveries are deep under the oceans and, at least with foreseeable technology, are economically and technically irrecoverable. For this and for other reasons, the Council has adopted a pessimistic view of the long-term prospects for oil as one of the principal forms of energy. Since the present authors have repeatedly attacked the oil industry, this pessimism might have been welcomed; unfortunately, long-term prospects rarely affect the behaviour and balance sheets of a profoundly short-termist form of capitalism. Not only may we see here an additional explanation for Bush's interest in Iraqi oil, but we also have to consider the web of interdependence between corporations. The oil industry is not alone, its principal customers are other corporations in the chain of purchase and distribution – even where share ownership may be interlocking. One important consequence of this is not only hegemonic control of the resources, but also an increasing tendency to ensure that they are sequestered in the interests of the indus-trialised states.

Table 4.3   GDP Projections

	Current Policies							
	GDP (billion US$)			*Growth Rate (% per year)*			*Index (95=1)*	
Region	*1995*	*2025*	*2050*	*95–25*	*25–50*	*95–50*	*2025*	*2050*
Africa	1,165	3,958	9,279	4.2	3.5	3.8	3.4	8.0
China	3,839	12,099	22,555	3.9	2.5	3.3	3.2	5.9
Latin America	2,858	7,449	14,071	3.2	2.6	2.9	2.6	4.9
Middle East	938	3,159	6,554	4.1	3.0	3.6	3.4	7.0
S & SE Asia	4,329	14,160	30,745	4.0	3.1	3.6	3.3	7.1
	Moderate Policy Reform							
Africa	1,165	6,381	16,427	5.8	3.9	4.9	5.5	14.1
China	3,839	13,762	25,368	4.3	2.5	3.5	3.6	6.6
Latin America	2,858	8,026	15,177	3.5	2.6	3.1	2.8	5.3
Middle East	938	3,501	7,383	4.5	3.0	3.8	3.7	7.9
S & SE Asia	4,329	17,013	36,417	4.7	3.1	3.9	3.9	8.4

Source: abstracted from Global Scenario Group, 1998, A-5.

Of the fuels immediately available for the purposes of develop-ment, coal is the least efficient and the most destructive, but it is also the cheapest and, if the task of making it relatively clean is ignored, then it is the simplest fuel to use in power generation. Asia holds about 25 per cent of the world's reserves, North America another 25 per cent and Europe somewhat more than 30 per cent. Africa, the continent most in need of energy resources, has about 6 per cent, but most of it is in South Africa, Botswana and Zimbabwe. Even if the reserves were adequate, for the foreseeable future distribution would be difficult. The production of electricity and, to a lesser degree, the production of steel have largely been the basis for industrialisation in developing countries, and in the past both have depended on burning coal. It is probable that much future development will take the same path, but, quite apart from environmental worries which, no matter how real, tend to be the preserve of citizens in the developed world, supplies are subject to the whims of the market. The US in particular is a major exporter, but is in the habit of suspending supplies whenever it considers the price to be too low – and other exporters will certainly follow that lead.[19] The issue of fuel for underdeveloped countries thus has two parts: east Asia, particularly China, has made extensive use of coal in its industrialisation, but is now moving towards natural gas; coal is not a realistic starting point for most of Africa nor, come to that, for the poorer states of Latin America where very little coal is to be found; the second part is, once again, the contradiction between development and the operation of the markets.

The WEC suggests that natural gas will be the most important and successful intermediate source of energy. It is the cleanest of the fossil fuels and the industry is considering ways of making it cleaner: coal produces 50 per cent more CO_2 equivalent than natural gas and oil produces 20 per cent more. There are 151.4 trillion cubic metres of known recoverable reserves and new reserves are frequently being discovered, particularly in places where the industry has already been searching for oil. Many other regions thought to contain reserves have yet to be fully explored; Bangladesh is an example, yet despite its underexploited resources, it derives over two thirds of its commercial energy from gas. The current geographical distribution of reserves is shown in Table 4.4. A substantial part of Europe's reserves are to be found in Russia, which is a net exporter of gas. We have no reason to doubt the WEC's assertion that companies in the gas business are trying to find ways to make it even cleaner, but the extent of that research and the purposes to which it is being put may be another issue. It is important to remember that major oil companies are also the corporations drilling for gas and their record in environmental concern is less than admirable. Once again we remark on Shell's record in Ogoniland, but a less dramatic, but still ruthless, refusal to countenance environmental objections to their activities may be seen in its ecologically destructive construction of a gas terminal in one of the more beautiful parts of the West of Ireland – supported, of course, by a supine government. We should treat any suggestion that TNC enterprise in drilling for gas is a public good with a little reserve.

Table 4.4   Distribution of Known Reserves of Natural Gas (%)

Africa	7.5
North America	5.2
South America	4.2
Asia	11.3
Europe	35.3
Middle East	35.2
Oceania	1.3

Source: WEC, *Survey of Energy Resources*, 2001.

Nonetheless, as both the Global Scenario Group and the WEC have said, natural gas could be used to fuel development and, with some effort, adequate infrastructure could be put into place and technology easily transferred. Difficulties in the way are twofold: gas, infrastructure and the technology are all in the control of the corporate sector and the world at large, at least so far as it is represented by the WSSD, wants to see development in the poorer states within the existing market system. In the case of the first difficulty, we have no reason to suppose that the corporations will temper their practices so far as to reduce their levels of expatriated profits by reducing costs to recipient nations. The second simply contains a contradiction: the centripetal nature of international markets is such that they can only survive by the *extraction* of profit; any dealing through them produces loss for the weakest partner. It is notorious that a great part of the difficulties in which developing countries find themselves is a product of the operations of these markets.

Natural gas may be plentiful, but it is still a fossil fuel, ultimately finite as to supplies and, although it is relatively clean, using it to replace oil and coal would certainly substantially reduce the rate of CO_2 emissions, but would continue to result in a net contribution to the problem of global warming. In the improbable event of development, even fuelled by natural gas, progressing to the point where the MDGs are met, its scale would suggest a sizeable addition to the emissions of carbon dioxide and other gasses. This additional burden is reflected in the predictions made by the Global Scenario Group and by *GEO 3* – both allow for an increase in the early stages. The one OECD state that has substantially reduced its emissions, without resorting to natural gas, is France and it has done so by opting for nuclear power generation. There is little point in rehearsing the dangers of this resource, they are too well known and opposition to it is considerable, well informed and vocal. The WEC, while remaining non-committal, is inclined not to dismiss the possibility of the further deployment of nuclear energy. It remarks that despite stagnation in the building of new plants in North America and Western Europe, there is a small building programme in the transitional states of Eastern Europe and a rapid expansion in East Asia. Nuclear power stations may now be built more quickly and cheaply than in the past, they cost less to run, new and partially successful research into nuclear waste disposal continues and much research into new reactor technologies is currently being undertaken. The major OECD states have many reasons, economic and political, for disliking the increased availability of nuclear technology. Economically it could undermine their hegemony and politically they see it as increasing the risk of the military use of its by-products. But, if the option becomes relatively cheap, then its use will be demanded by developing countries beyond those called 'transitional'; some of the poorest states, for example Malawi, are thought to possess substantial deposits of uranium and the Global Scenario Group suggests that Africa as a whole has 35 per cent of the world's reserves.[20]

If this development should take place, a further difficulty could emerge. The power industry is happiest with gigantic sources of energy, and this is particularly true of nuclear power; gigantic sources call for gigantic investment and in both current and foreseeable circumstances, this means handing over yet another major resource to the corporate sector. Developing states are unlikely to have the ability, or the political will, to ensure at least some state control. Partnerships for energy have been created, but, in general, the energy corporations have preferred to make their own arrangements, or, as in the case of oil, to maintain their interests intact. They have certainly not shown excessive enthusiasm in developing sustainable energy resources for poor countries. About three weeks after the Summit ended, the UN Department for Economic and Social Affairs triumphantly announced that: 'A ten year old organisation of nine electric utilities in Japan, Europe and North America, the "e7," entered into a series of agreements with the United Nations and its agencies during the World Summit on Sustainable Development aimed at expanding access by the poor to electricity.'[21] But e7 was formed at the Rio Summit ten years earlier and is hardly news; at present, it consists of: AEP (US), Electricité de France (France), Enel (Italy), Hydro-Quebec (Canada), Kansai Electric Power (Japan), Ontario Power Generation (Canada), RWE (Germany), Scottish Power (UK) and Tokyo Electric Power (Japan). By any standards this is a consortium with considerable economic muscle, but, at the time of writing, it lists only five small projects in Ecuador, Bolivia, Indonesia, Bhutan, Jordan and a sixth in the Niger's national park which touches on Burkino Faso and Benin as well as Niger – a performance which the present authors feel lacks lustre.

We have already remarked that the oil industry is also the natural gas industry, and we have little hope of serious reform which will drive oil corporations to the use of ecologically sound practices. The nuclear industry may be forced to clean up its act if it is to survive, but it, too, is increasingly controlled by power-generating corporations. In the final chapter of this book, we shall address the question of how such arrangements stand in the way of development and the achievement of the MDGs. Here it is enough to remind ourselves that rapid urbanisation means that an increasing number of the destitute are to be found in cities (see Table 4.5). Agricultural revolution, whether the move is towards either intensive or sustainable farming, will demand increased energy, but even greater demands will be made by the development both of industry and of urban living. Any attempt to deny the poor access to energy, either because it does not suit the balance sheet or because the Western middle classes are frightened (no matter how reasonably) of the consequences of expanding nuclear power, can only be interpreted by the poor as unwarrantable, dog-in-manger responses.

Table 4.5   Urbanisation (% of each population)

Region	1995	2025	2050
Africa	34	54	69
China	31	54	69
Latin America	74	84	90
Middle East	58	72	80
S & SE Asia	31	48	62

Source: Global Scenario Group, 1998.

5   Other Business

Clean water, essential for general survival as well as prophylaxis, is clearly one of the most important conditions for achieving the Millennium Development Goals. So too is producing the energy necessary for development, without which the goals are meaningless. We have devoted two chapters to them not only because of their centrality, but also because of the attention they were given by the Summit. Nonetheless, as a cursory glance at the *Plan of Implementation* will show, there were many more items on the agenda. Some were either dealt with very briefly, or were adjuncts to larger issues as, for example, in the cases of the demand for improved transport (paragraph 20) and for the improvement of marine safety (paragraph 33.*bis*). Both are plainly important, but both are dependent on agreements to larger frameworks. Other matters impinge more directly on everyone's lives, particularly on the lives of those surviving on the edge, or even just poor. Not all of these will be covered in the remainder of this chapter, only those listed as the central points of the agenda by the WEHAB Frameworks (see Chapter 2).

We have already commented on the problems posed by climate change and the fact that, even if it had been universally accepted, the Kyoto Protocol would have done very little in the way of amelioration. Its rejection as Draconian by US industry and its clients in the White House has successfully moved the battleground away from the inadequacy of the Protocol to getting it recognised and acted upon by other governments in the industrialised world. This is a move which, to a considerable extent, has effectively muffled protest at the deficiencies of the Protocol and paragraph 36 of the *Plan*, which calls for worldwide ratification, has little to offer apart from exhortation. But climate change is not the only product of the profligate and irresponsible consumption of energy, which also contributes to air and water pollution, acid deposits and ozone destruction (paragraph 37). Here the strongest proposal offered by the Summit is that states should 'facilitate implementation of the Montreal Protocol on Substances that Deplete the Ozone Layer by ensuring adequate replenishment of its funds by 2003/2005' (37.b).

The Montreal Protocol, first agreed in 1987, but subsequently modified, is to the 1985 Vienna Convention for the Protection of the Ozone Layer. It was an agreement that industrialised countries should stop producing halons by January 1994; it was also agreed that they should stop the production of chlorofluorocarbons (usually known as CFCs), carbon tetrachloride and methyl chloroform by January 1996. In the case of CFCs, initial exceptions were made so that enough could be produced to meet the essential needs generated by certain medical technologies and those of developing countries which could not substitute other agents. Alternatives to CFCs, principally hydrochlorofluorocarbons (HCFCs) and hydrofluorocarbons (HFCs) are also damaging, but less so; these were to be phased out more slowly until safe alternatives were introduced, and are to be abandoned completely by 2030. Developing countries were given a longer period in which to comply with the Montreal Protocol, but they are expected to do so by 2040. The *Plan*'s plea for money is ominous, since administrators of the Protocol are, in a sense, the enforcing body and are facing challenges from industry which claims that it is in breach of GATT regulations. If that challenge is pursued, then without adequate finance the Protocol's administration will fail. In passing, we should note that the Montreal Protocol was an agreement about a single issue, the ozone layer, with simple and achievable targets. That it is limping heavily and is in increasing danger of dying for lack of sustenance offers us little hope for an agreement like the Kyoto Protocol which, quite apart from US intransigence, has variable targets and is more complicated.

No further mention of acid deposits is made in the *Plan* and air pollution appears again only in the context of demanding that lead be phased out of petrol in order to reduce respiratory disease (paragraph 49). But pollution in general, which we must presume to include these two categories, is mentioned extensively throughout the document. The importance of reducing pollution and waste is listed as a necessary part of establishing sustainable consumption and, a little like gender equality, it is added to any topic to which it could possibly pertain. In both cases the reader is left with a faint impression of mantra rather than of meaning, but this is probably an unreasonable quibble. Much of the world's population is faced daily with the problems caused by pollution and it would seem to be indisputable that they should be addressed. How this is to be done is the point at which difficulties emerge and, in paragraph 18.b, dealing with the need to internalise environmental costs, the not infrequent condition appears. States are urged

> to promote the internalization of environmental costs and the use of economic instruments, taking into account the approach that the polluter should, in principle, bear the costs of pollution, with due regard to the public interest and without distorting international trade and investment.

'Public interest' is a notoriously slippery concept since a variety of publics differ about what is in their interests. This becomes an acute difficulty when we realise that much research into it is conducted by interested corporations who frequently own the means of communicating its content. The injunction not to distort trade and investment is the fatal condition; it simply reinforces, for example, the fossil fuel industry's substantial and successful efforts to prevent its polluting practices from being curtailed. Bush's capitulation to the environmentally destructive timber trade is another example.

The two principles set out in paragraph 18.b, the internalisation of environmental costs and payment by the polluter of the costs of cleaning up the pollution, are important. We should remind ourselves of what should be meant by these apparently admirable proposals. Environmental costs are incurred by processes or actions that damage the environment. Industrial production which, for example, releases polluting elements into the atmosphere, into water courses or seas and onto the land, or which generates noise, light and aesthetic pollution, is a case in point: the environment is savaged and we, who live in it, bear the costs. Business economists call such events 'externalities' and the apparent inability to put prices on them, together with the use of that particular word, makes it possible for them to be regarded as incidental, as someone else's problem.[1] The owners of industrial processes producing these effects would, in what they see as a perfect world, probably prefer not to do these things, but they operate in a competitive market and must, if they are to survive as producers not just of goods but of the far more vital returns on investment, keep their costs down. Those often mentioned bottom lines in company reports must show increasingly positive sums and they are based on business plans and balance sheets that work according to rigorous rules. At the root of the system lies a simple formula: every item in it must have a price and a calculated return; investment in plant, materials and personnel not only have direct costs, but the capital used in each of these categories has also to be paid for by way of interest. In a sense it is a descending chain: investment funds must be bought at a market price, but when money from those funds is disbursed, each item must show a return greater than its original cost. It is a curiously rigid system which is incapable of responding to environmental costs because it is notoriously difficult to put a price on, for example, air quality in domestic areas adjacent to a cement factory. When those states with governments susceptible to public pressure introduce regulation to control pollution, the accountants calculate the costs of compliance and add them to all those other costs which must show a return. This is to externalise, not to internalise, the cost of environmental damage; what is unquestionably not happening is payment by the polluter, but by the ordinary purchaser of the end product who is frequently unable to find a more environmentally friendly alternative.

One may watch with fascination the sleight of hand employed by manufacturers who sell polluting goods and services to a public without choice and then suggest that it is the purchaser who is polluting and who should bear the consequent costs. An example may be seen in the relentless increase in food packaging. If the real polluter paid, the profit line would be reduced significantly. We have already commented on another farcical, but deadly, version of this in the creation of an international financial market in carbon emission permits – the net result of which is not the reduction, but the more efficient spreading of what may yet prove to be the most catastrophic of all pollutions. Other less immediately lethal but still maleficent 'externalities' prevail. At the point of production health and safety are ignored until regulation and control, usually paid for with tax revenues, are introduced; at the point of social reproduction, the town and country planning, frequently resisted by industry as an impediment to what it sees as its efficiency, is also an externality to be charged to the public purse.

Despite rapid urbanisation (see Table 4.5), over half of the world's population is rural, most of them dependent on farming of one sort or another.[2] The *Plan* begins its recommendations for agriculture with the customary list of unexceptionable proposals: the MDGs are reaffirmed together with a reminder to states of 'their obligations under article 11 of the International Convention on Economic, Social and Cultural Rights' – a convention which must rank among the least enforced (paragraph 38.a). This optimism is followed by a clutch of quite sensible suggestions: 'integrated land management and water-use plans ... based on sustainable use of renewable resources' should be developed (paragraph 38.b); water resources should be protected and sensibly managed, land should be made more sustainably productive (paragraphs 38.c–d); land degradation, the participation of women, information systems and extension services for farmers, indigenous resource management, land and water rights and public finance for the sector should all be adopted, enhanced, promoted and increased (paragraphs 38.e–i). The rub comes in subclauses 38.k and l; in the first of these it is suggested that incentives should be offered to farmers who monitor and manage water resources and their use, but those incentives should be 'market-based'. Once again, the cat is positively ejected from the bag in the next sub-clause: 'Enhance access to existing markets and develop new markets for value-added agricultural products.' Paragraph 38, like many others, concerns farmers throughout the world and, for those in industrialised states, it may be taken as admonitory. But for farmers in the underdeveloped world, who lack the complex social and physical infrastructure available to their wealthier counterparts, and for whom any but the most rudimentary forms of food-processing are far beyond reach, that development of new markets will simply reinforce the peonage of contract farming.

If the MDGs, or even the more cautious ambitions of the Global Scenario Group, are to be achieved, then health is obviously hugely important; just as it is in all sustainable development. The WSSD made the point and the *Plan* reminds us (in paragraph 46) that it was also made ten years earlier in the Rio Declaration on Environment and Development. It is referring to Principle 1 of that Declaration, which, in turn, quotes chapter 6 of Agenda 21, paragraph 1: 'health and development are intimately interconnected ... Agenda 21 must address the primary health needs of the world's population, since they are integral to the achievement of the goals of sustainable development and primary environmental care.' Once again, the exhortations of the *Plan* are, in general, entirely reasonable: health education, affordable resources for health care, the marriage of allopathic and traditional practices and so on. Some important and already agreed targets are reaffirmed: 'by the year 2015, mortality rates for infants and children under 5 [are to be reduced] by two thirds, and maternal mortality rates by three quarters of the prevailing rate in 2000' (paragraph 47.f). An earnest, if ill-defined, task is set for health educationalists with, 'where appropriate' 'the involvement of United Nations agencies'; they are expected to achieve 'improved health literacy on a global basis by 2010', but what this might mean is not elaborated (paragraph 47.e).

A curious disjunction between paragraphs 47 and 48 is discernible. The latter is concerned with HIV/AIDS, but no connection is made between it and the targets for mortality rates. Nothing in the paragraph is objectionable, but, considering the scale of the phenomenon, it is very low key. Further references occur in paragraphs 54, 58, 94 and 111. The first of these is a general call for help for SIDS in acquiring the 'necessary drugs and technology in a sustainable and affordable manner to fight and control ... diseases, in particular HIV/AIDS, tuberculosis, diabetes, malaria and dengue fever'. Paragraph 58 occurs in part VIII which is devoted to the African continent, its sub-clause 58.b provides the same anodyne proposals as those in 54.b for SIDS. Not until we get to paragraph 94 do we find a more substantive proposal, in part IX, oddly entitled 'Means of Implementation' – odd simply because it is no such thing, but is principally a summary of what has gone before. That proposal is worth quoting in full, as it calls on states to:

> Address the public health problems affecting many developing and least developed countries, especially those resulting from HIV/AIDS, tuberculosis, malaria and other epidemics, while noting the importance of the Doha Declaration on the TRIPS Agreement and Public Health, in which it has been agreed that the TRIPS Agreement does not and should not prevent WTO members from taking measures to protect public health. Accordingly, while reiterating our commitment to the TRIPS Agreement, we reaffirm that the Agreement can and should be interpreted and implemented in a manner supportive of WTO members' right to protect public health and in particular to promote access to medicines for all.

In November 2001, a WTO Ministerial Conference was held in Doha; among its purposes was the reinforcement of the agreement known as TRIPS (Trade-Related Aspects of Intellectual Property Rights). That agreement was negotiated between the members of the WTO shortly after its establishment in Marrakesh in 1994; its purpose was to defend the rights of the owners of intellectual property. It spells out the sorts of thing it covers: copyright, trademarks, products identified by their place of origin (for example, Parmesan cheese), new or original industrial designs, patentable matter (the most important issue for the purposes of this discussion), undisclosed information and the control of 'anti-competitive practices in contractual licences'.[3] In its preamble, it makes a gesture towards poor countries by: 'Recognizing the special needs of the least-developed country Members in respect of maximum flexibility in the domestic implementation of laws and regulations to enable them to create a sound and viable technological base.'

The Doha conference added its mite in paragraph 44 of its Ministerial Declaration:

> We reaffirm that provisions for special and differential treatment are an integral part of the WTO Agreements. We note the concerns expressed regarding their operation in addressing specific constraints faced by developing countries, particularly least-developed countries. In that connection, we also note that some members have proposed a Framework Agreement on Special and Differential Treatment.

Earlier in the Declaration the delegates had asserted that:

> We stress the importance we attach to implementation and interpretation of the Agreement on Trade-Related Aspects of Intellectual Property Rights (TRIPS Agreement) in a manner supportive of public health, by promoting both access to existing medicines and research and development into new medicines.

Other protocols made the same promises and these were the basis for the campaign for the manufacture of cheap, generic medicines for those too poor to afford their commercial counterparts. A further agreement on the matter was negotiated. Even though it did not address the issue of those too poor to buy even the cheaper drugs, it was a victory, of a sort, for humanity.

Public opinion, within the most afflicted countries as well as in the industrialised world, had brought about this modest change through vigorous and vociferous campaigns. But these were waged against a recalcitrant and powerful industry which, well before the Doha Conference, had made clear its displeasure at any such agreement. It had partly lost the battle in the case of HIV/AIDS, but it was determined not to allow the general extension of the principle to all the other major scourges of acute poverty throughout the developing world and had demanded that the concession should be limited to malaria, TB and a few peculiarly African diseases. In December 2002 the corporations got their way when Cheney, Vice-President of the US, announced that the administration was rejecting the Doha position and the subsequent negotiations. This announcement followed intense lobbying by the US pharmaceutical industry and it means that poor countries will not be allowed either to manufacture or import badly needed cheaper medicines.[4]

This abandonment of the flimsy promises made at Doha must be added to the list of international agreements rejected by the Bush regime; in terms of its effect on the health of the world's poor, it may be even more destructive than that Protestant fundamentalist administration's ban on funding clinics which even so much as discuss abortion with their patients. But to return to the paragraph from the *Plan* with which we began this brief discussion of health, it is worth comparing it with the far more direct expression contained in the WEHAB group's Framework for Action on Health and the Environment, presented, at his request, to the UN Secretary General immediately before the Summit began:

> While poverty may cause people to become ill, it often means becoming poorer – both directly, because the poor have to spend a part of their small income to pay for treatment and medicines, and indirectly, because their choices become limited and they may be unable to secure a livelihood. (section 10)

In the case of southern Africa particularly, it makes the point that: 'In stark contrast to trends in other regions, children today in southern Africa can expect to live shorter lives than their grandparents.' It goes on to deal with the question of AIDS, but incorporates all the other diseases of poverty:

> Effective measures for a substantially scaled-up AIDS prevention effort, for example, that incorporates the education and empowerment of women include the following, among other components: accessible, inexpensive condoms; immediate treatment of other sexually transmitted infections; voluntary counselling and testing for HIV; prevention of mother-to-child transmission; ... *innovative new partnerships* to provide sustainable and affordable supplies of medicines and diagnostics. As with other diseases, effective care of people living with HIV/AIDS will require affordable drugs and strengthened health systems, including stable

and effective drug distribution, improved laboratory services and supportive health care staff. (section 11, emphasis added)

Apart from its unspecific reference to 'innovative new partnerships', WEHAB's framework is not hedged about with the conditions incorporated into the final *Plan of Implementation*. It is improbable that the framers of this much more direct demand were excluding public–private partnerships, but the Bush administration's destruction of the ambitions for public health in the developing world adds to the view that to think of such partnerships as a means of achieving the MDGs is little more than a pious hope.

Agriculture makes its first appearance in the *Plan* in paragraph 6, which is devoted to the eradication of poverty: 'actions at all levels' must be undertaken to, *inter alia*, 'provide access to agricultural resources for people living in poverty', to 'build basic rural infrastructure, diversify the economy and improve transportation' and to transfer 'sustainable agricultural techniques'. What might be meant by this is spelled out more fully in paragraph 38 which we discussed briefly in Chapter 2. Its eighteen sub-clauses present us with yet another list of good intentions: land and water management plans are to be 'integrated' allowing the 'sustainable use of renewable resources' and improvements in productivity; women's participation is to be enhanced; information systems are to be strengthened; the rights to the use of land and water should be codified and enforced. We have already commented, in Chapter 2, on the three sub-clauses on 'public sector finance', 'market-based incentives' and the vexed question of access to the undefined markets together with the ability of poor farmers to add value to their primary products. These are followed by a number of increasingly vague aspirations (see appendix B), but lurking among them is a plea to those states who have not yet ratified the International Treaty on Plant Genetic Resources for Food and Agriculture, agreed in November 2001, to do so.

The purpose of the Treaty is set out in its first article:

The objectives of this Treaty are the conservation and sustainable use of plant genetic resources for food and agriculture and the fair and equitable sharing of the benefits arising out of their use, in harmony with the Convention on Biological Diversity, for sustainable agriculture and food security.[5]

It is to do with the conservation of such resources, their equitable use and the reinforcement of the rights of people in their 'centres of origin'. It is a good and common-sensical treaty and its progress has been as rapid as it usually is in the case of obviously worthwhile endeavours. Of the seventy-eight states, plus the European Community, which participated in the formulation of the Treaty, only twelve so far have ratified it.[6] The US signed the Treaty in November 2000, but given the success that the pharmaceutical industry has achieved in that country, it might be rash to expect rapid ratification, or even to expect ratification at all. Britain signed in June 2000 with much publicity and signs of governmental pleasure, followed by masterly inaction. The importance of the Treaty to agriculture in the developing world is clear: article 5 begins with a commitment to surveying, collecting and conserving these resources; it then proposes the promotion 'or support, as appropriate, [for] farmers and local communities' efforts to manage and conserve on-farm their plant genetic resources for food and agriculture' (5.1.c). States which have signed the Treaty have also agreed to: 'Promote *in situ* conservation of wild crop relatives and wild plants for food production, including in protected areas, by supporting, *inter alia*, the efforts of indigenous and local communities' (5.1.d). Article 6 carries the point yet further in its suggestions for the use of genetic resources for food and agriculture: 'agricultural policies that promote ... the development and maintenance of diverse farming systems that enhance the sustainable use of agricultural biological diversity and other natural resources' (6.2.a). This is followed by a call for research which will 'benefit ... farmers, especially those who generate and use their own varieties and apply ecological principles in maintaining soil fertility and in combating diseases, weeds and pests' (6.2.b). Should we be left in any doubt about the general direction of the Treaty, the position is underlined by the commitment to promote 'plant breeding efforts which, with the participation of farmers, particularly in developing countries, strengthen the capacity to develop varieties particularly adapted to social, economic and ecological conditions, including in marginal areas' (6.2.c). In short it is a treaty designed to preserve and to make use of genetic resources, but also protect both the rights of people to their indigenous resources and to preserve the highly productive diversity in Third World farming. Such measures are anathema to agribusiness, since they would remove both substantial forms of production from its control and profitable resources that it might otherwise privatise under the TRIPS Agreement.

Biodiversity was the fifth central issue on the WSSD's agenda and its discussion was heavily conditioned by the effort to persuade states that had signed up to the CBD, which had a stormy birth leading up to and during the UNCED in June 1992; the Rio Summit almost foundered because of US opposition to the Convention. At the time, the destruction of the world's rainforests was a very popular cause; the loss of biological diversity (now usually referred to in the neologism 'biodiversity') was subsumed into it and the entire package constituted a major issue for the Rio Summit. This was interpreted, in the US administration's customary dysfunctional reasoning, as a direct onslaught on the standards of living in the US, by which, of course, it meant the profitability of some corporations. The president at the time was George Bush senior and a petulant abstentionism seems to run in the family since he, too, had threatened to withdraw from the Summit. Unlike his son, he was persuaded to cooperate, but part of the price was the evisceration of a convention which, in its draft, was already far from exigent.

At the heart of the difficulty then was, as it is now, the question of ownership and control of resources. In the draft of the Convention we find the recommendation that states should:

> Recognize and foster the traditional methods and the knowledge of indigenous people and their communities, emphasizing the particular role of women, relevant to the conservation of biological diversity and the sustainable use of biological resources, and ensure the opportunity for the participation of those groups in the economic and commercial benefits derived from the use of such traditional methods and knowledge. (paragraph 4.g)

That proved to be a brew far too heavy for the stomachs of the US administration and what the Convention finally contained was a far weaker provision:

> Subject to its national legislation [each state shall] respect, preserve and maintain knowledge, innovations and practices of indigenous and local communities embodying traditional lifestyles relevant for the conservation and sustainable use of biological diversity and promote their wider application with the approval and involvement of the holders of such knowledge, innovations and practices and encourage the equitable sharing of the benefits arising from the utilization of such knowledge, innovations and practices. (article 8.j)

Article 3 makes clear that the resources belong to the states in which they occur and the parties to the Convention make the dubious assumption that these states will 'respect, preserve and maintain [the] knowledge ... of indigenous and local communities' – yet another act of heroic piety. But even this anodyne recommendation was further adulterated in article 16:

Access to and transfer of technology referred to in paragraph 1 above to developing countries shall be provided and/or facilitated under fair and most favourable terms, including on concessional and preferential terms ... In the case of technology subject to patents and other intellectual property rights, such access and transfer shall be provided on terms *which recognize and are consistent with the adequate and effective protection of intellectual property rights.* (article 16, clauses 2 and 2.1; emphasis added)

In short, 'indigenous and local communities' (not people) will be respected, but will also have to pay the inflated prices that the ultimate technological products command.[7]

In January 2000, the Convention was modified by the Cartagena Protocol on Biosafety – a protocol first adumbrated in 1999 at Cartagena on the coast of Colombia and completed, a year later, in a subsequent meeting in Montreal. It is designed to protect biodiversity from the risks posed by genetically modified organisms produced by modern biotechnology – a purpose set out in its first article:

In accordance with the precautionary approach contained in Principle 15 of the Rio Declaration on Environment and Development, the objective of this Protocol is to contribute to ensuring an adequate level of protection in the field of the safe transfer, handling and use of living modified organisms resulting from modern biotechnology that may have adverse effects on the conservation and sustainable use of biological diversity, taking also into account risks to human health, and specifically focusing on transboundary movements.

To the casual reader, this would seem to be uncontentious stuff to be accepted alongside the modest requirements of the CBD – yet some large-sized feet are being dragged in the process of ratification. In the case of the Convention, the US joins Ireland (which was neither a party nor a signatory, but has an unenviable record of total disregard for its own biodiversity), Thailand and Tuvalu in failing to ratify; in the case of the more recent Protocol, so far forty countries have either ratified or are on the point of doing so and, once again, the most industrially powerful of nations are the most somnolent in their response.[8]

Difficulties lie not just in the repeated failure of the process of ratification, but also in the failure of the drafters to specify the objects of concern. Whether conservation refers to genes, species or ecologies or, indeed, to all three is not addressed; the consequence of this failure is a muddle behind which recalcitrant states can hide. The conservation and exploitation of genetic resources is, whatever the ultimate effects on society at large may be, a matter of science. Preserving species, as in the famous case of the panda, is a popular cause and it may affect the conservation of gene pools, but it is primarily a political issue. Ecological conservation concerns land and water and is directly affected by the implementation of the *Plan*'s frequent plea for the management and sustainable use of these fundamental resources. Each requires its own definition and its own processes, which should have been spelt out in the texts rather than put into the bundles of diversity and safety.

All this is the background to paragraph 42 of the *Plan of Implementation*; it is one of the longer passages and, quite possibly, its length is a consequence both of its importance and of the improbability of the acceptance of any of its proposals. Many of its twenty sub-clauses are unspecific; for example, actions must be taken at all levels to: '[i]ntegrate the objectives of the Convention into ... cross-sectoral programmes and policies' (42.a) or to '[p]romote the ... work under the Convention on the sustainable use on [*sic*] biological diversity' (42.b). Others come closer to a recognisable stance and the first few of those to do so (sub-clauses 42.e–i) are devoted to measures for ecological protection and preservation. Apart from the introductory section of the paragraph, it is not until 42.h that reference is made to people: 'financial and technical support to developing countries, including capacity-building [must be provided], in order to enhance indigenous and community-based biodiversity conservation efforts'. The text reverts briefly to ecological matters in urging the 'control [of] invasive alien species' (42.i), but returns, in 42.j, to societal concerns by urging the recognition, '[s]ubject to national legislation', of 'the rights of local and indigenous communities ... [the] holders of traditional knowledge, innovations and practices'. These communities are to be included in the 'decision and policy-making ... [in] the use of their traditional knowledge' (42.l). In sub-clause 42.n we come across the most substantive proposal: 'the wide implementation of and continued work on the Bonn Guidelines on Access to Genetic Resources and Fair and Equitable Sharing of Benefits [must be promoted]'.

The CBD had established 'The Ad Hoc Open-Ended Working Group on Access and Benefit-Sharing', which met, initially in Bonn, to draw up guidelines for the interpretation of the Convention and of the Cartagena Protocol – they are known as 'the Bonn Guidelines'. They propose the establishment of 'competent national authorities' to deal with the issues surrounding the exploitation of biological resources and indigenous knowledge and to secure the 'informed consent' of the indigenous communities to that exploitation. In setting out the responsibilities of those authorities, the guidelines make a small but crucial change in emphasis: the 'contracting parties' (that is, to the Convention) 'are [the] countries of origin of genetic resources, or *other Parties which have acquired the genetic resources* in accordance with the Convention' (paragraph 14.a, emphasis added), and it is they who must make the decisions and agreements. No matter what attempts might be made to ensure the informed consent of the indigenous communities, the fox would seem to have been made welcome to the hen-coop. That impression is reinforced in 14.b.vi when the parties to the Convention are urged to: 'As much as possible endeavour to carry out their use of the genetic resources in, and with the participation of, the providing country.'

If we return to the *Plan* we find, yet again, that underlying contradiction between the campaign to achieve the MDGs and the realities of international agreements. In paragraph 42.r manic equivocations mount up:

> With a view to enhancing synergy and mutual supportiveness, taking into account the decisions under the relevant agreements, promote the discussions, without prejudging their outcome, with regard to the relationships between the Convention and agreements related to international trade and intellectual property rights, as outlined in the Doha Ministerial Declaration.

Here, lurking in the sludge of the *Plan's* prose, we may detect that capitulation to the TNC's programme which was embodied in George Bush junior's rejection of even the modest concessions made to the poor at Doha.

6   Development and Duplicity

In our introductory chapter we expressed our reservations about INGO responses to the WSSD. We said that they were mistaken in complaining about the lack of targets and had given insufficient attention to the surprising fact that the Summit has actually taken place despite the posturing and bellicosity of the Bush plutocracy. But not everything can be laid at the door of that regime. Bush is not alone: several OECD governments, together with the Bretton Woods international financial institutions, have vested interests in not being overspecific in the matters of either the eradication of poverty or the future development of poor countries. At the root of the INGO responses lies a certain disingenuity, since it had been clear for some considerable time before the event that enforceable targets of any kind, apart from the less than totally convincing MDGs, could not be set. In the WSSD, as in all other summits, there is a degree of theatricality since much of the bargaining takes place before the event, and we have already noted the dismal story of the preparatory committees. The WEHAB proposals were tangential to the limping committee documents and were an ungenial argument for the most optimistic results possible in the circumstances. In acting as if a major reversal of the outcomes of the committees was possible at the Summit itself, the INGOs were simply adding their bit-parts to the performance. There are politics here to which we must return.

Behind the WSSD there is a long history, not just of summits, but of countless other 'high level' meetings in which earnest people have addressed one another on the subject of worldwide poverty – the present authors have attended several of them. In each case academics, members of NGOs, senior politicians and civil servants and a suitably small body of representatives from the Third World are brought together. The latter are usually carefully chosen to avoid upsetting too many susceptibilities, although fortunately the organisers frequently either get that selection wrong or have among themselves the occasional subversive – alternative voices are sometimes heard.[1] Poverty is still a grotesque blight in a world of plenty, but these meetings, designed to alleviate that blight, have gradually changed their agendas, even if they have had little discernible effect on the problem. Early agendas formed by the warriors of the Cold War or which were blatantly neo-colonial in intent were very important, often dominant, but it is possible to describe changes nonetheless.

To begin with, parodic versions of the Marshall plan were put in place for poor countries, loans were made, some technological help was given and the supposition was that the recipients would, with this bounty and through honest toil, bring themselves into the contemporary world and repay the loans.[2] Somehow, this was to be achieved despite very extensive protectionism by the states of the industrialised world. During this early period, we can also see that thinking about disaster tended only to encompass 'natural' catastrophies – drought, flood, earthquake and the like; effort devoted to relieving people affected by them was confined to the provision of temporary welfare until their communities were rehabilitated. Neither of these approaches bore much relation to reality, but they were the models on which theory was based and 'aid' was advanced. From the beginning of this history it was necessary to put quotation marks around 'aid', simply because most of it was in the form of profitable investment by finance, industry and some states – a point well argued by Teresa Hayter more than thirty years ago.[3] Many subsequent mutations have taken us through, for example, debt relief, including the infamous 'debt-for-nature-swaps'; linking poverty with environmental degradation (frequently mistakenly); the campaign to get local livelihoods treated with the same enthusiasm as investment in massive developmental infrastructure. There are very many more, but the most important, and probably the most destructive of all changes has been the 'marketisation' of development.

Similar mutations took place in thinking about humanitarian assistance: the most important was the recognition of the distinction between acute and chronic emergencies. The first of these might be natural, but it is always necessary to keep in mind the frequency with which a 'natural' disaster can be triggered by human activity or intervention; the second is the recurrent or continuous emergency caused either by international or internecine conflict, or by, for example, the six year drought in Africa.[4] A crude distinction has also been made between the kinds of response called for by each sort of catastrophe: acute emergencies frequently demand a radical first-aid operation, but chronic emergencies call for investment in rebuilding livelihoods and establishing some degree of security.[5] Later thinking about these distinctions has become more sophisticated and, outside the foreign ministries of the industrialised states, the role played by the developed world in responding to such crises is now frequently recognised as counter-productive. Another canard which has lingered on through several of the mutations in thinking, both about developmental and humanitarian assistance, is the very dubious, quasi-philanthropic and Malthusian theory that too great a liberality towards the destitute runs the danger of creating dependency.

Not all changes have been so negative, the most important of them all has been the open politicisation of development theory; it was, of course, always political, but the widespread understanding of that politics was inhibited by a comforting shroud of benevolence. To a considerable degree, the present writers would argue that the establishment of the MDGs is one consequence of this change. The process would seem to be incremental as well as spasmodic and a parallel may decently be drawn between it and the fitful start of the International Criminal Court (ICC). US, Chinese and Indian determination that their home-grown war criminals should not be accountable, and British ambivalence (as in the fudging of issues over Pinochet), were all among the difficulties leading up to the Rome Statute of 1998 which, once ratified by the necessary sixty states, brought the ICC into legal existence.[6] Hamstrung it may be, but that Court now exists and the ground of the battle has shifted from the fight to create it to the fight to get recalcitrant states to recognise it (we are tempted to use the adjective 'rogue', but that, of course, would be malicious). Like the Kyoto Protocol, the MDGs are ludicrously inadequate, but few doubt that their achievement would significantly alter the political landscape. Parallels with the ICC, which exists compromised by concessions made in the attempt to meet the rejectionists' demands and unable to protect half of the world's population, are obvious. The goals have been set, they have frequently been reaffirmed, there is a handful of states willing to put in place whatever measures are called for, but there is little movement because the actions of the bellicose refuseniks in Washington and the lassitude of several other states have ensured, at least for the time being, that they are off the agenda.

That the MDGs should be thus delayed eight years after their establishment, makes their achievement by 2015, at best, improbable. It was because they foresaw these doldrums that the Global Scenario Group proposed a more viable timetable: 'reducing the incidence of hunger, unsafe water and illiteracy by half by 2025 and in half again by 2050, based on 1995 figures'.[7] But that viability is based on some strictly political assumptions which are now open to serious doubt.

We referred, in Chapter 1, to the Group's earlier work, *Branch Points*, in which it set out three possible underlying and macrocosmic social trajectories, describing them as Conventional Worlds, Barbarisation and Great Transition. It presented them as choices facing the world in general and industrialised states in particular. Conventional Worlds is the shorthand phrase for the liberal-democratic, capitalist society with which we are familiar and is the position from which choice could be made. The Group suggested that as matters stood, it was possible for developed societies to entrench themselves in self-interested fortress nation ghettos with all the repressive responses entailed in such a choice. These societies could also decide to tinker with the existing systems and make do with business as before, the tinkering would have to become more constant as the faults in it became more apparent. But the Group also saw the current tensions and international difficulties of the time as creating the opportunity for real change to a more just and sustainable society – a change which they called Great Transition.

In its later work, *Bending the Curve*, the Group was less optimistic and concentrated on what might happen if conventional positions prevailed and how their occupiers might be compelled, or persuaded, to adjust in the face of both natural and political *force majeure*. But the Group's optimism was recovered in its next publication, *Great Transition*, which began by describing what it saw as the new 'Planetary Phase' into which the world has now entered.[8] That expression, or concept, is essentially the humanist alternative to the concept of market globalisation and the Group lists the obvious events and processes that gave rise to the situation which, in different ways, both expressions embody. These are the major global environmental changes and dangers, the revolution in communications and information technology, the end of the Cold War which led to the possibility of 'a hegemonic world capitalist system', economic integration, the rise of international institutions (TNCs, the Bretton Woods organisations, INGOs, even global terrorists) and the deregulation of production, trade and finance. Few would quarrel with the proposition that the Planetary Phase has begun, but, the Group points out, no matter how accelerated events have become, the ultimate directions it takes have yet to be seen.[9] The web of events which lead to particular geo-political or economic directions is, of course, hugely complicated and directions do not usually emerge as neat, systematic social and economic arrangements. It is also the case that the concept of the Planetary Phase (or of globalisation) is itself a simplification of complex and frequently contradictory pressures: for example, the role of the nation state in such an order is far from clear; another instance may be seen in the UN, the institution of assembled member states, not of global or globalising capital which actually sees the UN as an impediment. Between an inchoate planetary order and its greater formalisation the Group sees ground for persuasion and hope.

This optimism is tempered by the recognition, spelled out in *Bending the Curve*, that the path to transition starts with the contemporary conventional world and may, with policy reforms imposed by environmental reality and political pressure, continue along something like its present path. However ultimate goals may be conceived, this means that the immediate future holds, at best, repeated battles over reforms, aimed at prising the capitalist world away from its myopic absorption with balance sheets, before it produces yet greater human misery and even more catastrophic environmental damage. In *Great Transition*, the Global Scenario Group suggests that these battles will be fought through democratic means by '[c]ivil society and engaged citizens [who] become critical sources of change for the new values of *Great Transitions*'. We have expressed our reservations about the concept of 'civil society' elsewhere and, following Marx in his attack on Proudhon, regard it largely as the reproduction of the state in which it operates.[10] We may put that criticism aside for the moment and may even accept, in this case, the Group's assumptions. But to rely on 'civil society and engaged citizens' to force the necessary changes does seem to mean reliance on a frail reed – they may be worthy agents, but their record in such matters is not scintillating.

Democracies are transforming themselves into market states, commonly adopting the semi-literate and obfuscating jargon of the corporate world, and pretending that their decisions, now made by parliaments and civil servants posing as boards of directors, are the product of inexorable market forces. Despite this folly, forcing change is essentially a political act and the *soi-disant* civil society, much of it largely dependent on the very governments it is supposed to influence, eschews politics. Engaged citizens have a distinguished record in particular kinds of single issue campaign, but are not famous for their successes in more complex political issues. One example of massive effort making very little difference, either in national or in international politics, may be seen in the Campaign for Nuclear Disarmament. This is not to decry the campaign, it has been crucial in raising international public awareness, and it has also made life a lot harder for the obtuse nuclear warriors, but it has failed in its principal aim, which was to make a serious dent in the genocidal proclivities of those states, like the US, prepared to use the nuclear threat. The activities of engaged citizens are an essential ingredient of any democratic opposition, but without coherent political programmes they can expect only to compel tinkering with social and environmental problems and not the degree of change for which the Global Scenario Group makes such a strong case.

The instability of societies ruling with, or ruled by, market forces is pithily described by the Group: 'social and economic stability of [the] world would be compromised. A combination of factors – persistence of global poverty, continued inequity among and within nations and degradation of environmental resources – would undermine social cohesion, stimulate migration and weaken international security.'[11] The Group suggests that such unstable societies could continue for a long time, surviving intermittent environmental crises, social unrest and threats to security. But the consequence of their failure substantially to modify their policies could lead, on the one hand, to successful opposition which might compel change or, on the other, it could lead to crises increasing in number and ferocity and ending in catastrophe. As arguments for major changes in policy, these propositions are irresistible, but important questions are evaded by presenting such changes as a choice that society can make, the most obvious of which is who, exactly, makes the choice and how do they enforce it? In lauding the efforts of the engaged, the Group has barely taken into account the rise of a Hydra-like hegemony – the unholy combination of powerful market states, including a new imperial power, and their TNCs.

This brief account of the Global Scenario Group's heroic attempt at rationality, and what the present authors see as its shortcomings in the face of the exponential increase in the power of finance capital since the Second World War, also serves as an account of the circumstances in which the Johannesburg Summit was held. The principal, and crucial, difference between the Group and the plenipotentiaries at the Summit lies in their respective attitudes: the Group sees the emergence of market states as, at least, dangerous and probably disastrous; most, if not all, the governmental participants in the Summit insist that market globalisation is the only possible route to take. That position entails a remarkable shift in perspective in the consideration of both poverty and the environment. It has been described by Timothy W. Luke in an otherwise interesting article in *CNS*, rendered almost unintelligible by the author's fitful abuse and frequent grammatical misuse of his native language. It is entitled 'The Practices of Adaptive and Collaborative Environmental Management: a Critique.'[12] This kind of environmental management, known as ACEM, has become immensely popular among those working in the field; it is a formalisation of all those virtuous recommendations for participatory control of development, resources and governance. At first glance, its fundamental propositions seem to be unexceptionable, of course people should own and control their natural resources and participate in their development. Much ink has been spilled, including by the present authors, in urging just that. Luke points to fundamental flaws in these suggestions which have remained largely unexamined. ACEM operates entirely within the ambit of the market's view of the world and treats the environment as the repository of 'natural resources' which must be managed to the benefit of all those included in that nebulous category labelled 'stakeholders'; Luke calls this process 'resourcifying' nature. Management is the process by which the extraction of resources can be maintained, that is, made sustainable, and ecologies are defined in relation to the spatial arrangements of human habitation and as the bearers of good things. Collaboration in managing the environment, in this understanding, is dependent on the acceptance of the preeminence of the market as the main arbiter of human relations. The repeated insistence on the participatory management of resources throughout the *Plan of Implementation* is just such an acceptance and turns on concepts encapsulated in ACEM. It is a small step, taken by the WSSD, from this view of the environment to the conviction that only through the efficient management of its productivity, and by making world markets accessible to everyone, can poverty be alleviated.

ACEM, like globalisation, is reductionist – both limit analyses of the necessarily infinite complexity of what constitutes the world to a few simple and rigid principles and categories. Chief among these is that virtually everything is negotiable through some form of trading. But trade is not a matter of useful exchange, it is entirely based on continued increases in profit – an increase which, with questionable logic, is supposed to continue ad infinitum. Competition in the markets is the method by which profit is extracted and, no matter how tempered, inevitably results in winners and losers. For example, at the time of writing, stock markets are going through a period in which 'aggressive take-overs' are increasingly common; these are consequences of stock market rules which demand that once certain investment conditions arise, companies are open game for other, predatory, corporations. It is a process, designed to protect the profits of shareholders, which normally results in 'efficiencies', cost savings directed at increasing profitability, usually at the expense of the staff of both corporations in a process euphemistically referred to as 'down-sizing'. Other losers are obvious, the MDGs were intended to relieve their problems, but the system proposed for cure can, by its nature, only make matters worse.

Even the Global Scenario Group has not considered the questions in quite these terms, not surprisingly, since it, too, produced its analyses with the Summit in mind – the object of its work was, at least in part, to add to the voices attempting to persuade the Summit to adopt sensible environmental measures and to come up with practical ways in which to meet the MDGs. The last of its three publications to this end appeared shortly after the events in New York of 11 September 2001 – it would have been impossible for them to have incorporated the effects of the attack into their work before it went to press. Those effects probably included the support for the Republican party in the mid-term elections, which gave Bush the power he needed to launch his subsequent unilateral and corporation driven programme. We have already mentioned the role of his alliances in the rejection of the Kyoto Protocol and the abandonment of the Doha promises of cheap drugs for people too poor to pay their inflated prices. But these are both symptoms of a far larger phenomenon, the descent into the Barbarisation suggested, by the Group, as one possible trajectory that the powerful states of the world might follow.

Barbarisation is presented, in *Great Transition*, in slightly apocalyptic terms, the cross-head in the relevant chapter reads 'Barbarization and the Abyss'.[13] The word is used to describe a world in which those in power have heard the environmental warnings and are aware of the world's massive inequalities, but have ignored them in favour of the pursuit of profit and economic dominance. Market forces, with the divisiveness and suffering which accompany their unregulated practices, become the sole societal rule. The yet greater damage this would wreak on weaker economies will cause more widespread collapses of states, similar to several seen on the continent of Africa in the twentieth century, and would add substantially to world economic misery. This, in turn, would lead to instability and to immense numbers of economic refugees who would be rejected by the industrialised world. Hatches would be battened down and fortress states, or groups of states, would come into existence and be racked by paranoid fears of terrorism and, to a small extent, actual terrorist activities. Engagement with poorer states would be limited to a few clients, preferably with some coveted resource or another, which would act as security buffers and become 'privileged enclaves to maintain control over the disenfranchized'.

In an excellent summary of Barbarisation, the Group remarks that:

> The mantra of economic growth, trade liberalization and structural adjustment continues to be heard in the halls of global governance organizations, such as the WTO, the boardrooms of transnational corporations and corridors of national governments. The old ideology of individualism and consumerism flourishes anew, but with a greater respect for the legitimacy of government ... as an activist partner in enforcing a global market regime.[14]

That enforcement overrides concern both for the environment and for worldwide poverty; the refusal to countenance any other economic formulation results not only in the failure even to manage matters like the sustainable use of water, growing hunger and disease control, but also in the failure to assist the excluded. The Group sees this neglect as resulting in an anarchy which would encourage the appearance of 'powerful global syndicates able to field fearsome fighting units in their battle against international policing'. The prophetic tone of this picture continues:

> The forces of global order take action ... [and] form the self-styled Alliance for Global Salvation. Using a revamped United Nations as their platform a state of planetary emergency is declared. A campaign of overwhelming force, rough justice and draconian police measures sweeps through hot spots of conflict and discontent ... A system of global dualism – some call it a *Fortress World*, others Planetary Apartheid – emerges from the crisis.[15]

It all sounds depressingly familiar and the Group was astonishingly prescient; two years after the publication of its apparently remote fear that this trajectory might be followed, we find that the Bush administration, supported by its British accomplices, has already happily embarked upon it. The gallop towards Barbarisation did not spring fully armed from the head of President Bush, obviously its roots are much earlier than his dubious election and they are evident in, for example, the history of inaction between the Rio and Johannesburg Summits, followed by the latter's weak *Plan of Implementation*. The people for whom the Summits and other gatherings devised all those wonderful managerial and market prescriptions are largely outside the magic dominant circle, and it is that exclusion which gives us the key to understanding the implacability, not only of the global marketeers, but also of the major bellicose states. In his remarkable book *Homo Sacer*, the Italian philosopher Giorgio Agamben analyses the relationship between sovereignty and what he calls 'bare life'. His argument begins with a classical Greek distinction between *zoë*, 'the simple fact of living common to all living beings (animals, men, or gods)', and *bios*, 'the form of living proper to an individual or a group'.[16] Further distinctions, made by both Plato and Aristotle, are described by Agamben, but they belong to a fuller version of his argument than we need here. Sovereignty refers to ordered societal relationships of governance within a state which permit the achievement of an ordinary good life by those who live in it (*bios*). Agamben remarks that 'what characterizes modern politics is not so much the inclusion of *zoë* in the *polis* ... [but that] the realm of bare life – which is originally situated at the margins of the political order – gradually begins to coincide with the political realm'.[17] The form of that order may vary in all the familiar ways, from monarchy to open democracy and all points between, but, whatever its form, its citizens are subject to the legal and political power which validates its order. In contemporary states this produces 'modern democracy's specific aporia: it wants to put the freedom and happiness of men [*sic*] into play on the very place – "bare life" – that marked their subjection'.[18] 'Bare life' is not simply the abstract noun for life, but applies simultaneously to those included and excluded from the *polis*. It is 'the life of *homo sacer* (sacred man), who *may be killed and yet not sacrificed*'.[19] This concept is borrowed from ancient Roman law, which incorporates human life within the juridical order – law – in which 'violence ... [is] a primordial juridical fact'.[20] This gives rise, not only to Agamben's powerful arguments, but also to an important debate with Michel Foucault. For our purposes we need only to follow the processes of inclusion and exclusion which spring from this aporia. A further and, in this discourse, important distinction is made: those who are sacred may be killed, but not sacrificed; the excluded may be killed, but it is not a crime.

Sovereign power is not, of course, an undifferentiated phenomenon, in particular it may be more, or less, flexible in its self-understanding and the major gauge of its flexibility is its reaction to those within its realm who refuse to be assimilated – Jews, Roma and Travellers, people of another colour or from radically different societies and political and cultural dissidents are all examples.[21] Agamben's argument is richer and more complex than the reductive fillet that we have adopted here, but its application to our present concerns is obvious. Bush's 'axis of evil' (a term derived from Reagan, who described the Soviet Union as an 'empire of evil') is the most blatant example of exclusion, the denial of *bios* to those he determines as the opponents in a world that he is attempting to control by US hegemony. At first sight 'evil' sounds like an infantile categorisation, but it has substantial consequences. Among them, as Gilbert Achcar has pointed out, is the revival, in yet more poisonous form, of McCarthyist witchhunts – even internal dissidents become 'anti-American', particularly if they advance the possibility that the US's murderous career through the second half of the twentieth century may, at least in part, account for the hatred that led to 11 September.[22]

By any civilised standard, the British–US insistence on continuing the sanctions imposed on Iraq and the constant bombing of that country are crimes against humanity. But in the barbaric mores of the US and Britain, the victims, the ordinary and largely impover-ished citizens of Iraq, are the excluded whom it is not a crime to kill. The sanctions and the war are among the most salient of contem-porary events reducing others to 'bare life', but other instances are commonly to be found. Nazism's Final Solution, in which 'the Jews ... [were] the representatives *par excellence* and almost the living symbol ... of the bare life that modernity necessarily creates within itself', was the most notorious and extreme example in recent history.[23] It is one of the tragedies of the modern world that Israel is now, in turn, making Palestinians into 'the living symbol ... of the bare life'.

There are less obvious places in which the phenomenon occurs. It may be seen, of course, in the US administration's rejectionist positions to which we have already referred, if only because the abrogation of treaties (particularly environmental treaties) is frequently the advancement of domestic interests over the irrelevant interests of the remainder of the world. The combination of unilat-eralism and bellicosity by the world's most powerful state could not but influence the working of the WSSD and largely accounts for the depressingly aspirational *Plan of Implementation* as opposed to an attempt actively to incorporate poor states and their people into the international body politic (*bios*). Interlaced with all these events is a far more general and polymorphous exclusion. It comes from the fundamental relationships of inequality; for example, in any given state the rich and powerful are separated from others and occupy a material world for which the most popular adjective is 'exclusive'. Class, when used self-referentially either explicitly or implicitly, is invariably a category that excludes lesser mortals; economic status, codes of conduct and language are the defining signs of the good life and all of them have, in some sense, the quality of law. It is possible to be benevolent to the poor, but not to include them.

The very fact of using 'the poor' as a group definition, as a collective noun, as we have throughout this book, runs the danger of reproducing that exclusion. More importantly, it is necessary to understand how the wealthy sovereign deals with those deprived not only of economic power, but of membership of the *polis*. We have written elsewhere about the function of humanitarian assistance in the political agendas of the states and international institutions which provide it.[24] Agamben introduces another important distinction into that debate when he remarks that: 'The separation between humanitarianism and politics ... is the extreme phase of the separation of the rights of man from the rights of the citizen ... [H]umanitarian organizations ... can only grasp human life in the figure of bare or sacred life, and therefore, despite themselves, maintain a secret solidarity with the very powers they ought to fight.'[25] But, of course, the concept of 'development' is subject to the same criticism, since, as it is presently conceived, its purpose is the elimination of an alternative to globalised markets by incorporating whomever the system can absorb, while propping up in bare life, or completely neglecting, the remainder.

We return to our early proposition that the fuss created by the INGOs over the failure of the WSSD to establish targets and timetables is, at least, suspect. In what Agamben describes as 'the civil war that divides the peoples and the cities of the earth', it is difficult to disentangle the Summit from the barbaric trajectory described by the Global Scenario Group and demonstrated in Bush's demented environmental policies.[26] In that context, targets and timetables become instruments of control in the hands of the barbarians, confirmed in the mantras of the *Plan* to do with resources, their management and their absorption into the market. Luke's point coincides with parts of Agamben's analysis – treating the environment solely as a parcel of useable resources is a symptom of capitalism's bipolarity. Not the least because of the refusal to dislodge the warlords of Afghanistan after their war, the Bush–Blair determination that the only way of unseating Saddam Hussein is by killing large numbers of the people he is oppressing is a remarkable example of the point that we have been making. There can be no lively hope that war crimes of that sort are likely to improve matters for the survivors in Iraq, any more than they did in Afghanistan. Making the world safe for finance capital and securing the hegemonies of the three principal capitalist blocs (US, EU and Japan) is the long-term aim.

If the Bush–Blair programme succeeds, the United Nations will either become the servant of capital or simply a diplomatic talking shop. Yet flawed as the agreements it has sponsored may be, they can serve as a basis, at least, for restraining the gallop to destruction by the globalising market forces (a better phrase for them would be the determined seekers after profit).

The UN may become, as Colin Powell so charmingly expresses it, 'irrelevant' – at least to US interests and not just in the matter of Iraq; for the rest of the world it may yet prove to be more resilient than the fevered imaginations of White House functionaries would allow. The WSSD may have been both craven and flatulent. But neither US imperialism, nor the ambivalence of all other nation states in the face of market ideology, can completely erase the achievements represented in cautious, but, nonetheless progressive treaties made, largely under the auspices of the UN, since the end of the Second World War. Politics, not targets, is the issue and until 'civil society' recognises this and acts on that recognition, it will continue to be part of the problem.

Appendix A[*]
The Johannesburg Declaration
on Sustainable Development

FROM OUR ORIGINS TO THE FUTURE

1.   We, the representatives of the peoples of the world, assembled at the World Summit on Sustainable Development in Johannesburg, South Africa from 2–4 September 2002, reaffirm our commitment to sustainable development.

2.   We commit ourselves to build a humane, equitable and caring global society cognizant of the need for human dignity for all.

3.   At the beginning of this Summit, the children of the world spoke to us in a simple yet clear voice that the future belongs to them, and accordingly challenged all of us to ensure that through our actions they will inherit a world free of the indignity and indecency occasioned by poverty, environmental degradation and patterns of unsustainable development.

4.   As part of our response to these children, who represent our collective future, all of us, coming from every corner of the world, informed by different life experiences, are united and moved by a deeply-felt sense that we urgently need to create a new and brighter world of hope.

5.   Accordingly, we assume a collective responsibility to advance and strengthen the interdependent and mutually reinforcing pillars of sustainable development – economic development, social development and environmental protection – at local, national, regional and global levels.

6.   From this Continent, the Cradle of Humanity we declare, through the Plan of Implementation and this Declaration, our responsibility to one another, to the greater community of life and to our children.

7.   Recognizing that humankind is at a crossroad, we have united in a common resolve to make a determined effort to respond positively to the need to produce a practical and visible plan that should bring about poverty eradication and human development.

[*] These texts were downloaded from www.johannesburgsummit.org

FROM STOCKHOLM TO RIO DE JANEIRO TO JOHANNESBURG

8.   Thirty years ago, in Stockholm, we agreed on the urgent need to respond to the problem of environmental deterioration. Ten years ago, at the United Nations Conference on Environment and Development, held in Rio de Janeiro, we agreed that the protection of the environment, and social and economic development are fundamental to sustainable development, based on the Rio Principles. To achieve such development, we adopted the global programme, Agenda 21, and the Rio Declaration, to which we reaffirm our commitment. The Rio Summit was a significant milestone that set a new agenda for sustainable development.

9.   Between Rio and Johannesburg the world's nations met in several major conferences under the guidance of the United Nations, including the Monterrey Conference on Finance for Development, as well as the Doha Ministerial Conference. These conferences defined for the world a comprehensive vision for the future of humanity.

10.   At the Johannesburg Summit we achieved much in bringing together a rich tapestry of peoples and views in a constructive search for a common path, towards a world that respects and implements the vision of sustainable development. Johannesburg also confirmed that significant progress has been made towards achieving a global consensus and partnership among all the people of our planet.

THE CHALLENGES WE FACE

11.   We recognize that poverty eradication, changing consumption and production patterns, and protecting and managing the natural resource base for economic and social development are overarching objectives of, and essential requirements for sustainable development.

12.   The deep fault line that divides human society between the rich and the poor and the ever-increasing gap between the developed and developing worlds pose a major threat to global prosperity, security and stability.

13.   The global environment continues to suffer. Loss of biodiversity continues, fish stocks continue to be depleted, desertification claims more and more fertile land, the adverse effects of climate change are already evident, natural disasters are more frequent and more devastating and developing countries more vulnerable, and air, water and marine pollution continue to rob millions of a decent life.

14.   Globalization has added a new dimension to these challenges. The rapid integration of markets, mobility of capital and significant increases in investment flows around the world have opened new challenges and opportunities for the pursuit of sustainable development. But the benefits and costs

of globalization are unevenly distributed, with developing countries facing special difficulties in meeting this challenge.

15.   We risk the entrenchment of these global disparities and unless we act in a manner that fundamentally changes their lives, the poor of the world may lose confidence in their representatives and the democratic systems to which we remain committed, seeing their representatives as nothing more than sounding brass or tinkling cymbals.

OUR COMMITMENT TO SUSTAINABLE DEVELOPMENT

16.   We are determined to ensure that our rich diversity, which is our collective strength, will be used for constructive partnership for change and for the achievement of the common goal of sustainable development.

17.   Recognizing the importance of building human solidarity, we urge the promotion of dialogue and cooperation among the world's civilizations and peoples, irrespective of race, disabilities, religion, language, culture and tradition.

18.   We welcome the Johannesburg Summit focus on the indivisibility of human dignity and are resolved through decisions on targets, timetables and partnerships to speedily increase access to basic requirements such as clean water, sanitation, adequate shelter, energy, health care, food security and the protection of biodiversity. At the same time, we will work together to assist one another to have access to financial resources, benefit from the opening of markets, ensure capacity building, use modern technology to bring about development, and make sure that there is technology transfer, human resource development, education and training to banish forever underdevelopment.

19.   We reaffirm our pledge to place particular focus on, and give priority attention to, the fight against the worldwide conditions that pose severe threats to the sustainable development of our people. Among these conditions are: chronic hunger; malnutrition; foreign occupation; armed conflicts; illicit drug problems; organized crime; corruption; natural disasters; illicit arms trafficking; trafficking in persons; terrorism; intolerance and incitement to racial, ethnic, religious and other hatreds; xenophobia; and endemic, communicable and chronic diseases, in particular HIV/AIDS, malaria and tuberculosis.

20.   We are committed to ensure that women's empowerment and emancipation, and gender equality are integrated in all activities encompassed within Agenda 21, the Millennium Development Goals and the Johannesburg Plan of Implementation.

21.   We recognize the reality that global society has the means and is endowed with the resources to address the challenges of poverty eradication and sustainable development confronting all humanity. Together we will take extra steps to ensure that these available resources are used to the benefit of humanity.

22.   In this regard, to contribute to the achievement of our development goals and targets, we urge developed countries that have not done so to make concrete efforts towards the internationally agreed levels of Official Development Assistance.

23.   We welcome and support the emergence of stronger regional groupings and alliances, such as the New Partnership for Africa's Development (NEPAD), to promote regional cooperation, improved international cooperation and promote sustainable development.

24.   We shall continue to pay special attention to the developmental needs of Small Island Developing States and the Least Developed Countries.

25.   We reaffirm the vital role of the indigenous peoples in sustainable development.

26.   We recognize sustainable development requires a long-term perspective and broad-based participation in policy formulation, decision-making and implementation at all levels. As social partners we will continue to work for stable partnerships with all major groups respecting the independent, important roles of each of these.

27.   We agree that in pursuit of their legitimate activities the private sector, both large and small companies, have a duty to contribute to the evolution of equitable and sustainable communities and societies.

28.   We also agree to provide assistance to increase income generating employment opportunities, taking into account the International Labour Organization (ILO) Declaration of Fundamental Principles and Rights at Work.

29.   We agree that there is a need for private sector corporations to enforce corporate accountability. This should take place within a transparent and stable regulatory environment.

30.   We undertake to strengthen and improve governance at all levels, for the effective implementation of Agenda 21, the Millennium Development Goals and the Johannesburg Plan of Implementation.

MULTILATERALISM IS THE FUTURE

31.   To achieve our goals of sustainable development, we need more effective, democratic and accountable international and multilateral institutions.

32.   We reaffirm our commitment to the principles and purposes of the UN Charter and international law as well as the strengthening of multilateralism. We support the leadership role of the United Nations as the most universal and representative organization in the world, which is best placed to promote sustainable development.

33.   We further commit ourselves to monitor progress at regular intervals towards the achievement of our sustainable development goals and objectives.

MAKING IT HAPPEN!

34.   We are in agreement that this must be an inclusive process, involving all the major groups and governments that participated in the historic Johannesburg Summit.

35.   We commit ourselves to act together, united by a common determination to save our planet, promote human development and achieve universal prosperity and peace.

36.   We commit ourselves to the Johannesburg Plan of Implementation and to expedite the achievement of the time-bound, socio-economic and environmental targets contained therein.

37.   From the African continent, the Cradle of Humankind, we solemnly pledge to the peoples of the world, and the generations that will surely inherit this earth, that we are determined to ensure that our collective hope for sustainable development is realized.

We express our deepest gratitude to the people and the Government of South Africa for their generous hospitality and excellent arrangements made for the World Summit on Sustainable Development.

Appendix B
World Summit on Sustainable Development Plan of Implementation

I. INTRODUCTION

1.   The United Nations Conference on Environment and Development (UNCED), held in Rio de Janeiro in 1992, provided the fundamental principles and the programme of action for achieving sustainable development. We strongly reaffirm our commitment to the Rio principles, the full implementation of Agenda 21 and the Programme for the Further Implementation of Agenda 21. We also commit ourselves to achieving the internationally agreed development goals, including those contained in the United Nations Millennium Declaration and in the outcomes of the major United Nations conferences and international agreements since 1992.

2.   The present plan of implementation will further build on the achievements made since UNCED and expedite the realization of the remaining goals. To this end, we commit ourselves to undertaking concrete actions and measures at all levels and to enhancing international cooperation, taking into account the Rio Principles, including, inter alia, the principle of common but differentiated responsibilities as set out in principle 7 of the Rio Declaration on Environment and Development. These efforts will also promote the integration of the three components of sustainable development – economic development, social development and environmental protection – as interdependent and mutually reinforcing pillars. Poverty eradication, changing unsustainable patterns of production and consumption, and protecting and managing the natural resource base of economic and social development are overarching objectives of, and essential requirements for, sustainable development.

3.   We recognize that the implementation of the outcomes of the Summit should benefit all, particularly women, youth, children and vulnerable groups. Furthermore, the implementation should involve all relevant actors through partnerships, especially between Governments of the North and South, on the one hand, and between Governments and major groups, on the other, to achieve the widely shared goals of sustainable development. As reflected in the Monterrey Consensus, such partnerships are key to pursuing sustainable development in a globalizing world.

4.   Good governance within each country and at the international level is essential for sustainable development. At the domestic level, sound environ-

mental, social and economic policies, democratic institutions responsive to the needs of the people, the rule of law, anti-corruption measures, gender equality and an enabling environment for investment are the basis for sustainable development. As a result of globalization, external factors have become critical in determining the success or failure of developing countries in their national efforts. The gap between developed and developing countries points to the continued need for a dynamic and enabling international economic environment supportive of international cooperation, particularly in the areas of finance, technology transfer, debt and trade, and full and effective participation of developing countries in global decision-making, if the momentum for global progress towards sustainable development is to be maintained and increased.

5.   Peace, security, stability and respect for human rights and fundamental freedoms, including the right to development, as well as respect for cultural diversity, are essential for achieving sustainable development and ensuring that sustainable development benefits all.

5.bis   We acknowledge the importance of ethics for sustainable development, and therefore we emphasize the need to consider ethics in the implementation of Agenda 21.

II. POVERTY ERADICATION

6.   Eradicating poverty is the greatest global challenge facing the world today and an indispensable requirement for sustainable development, particularly for developing countries. Although each country has the primary responsibility for its own sustainable development and poverty eradication and the role of national policies and development strategies cannot be overemphasized, concerted and concrete measures are required at all levels to enable developing countries to achieve their sustainable development goals as related to the internationally agreed poverty-related targets and goals, including those contained in Agenda 21, the relevant outcomes of other United Nations conferences and the United Nations Millennium Declaration. This would include actions at all levels to:

(a)   Halve, by the year 2015, the proportion of the world's people whose income is less than $1 a day and the proportion of people who suffer from hunger and, by the same date, to halve the proportion of people without access to safe drinking water;

(b)   Establish a world solidarity fund to eradicate poverty and to promote social and human development in the developing countries pursuant to modalities to be determined by the General Assembly, while stressing the voluntary nature of the contributions, the need to avoid duplication of existing United Nations funds, and encouraging the role of the private sector and individual citizens relative to Governments in funding the endeavours;

(c) Develop national programmes for sustainable development and local and community development, where appropriate within country-owned poverty reduction strategies, to promote the empowerment of people living in poverty and their organizations. These programmes should reflect their priorities and enable them to increase access to productive resources, public services and institutions, in particular land, water, employment opportunities, credit, education and health;

(d) Promote women's equal access to and full participation, on the basis of equality with men, in decision-making at all levels, mainstreaming gender perspectives in all policies and strategies, eliminating all forms of violence and discrimination against women, and improving the status, health and economic welfare of women and girls through full and equal access to economic opportunity, land, credit, education and health-care services;

(e) Develop policies and ways and means to improve access by indigenous people and their communities to economic activities, and increase their employment through, where appropriate, such measures as training, technical assistance and credit facilities. Recognize that traditional and direct dependence on renewable resources and ecosystems, including sustainable harvesting, continues to be essential to the cultural, economic and physical well-being of indigenous people and their communities;

(f) Deliver basic health services for all and reduce environmental health threats, taking into account the special needs of children and the linkages between poverty, health and environment, with provision of financial resources, technical assistance and knowledge transfer to developing countries and countries with economies in transition;

(g) Ensure that children everywhere, boys and girls alike, will be able to complete a full course of primary schooling and will have equal access to all levels of education;

(h) Provide access to agricultural resources for people living in poverty, especially women and indigenous communities, and promote, as appropriate, land tenure arrangements that recognize and protect indigenous and common property resource management systems;

(i) Build basic rural infrastructure, diversify the economy and improve transportation and access to markets, market information and credit for the rural poor to support sustainable agriculture and rural development;

(j) Transfer basic sustainable agricultural techniques and knowledge, including natural resource management, to small and medium-scale farmers, fishers and the rural poor, especially in developing countries, including through multi-stakeholder approaches and public–private partnerships aimed at increasing agriculture production and food security;

(k) Increase food availability and affordability, including through harvest and food technology and management, as well as equitable and efficient distribution systems, by promoting, for example, community-based partnerships linking urban and rural people and enterprises;

(l) Combat desertification and mitigate the effects of drought and floods through such measures as improved use of climate and weather information and forecasts, early warning systems, land and natural resource management, agricultural practices and ecosystem conservation in order to reverse current trends and minimize degradation of land and water resources, including through the provision of adequate and predictable financial resources to implement the United Nations Convention to Combat Desertification in Those Countries Experiencing Serious Drought and/or Desertification, particularly in Africa, as one of the tools for poverty eradication;

(m) Increase access to sanitation to improve human health and reduce infant and child mortality, prioritizing water and sanitation in national sustainable development strategies and poverty reduction strategies where they exist.

7.   The provision of clean drinking water and adequate sanitation is necessary to protect human health and the environment. In this respect, we agree to halve, by the year 2015, the proportion of people who are unable to reach or to afford safe drinking water (as outlined in the Millennium Declaration) and the proportion of people who do not have access to basic sanitation, which would include actions at all levels to:

(a) Develop and implement efficient household sanitation systems;

(b) Improve sanitation in public institutions, especially schools;

(c) Promote safe hygiene practices;

(d) Promote education and outreach focused on children, as agents of behavioural change;

(e) Promote affordable and socially and culturally acceptable technologies and practices;

(f) Develop innovative financing and partnership mechanisms;

(g) Integrate sanitation into water resources management strategies.

8.   Take joint actions and improve efforts to work together at all levels to improve access to reliable and affordable energy services for sustainable devel-

opment sufficient to facilitate the achievement of the millennium development goals, including the goal of halving the proportion of people in poverty by 2015, and as a means to generate other important services that mitigate poverty, bearing in mind that access to energy facilitates the eradication of poverty. This would include actions at all levels to:

(a) Improve access to reliable, affordable, economically viable, socially acceptable and environmentally sound energy services and resources, taking into account national specificities and circumstances, through various means, such as enhanced rural electrification and decentralized energy systems, increased use of renewables, cleaner liquid and gaseous fuels and enhanced energy efficiency, by intensifying regional and international cooperation in support of national efforts, including through capacity-building, financial and technological assistance and innovative financing mechanisms, including at the micro and meso levels, recognizing the specific factors for providing access to the poor;

(b) Improve access to modern biomass technologies and fuelwood sources and supplies, and commercialize biomass operations, including the use of agricultural residues, in rural areas and where such practices are sustainable;

(c) Promote a sustainable use of biomass and, as appropriate, other renewable energies through improvement of current patterns of use, such as management of resources, more efficient use of fuelwood and new or improved products and technologies;

(d) Support the transition to the cleaner use of liquid and gaseous fossil fuels, where considered more environmentally sound, socially acceptable and cost-effective;

(e) Develop national energy policies and regulatory frameworks that will help to create the necessary economic, social and institutional conditions in the energy sector to improve access to reliable, affordable, economically viable, socially acceptable and environmentally sound energy services for sustainable development and poverty eradication in rural, peri-urban and urban areas;

(f) Enhance international and regional cooperation to improve access to reliable, affordable, economically viable, socially acceptable and environmentally sound energy services, as an integral part of poverty reduction programmes, by facilitating the creation of enabling environments and addressing capacity-building needs, with special attention to rural and isolated areas, as appropriate;

(g) Assist and facilitate on an accelerated basis, with the financial and technical assistance of developed countries, including through public–private partnerships, the access of the poor to reliable, affordable, economically viable, socially acceptable and environmentally sound energy services, taking into account the instrumental role of developing national policies on energy for sustainable development, bearing in mind that in developing countries sharp increases in energy services are required to improve the standards of living of their populations and that energy services have positive impacts on poverty eradication and improve standards of living.

9.   Strengthen the contribution of industrial development to poverty eradication and sustainable natural resource management. This would include actions at all levels to:

(a) Provide assistance and mobilize resources to enhance industrial productivity and competitiveness as well as industrial development in developing countries, including the transfer of environmentally sound technologies on preferential terms, as mutually agreed;

(b) Provide assistance to increase income-generating employment opportunities, taking into account the International Labour Organization (ILO) Declaration on Fundamental Principles and Rights at Work;

(c) Promote the development of micro, small and medium-sized enterprises, including by means of training, education and skill enhancement, with a special focus on agro-industry as a provider of livelihoods for rural communities;

(d) Provide financial and technological support, as appropriate, to rural communities of developing countries to enable them to benefit from safe and sustainable livelihood opportunities in small-scale mining ventures;

(e) Provide support to developing countries for the development of safe low-cost technologies that provide or conserve fuel for cooking and water heating;

(f) Provide support for natural resource management for creating sustainable livelihoods for the poor.

10.   By 2020, achieve a significant improvement in the lives of at least 100 million slum dwellers, as proposed in the 'Cities without slums' initiative. This would include actions at all levels to:

(a) Improve access to land and property, to adequate shelter and to basic services for the urban and rural poor, with special attention to female heads of household;

(b) Use low-cost and sustainable materials and appropriate technologies for the construction of adequate and secure housing for the poor, with financial and technological assistance to developing countries, taking into account their culture, climate, specific social conditions and vulnerability to natural disasters;

(c) Increase decent employment, credit and income for the urban poor, through appropriate national policies, promoting equal opportunities for women and men;

(d) Remove unnecessary regulatory and other obstacles for microenterprises and the informal sector;

(e) Support local authorities in elaborating slum upgrading programmes within the framework of urban development plans and facilitate access, particularly for the poor, to information on housing legislation.

11.   Take immediate and effective measures to eliminate the worst forms of child labour as defined in ILO Convention No. 182, and elaborate and implement strategies for the elimination of child labour that is contrary to accepted international standards.

12.   Promote international cooperation to assist developing countries, upon request, in addressing child labour and its root causes, inter alia, through social and economic policies aimed at poverty conditions, while stressing that labour standards should not be used for protectionist trade purposes.

III. CHANGING UNSUSTAINABLE PATTERNS OF CONSUMPTION AND PRODUCTION

13.   Fundamental changes in the way societies produce and consume are indispensable for achieving global sustainable development. All countries should promote sustainable consumption and production patterns, with the developed countries taking the lead and with all countries benefiting from the process, taking into account the Rio principles, including, inter alia, the principle of common but differentiated responsibilities as set out in principle 7 of the Rio Declaration on Environment and Development. Governments, relevant international organizations, the private sector and all major groups should play an active role in changing unsustainable consumption and production patterns. This would include the actions at all levels set out below.

14.   Encourage and promote the development of a 10-year framework of programmes in support of regional and national initiatives to accelerate the shift towards sustainable consumption and production to promote social and economic development within the carrying capacity of ecosystems by addressing and, where appropriate, delinking economic growth and environmental degradation through improving efficiency and sustainability in the use of resources and production processes, and reducing resource degradation, pollution and waste. All countries should take action, with developed countries taking the lead, taking into account the development needs and capabilities of developing countries through mobilization, from all sources,

of financial and technical assistance and capacity-building for developing countries. This would require actions at all levels to:

(a) Identify specific activities, tools, policies, measures and monitoring and assessment mechanisms, including, where appropriate, life-cycle analysis and national indicators for measuring progress, bearing in mind that standards applied by some countries may be inappropriate and of unwarranted economic and social cost to other countries, in particular developing countries;

(b) Adopt and implement policies and measures aimed at promoting sustainable patterns of production and consumption, applying, inter alia, the polluter-pays principle described in principle 16 of the Rio Declaration on Environment and Development;

(c) Develop production and consumption policies to improve the products and services provided, while reducing environmental and health impacts, using, where appropriate, science-based approaches, such as life-cycle analysis;

(d) Develop awareness-raising programmes on the importance of sustainable production and consumption patterns, particularly among youth and the relevant segments in all countries, especially in developed countries, through, inter alia, education, public and consumer information, advertising and other media, taking into account local, national and regional cultural values;

(e) Develop and adopt, where appropriate, on a voluntary basis, effective, transparent, verifiable, non-misleading and non-discriminatory consumer information tools to provide information relating to sustainable consumption and production, including human health and safety aspects. These tools should not be used as disguised trade barriers;

(f) Increase eco-efficiency, with financial support from all sources, where mutually agreed, for capacity-building, technology transfer and exchange of technology with developing countries and countries with economies in transition, in cooperation with relevant international organizations.

15.   Increase investment in cleaner production and eco-efficiency in all countries through, inter alia, incentives and support schemes and policies directed at establishing appropriate regulatory, financial and legal frameworks. This would include actions at all levels to:

(a) Establish and support cleaner production programmes and centres and more efficient production methods by providing, inter alia, incentives and capacity-building to assist enterprises, especially small and medium-sized enterprises and particularly in developing countries, in improving productivity and sustainable development;

(b) Provide incentives for investment in cleaner production and eco-efficiency in all countries, such as state-financed loans, venture capital, technical assistance and training programmes for small and medium-sized companies while avoiding trade-distorting measures inconsistent with WTO rules;

(c) Collect and disseminate information on cost-effective examples in cleaner production, eco-efficiency and environmental management, and promote the exchange of best practices and know-how on environmentally sound technologies between public and private institutions;

(d) Provide training programmes to small and medium-sized enterprises on the use of information and communication technologies.

16. Integrate the issue of production and consumption patterns into sustainable development policies, programmes and strategies, including, where applicable, into poverty reduction strategies.

17. Enhance corporate environmental and social responsibility and accountability. This would include actions at all levels to:

(a) Encourage industry to improve social and environmental performance through voluntary initiatives, including environmental management systems, codes of conduct, certification and public reporting on environmental and social issues, taking into account such initiatives as the International Organization for Standardization (ISO) standards and Global Reporting Initiative guidelines on sustainability reporting, bearing in mind principle 11 of the Rio Declaration on Environment and Development;

(b) Encourage dialogue between enterprises and the communities in which they operate and other stakeholders;

(c) Encourage financial institutions to incorporate sustainable development considerations into their decision-making processes;

(d) Develop workplace-based partnerships and programmes, including training and education programmes.

18. Encourage relevant authorities at all levels to take sustainable development considerations into account in decision-making, including on national and local development planning, investment in infrastructure, business development and public procurement. This would include actions at all levels to:

(a) Provide support for the development of sustainable development strategies and programmes, including in decision-making on investment in infrastructure and business development;
(b) Continue to promote the internalization of environmental costs and the use of economic instruments, taking into account the approach

that the polluter should, in principle, bear the costs of pollution, with due regard to the public interest and without distorting international trade and investment;

(c) Promote public procurement policies that encourage development and diffusion of environmentally sound goods and services;

(d) Provide capacity-building and training to assist relevant authorities with regard to the implementation of the initiatives listed in the present paragraph;

(e) Use environmental impact assessment procedures.

*   *   *

19.   Call upon Governments, as well as relevant regional and international organizations and other relevant stakeholders, to implement, taking into account national and regional specificities and circumstances, the recommendations and conclusions of the Commission on Sustainable Development concerning energy for sustainable development adopted at its ninth session, including the issues and options set out below, bearing in mind that in view of the different contributions to global environmental degradation, States have common but differentiated responsibilities. This would include actions at all levels to:

(a) Take further action to mobilize the provision of financial resources, technology transfer, capacity-building and the diffusion of environmentally sound technologies according to the recommendations and conclusions of the Commission on Sustainable Development as contained in section A, paragraph 3, and section D, paragraph 30, of its decision 9/1 on energy for sustainable development;

(b) Integrate energy considerations, including energy efficiency, affordability and accessibility, into socio-economic programmes, especially into policies of major energy-consuming sectors, and into the planning, operation and maintenance of long-lived energy consuming infrastructures, such as the public sector, transport, industry, agriculture, urban land use, tourism and construction sectors;

(c) Develop and disseminate alternative energy technologies with the aim of giving a greater share of the energy mix to renewable energies, improving energy efficiency and greater reliance on advanced energy technologies, including cleaner fossil fuel technologies;

(d) Combine, as appropriate, the increased use of renewable energy resources, more efficient use of energy, greater reliance on advanced energy technologies, including advanced and cleaner fossil fuel technologies, and the sustainable use of traditional energy resources, which could meet the growing need for energy services in the longer term to achieve sustainable development;

(e) Diversify energy supply by developing advanced, cleaner, more efficient, affordable and cost-effective energy technologies, including fossil fuel technologies and renewable energy technologies, hydro included, and their transfer to developing countries on concessional terms as mutually agreed. With a sense of urgency, substantially increase the global share of renewable energy sources with the objective of increasing its contribution to total energy supply, recognizing the role of national and voluntary regional targets as well as initiatives, where they exist, and ensuring that energy policies are supportive to developing countries' efforts to eradicate poverty, and regularly evaluate available data to review progress to this end;

(f) Support efforts, including through provision of financial and technical assistance to developing countries, with the involvement of the private sector, to reduce flaring and venting of gas associated with crude oil production;

(g) Develop and utilize indigenous energy sources and infrastructures for various local uses and promote rural community participation, including local Agenda 21 groups, with the support of the international community, in developing and utilizing renewable energy technologies to meet their daily energy needs to find simple and local solutions;

(h) Establish domestic programmes for energy efficiency, including, as appropriate, by accelerating the deployment of energy efficiency technologies, with the necessary support of the international community;

(i) Accelerate the development, dissemination and deployment of affordable and cleaner energy efficiency and energy conservation technologies, as well as the transfer of such technologies, in particular to developing countries, on favourable terms, including on concessional and preferential terms, as mutually agreed;

(j) Recommend that international financial institutions and other agencies' policies support developing countries, as well as countries with economies in transition, in their own efforts to establish policy and regulatory frameworks which create a level playing field between the following: renewable energy, energy efficiency, advanced energy technologies, including advanced and cleaner fossil fuel technologies, and centralized, distributed and decentralized energy systems;

(k) Promote increased research and development in the field of various energy technologies, including renewable energy, energy efficiency and advanced energy technologies, including advanced and cleaner fossil fuel technologies, both nationally and through international collaboration; strengthen national and regional research and development institutions/centres on reliable, affordable, economically viable, socially acceptable and environmentally sound energy for sustainable development;

(l) Promote networking between centres of excellence on energy for sustainable development, including regional networks, by linking competent centres on energy technologies for sustainable development that could support and promote efforts at capacity-building and technology transfer activities, particularly of developing countries, as well as serve as information clearing houses;

(m) Promote education to provide information for both men and women about available energy sources and technologies;

(n) Utilize financial instruments and mechanisms, in particular the Global Environment Facility (GEF), within its mandate, to provide financial resources to developing countries, in particular least developed countries and small island developing States, to meet their capacity needs for training, technical know-how and strengthening national institutions in reliable, affordable, economically viable, socially acceptable and environmentally sound energy, including promoting energy efficiency and conservation, renewable energy and advanced energy technologies, including advanced and cleaner fossil fuel technologies;

(o) Support efforts to improve the functioning, transparency and information about energy markets with respect to both supply and demand, with the aim of achieving greater stability and predictability and to ensure consumer access to reliable, affordable, economically viable, socially acceptable and environmentally sound energy services;

(p) Policies to reduce market distortions would promote energy systems compatible with sustainable development through the use of improved market signals and by removing market distortions, including restructuring taxation and phasing out harmful subsidies, where they exist, to reflect their environmental impacts, with such policies taking fully into account the specific needs and conditions of developing countries with the aim of minimizing the possible adverse impacts on their development;

(q) Take action, where appropriate, to phase out subsidies in this area that inhibit sustainable development, taking fully into account the specific conditions and different levels of development of individual countries and considering their adverse effect, particularly on developing countries;

(r) Governments are encouraged to improve the functioning of national energy markets in such a way that they support sustainable development, overcome market barriers and improve accessibility, taking fully into account that such policies should be decided by each country, and that its own characteristics and capabilities and level of development should be considered, especially as reflected in national sustainable development strategies, where they exist;

(s) Strengthen national and regional energy institutions or arrangements for enhancing regional and international cooperation on energy for sustainable development, in particular to assist developing countries in their domestic efforts to provide reliable, affordable, economically viable, socially acceptable and environmentally sound energy services to all sections of their populations;

(t) Countries are urged to develop and implement actions within the framework of the ninth session of the Commission on Sustainable Development, including through public–private partnerships, taking into account the different circumstances of countries, based on lessons learned by Governments, international institutions and stakeholders and including business and industry, in the field of access to energy, including renewable energy and energy-efficiency and advanced energy technologies, including advanced and cleaner fossil fuel technologies;

(u) Promote cooperation between international and regional institutions and bodies dealing with different aspects of energy for sustainable development within their existing mandate, bearing in mind paragraph 46 (h) of the Programme of Action for the Further Implementation of Agenda 21, strengthening, as appropriate, regional and national activities for the promotion of education and capacity-building regarding energy for sustainable development;

(v) Strengthen and facilitate, as appropriate, regional cooperation arrangements for promoting cross-border energy trade, including the interconnection of electricity grids and oil and natural gas pipelines;

(w) Strengthen and, where appropriate, facilitate dialogue forums among regional, national and international producers and consumers of energy.

*   *   *

20.   Promote an integrated approach to policy-making at the national, regional and local levels for transport services and systems to promote sustainable development, including policies and planning for land use, infrastructure, public transport systems and goods delivery networks, with a view to providing safe, affordable and efficient transportation, increasing energy efficiency, reducing pollution, reducing congestion, reducing adverse health effects and limiting urban sprawl, taking into account national priorities and circumstances. This would include actions at all levels to:

(a) Implement transport strategies for sustainable development, reflecting specific regional, national and local conditions, so as to improve the affordability, efficiency and convenience of transportation, as well as improving urban air quality and health, and reduce greenhouse gas emissions, including through the development of better vehicle technologies that are more environmentally sound, affordable and socially acceptable;

(b) Promote investment and partnerships for the development of sustainable, energy efficient multi-modal transportation systems, including public mass transportation systems and better transportation systems in rural areas, with technical and financial assistance for developing countries and countries with economies in transition.

*   *   *

21.   Prevent and minimize waste and maximize reuse, recycling and use of environmentally friendly alternative materials, with the participation of government authorities and all stakeholders, in order to minimize adverse effects on the environment and improve resource efficiency, with financial, technical and other assistance for developing countries. This would include actions at all levels to:

(a) Develop waste management systems, with highest priorities placed on waste prevention and minimization, reuse and recycling, and environmentally sound disposal facilities, including technology to recapture the energy contained in waste, and encourage small-scale waste-recycling initiatives that support urban and rural waste management and provide income-generating opportunities, with international support for developing countries;

(b) Promote waste prevention and minimization by encouraging production of reusable consumer goods and biodegradable products and developing the infrastructure required.

*   *   *

22.   Renew the commitment, as advanced in Agenda 21, to sound management of chemicals throughout their life cycle and of hazardous wastes for sustainable development and for the protection of human health and the environment, inter alia, aiming to achieve by 2020 that chemicals are used and produced in ways that lead to the minimization of significant adverse effects on human health and the environment, using transparent science-based risk assessment procedures and science-based risk management procedures, taking into account the precautionary approach, as set out in principle 15 of the Rio Declaration on Environment and Development, and support developing countries in strengthening their capacity for the sound management of chemicals and hazardous wastes by providing technical and financial assistance. This would include actions at all levels to:

(a) Promote the ratification and implementation of relevant international instruments on chemicals and hazardous waste, including the Rotterdam Convention on Prior Informed Consent Procedures for Certain Hazardous Chemicals and Pesticides in International Trade so that it can enter into force by 2003 and the Stockholm Convention on Persistent Organic Pollutants so that it can enter into force by 2004, and encourage and improve coordination as well as supporting developing countries in their implementation;

(b) Further develop a strategic approach to international chemicals management based on the Bahia Declaration and Priorities for Action beyond 2000 of the Intergovernmental Forum on Chemical Safety (IFCS) by 2005, and urge that the United Nations Environment Programme (UNEP), IFCS, other international organizations dealing with chemical management, and other relevant international organizations and actors closely cooperate in this regard, as appropriate;

(c) Encourage countries to implement the new globally harmonized system for the classification and labelling of chemicals as soon as possible with a view to having the system fully operational by 2008;

(d) Encourage partnerships to promote activities aimed at enhancing environmentally sound management of chemicals and hazardous wastes, implementing multilateral environmental agreements, raising awareness of issues relating to chemicals and hazardous waste, and encouraging the collection and use of additional scientific data;

(e) Promote efforts to prevent international illegal trafficking of hazardous chemicals and hazardous wastes and to prevent damage resulting from the transboundary movement and disposal of hazardous wastes in a manner consistent with obligations under relevant international instruments, such as the Basel Convention on the Control of Transboundary Movements of Hazardous Wastes and Their Disposal;

(f) Encourage development of coherent and integrated information on chemicals, such as through national pollutant release and transfer registers;

(g) Promote reduction of the risks posed by heavy metals that are harmful to human health and the environment, including through a review of relevant studies, such as the UNEP global assessment of mercury and its compounds.

IV. PROTECTING AND MANAGING THE NATURAL RESOURCE BASE OF ECONOMIC AND SOCIAL DEVELOPMENT

23.   Human activities are having an increasing impact on the integrity of ecosystems that provide essential resources and services for human well-being

and economic activities. Managing the natural resources base in a sustainable and integrated manner is essential for sustainable development. In this regard, to reverse the current trend in natural resource degradation as soon as possible, it is necessary to implement strategies which should include targets adopted at the national and, where appropriate, regional levels to protect ecosystems and to achieve integrated management of land, water and living resources, while strengthening regional, national and local capacities. This would include actions at all levels to:

24.   Launch a programme of actions, with financial and technical assistance, to achieve the millennium development goal on safe drinking water. In this respect, we agree to halve, by the year 2015, the proportion of people who are unable to reach or to afford safe drinking water as outlined in the Millennium Declaration and the proportion of people without access to basic sanitation, which would include actions at all levels to:

(a)   Mobilize international and domestic financial resources at all levels, transfer technology, promote best practice and support capacity-building for water and sanitation infrastructure and services development, ensuring that such infrastructure and services meet the needs of the poor and are gender-sensitive;

(b)   Facilitate access to public information and participation, including by women, at all levels, in support of policy and decision-making related to water resources management and project implementation;

(c)   Promote priority action by Governments, with the support of all stakeholders, in water management and capacity-building at the national level and, where appropriate, at the regional level, and promote and provide new and additional financial resources and innovative technologies to implement chapter 18 of Agenda 21;

(d)   Intensify water pollution prevention to reduce health hazards and protect ecosystems by introducing technologies for affordable sanitation and industrial and domestic wastewater treatment, by mitigating the effects of groundwater contamination, and by establishing, at the national level, monitoring systems and effective legal frameworks;

(e)   Adopt prevention and protection measures to promote sustainable water use and to address water shortages.

25.   Develop integrated water resources management and water efficiency plans by 2005, with support to developing countries, through actions at all levels to:

(a)   Develop and implement national/regional strategies, plans and programmes with regard to integrated river basin, watershed and groundwater management, and introduce measures to improve the efficiency of water infrastructure to reduce losses and increase recycling of water;

(b) Employ the full range of policy instruments, including regulation, monitoring, voluntary measures, market and information-based tools, land-use management and cost recovery of water services, without cost recovery objectives becoming a barrier to access to safe water by poor people, and adopt an integrated water basin approach;

(c) Improve the efficient use of water resources and promote their allocation among competing uses in a way that gives priority to the satisfaction of basic human needs and balances the requirement of preserving or restoring ecosystems and their functions, in particular in fragile environments, with human domestic, industrial and agriculture needs, including safeguarding drinking water quality;

(d) Develop programmes for mitigating the effects of extreme water-related events;

(e) Support the diffusion of technology and capacity-building for non-conventional water resources and conservation technologies, to developing countries and regions facing water scarcity conditions or subject to drought and desertification, through technical and financial support and capacity-building;

(f) Support, where appropriate, efforts and programmes for energy-efficient, sustainable and cost-effective desalination of seawater, water recycling and water harvesting from coastal fogs in developing countries, through such measures as technological, technical and financial assistance and other modalities;

(g) Facilitate the establishment of public–private partnerships and other forms of partnership that give priority to the needs of the poor, within stable and transparent national regulatory frameworks provided by Governments, while respecting local conditions, involving all concerned stakeholders, and monitoring the performance and improving accountability of public institutions and private companies.

26.   Support developing countries and countries with economies in transition in their efforts to monitor and assess the quantity and quality of water resources, including through the establishment and/or further development of national monitoring networks and water resources databases and the development of relevant national indicators.

27.   Improve water resource management and scientific understanding of the water cycle through cooperation in joint observation and research, and for this purpose encourage and promote knowledge-sharing and provide capacity-building and the transfer of technology, as mutually agreed,

including remote-sensing and satellite technologies, particularly to developing countries and countries with economies in transition.

28.   Promote effective coordination among the various international and intergovernmental bodies and processes working on water-related issues, both within the United Nations system and between the United Nations and international financial institutions, drawing on the contributions of other international institutions and civil society to inform intergovernmental decision-making; closer coordination should also be promoted to elaborate and support proposals and undertake activities related to the International Year of Freshwater 2003 and beyond.

*   *   *

29.   Oceans, seas, islands and coastal areas form an integrated and essential component of the Earth's ecosystem and are critical for global food security and for sustaining economic prosperity and the well-being of many national economies, particularly in developing countries. Ensuring the sustainable development of the oceans requires effective coordination and cooperation, including at the global and regional levels, between relevant bodies, and actions at all levels to:

(a)   Invite States to ratify or accede to and implement the United Nations Convention on the Law of the Sea, which provides the overall legal framework for ocean activities;

(b)   Promote the implementation of chapter 17 of Agenda 21 which provides the programme of action for achieving the sustainable development of oceans, coastal areas and seas through its programme areas of integrated management and sustainable development of coastal areas, including exclusive economic zones; marine environmental protection; sustainable use and conservation of marine living resources; addressing critical uncertainties for the management of the marine environment and climate change; strengthening international, including regional, cooperation and coordination; and sustainable development of small islands;

(c)   Establish an effective, transparent and regular inter-agency coordination mechanism on ocean and coastal issues within the United Nations system;

(d)   Encourage the application by 2010 of the ecosystem approach, noting the Reykjavik Declaration on Responsible Fisheries in the Marine Ecosystem and decision 5/6 of the Conference of Parties to the Convention on Biological Diversity;

(e)   Promote integrated, multidisciplinary and multisectoral coastal and ocean management at the national level, and encourage and assist coastal States in developing ocean policies and mechanisms on integrated coastal management;

(f) Strengthen regional cooperation and coordination between the relevant regional organizations and programmes, the UNEP regional seas programmes, regional fisheries management organizations and other regional science, health and development organizations;

(g) Assist developing countries in coordinating policies and programmes at the regional and subregional levels aimed at the conservation and sustainable management of fishery resources, and implement integrated coastal area management plans, including through the promotion of sustainable coastal and small-scale fishing activities and, where appropriate, the development of related infrastructure;

(h) Take note of the work of the open-ended informal consultative process established by the United Nations General Assembly in its resolution 54/33 in order to facilitate the annual review by the Assembly of developments in ocean affairs and the upcoming review of its effectiveness and utility to be held at its fifty-seventh session under the terms of the above-mentioned resolution.

30.   To achieve sustainable fisheries, the following actions are required at all levels:

(a) Maintain or restore stocks to levels that can produce the maximum sustainable yield with the aim of achieving these goals for depleted stocks on an urgent basis and where possible not later than 2015;

(b) Ratify or accede to and effectively implement the relevant United Nations and, where appropriate, associated regional fisheries agreements or arrangements, noting in particular the Agreement for the Implementation of the Provisions of the United Nations Convention on the Law of the Sea of 10 December 1982 relating to the Conservation and Management of Straddling Fish Stocks and Highly Migratory Fish Stocks and the 1993 Agreement to Promote Compliance with International Conservation and Management Measures by Fishing Vessels on the High Seas;

(c) Implement the 1995 Code of Conduct for Responsible Fisheries, taking note of the special requirements of developing countries as noted in its article 5, and the relevant Food and Agriculture Organization of the United Nations (FAO) international plans of action and technical guidelines;

(d) Urgently develop and implement national and, where appropriate, regional plans of action, to put into effect the FAO international plans of action, in particular the international plan of action for the management of fishing capacity by 2005 and the international plan of action to prevent, deter and eliminate illegal, unreported and unregulated fishing by 2004. Establish effective monitoring, reporting and enforcement, and control of fishing vessels, including by flag States, to further the international plan of action to prevent, deter and eliminate illegal, unreported and unregulated fishing;

(e) Encourage relevant regional fisheries management organizations and arrangements to give due consideration to the rights, duties and interests of coastal States and the special requirements of developing States when addressing the issue of the allocation of share of fishery resources for straddling stocks and highly migratory fish stocks, mindful of the provisions of the United Nations Convention on the Law of the Sea and the Agreement for the Implementation of the Provisions of the United Nations Convention on the Law of the Sea of 10 December 1982 Relating to the Conservation and Management of Straddling Fish Stocks and Highly Migratory Fish Stocks, on the high seas and within exclusive economic zones;

(f) Eliminate subsidies that contribute to illegal, unreported and unregulated fishing and to over-capacity, while completing the efforts undertaken at WTO to clarify and improve its disciplines on fisheries subsidies, taking into account the importance of this sector to developing countries;

(g) Strengthen donor coordination and partnerships between international financial institutions, bilateral agencies and other relevant stakeholders to enable developing countries, in particular the least developed countries and small island developing States and countries with economies in transition, to develop their national, regional and subregional capacities for infrastructure and integrated management and the sustainable use of fisheries;

(h) Support the sustainable development of aquaculture, including small-scale aquaculture, given its growing importance for food security and economic development.

31.   In accordance with chapter 17 of Agenda 21, promote the conservation and management of the oceans through actions at all levels, giving due regard to the relevant international instruments to:

(a) Maintain the productivity and biodiversity of important and vulnerable marine and coastal areas, including in areas within and beyond national jurisdiction;

(b) Implement the work programme arising from the Jakarta Mandate on the Conservation and Sustainable Use of Marine and Coastal Biological Diversity of the Convention on Biological Diversity, including through the urgent mobilization of financial resources and technological assistance and the development of human and institutional capacity, particularly in developing countries;

(c) Develop and facilitate the use of diverse approaches and tools, including the ecosystem approach, the elimination of destructive fishing practices, the establishment of marine protected areas consistent with international law and based on scientific information, including representative networks by 2012 and time/area closures for the protection of nursery grounds and periods, proper coastal land use; and watershed planning and the integration of marine and coastal areas management into key sectors;

(d) Develop national, regional and international programmes for halting the loss of marine biodiversity, including in coral reefs and wetlands;

(e) Implement the RAMSAR Convention, including its joint work programme with the Convention on Biological Diversity, and the programme of action called for by the International Coral Reef Initiative to strengthen joint management plans and international networking for wetland ecosystems in coastal zones, including coral reefs, mangroves, seaweed beds and tidal mud flats.

32.   Advance implementation of the Global Programme of Action for the Protection of the Marine Environment from Land-based Activities and the Montreal Declaration on the Protection of the Marine Environment from Land-based Activities, with particular emphasis in the period 2002–2006 on municipal wastewater, the physical alteration and destruction of habitats, and nutrients, by actions at all levels to:

(a) Facilitate partnerships, scientific research and diffusion of technical knowledge; mobilize domestic, regional and international resources; and promote human and institutional capacity-building, paying particular attention to the needs of developing countries;

(b) Strengthen the capacity of developing countries in the development of their national and regional programmes and mechanisms to mainstream the objectives of the Global Programme of Action and to manage the risks and impacts of ocean pollution;

(c) Elaborate regional programmes of action and improve the links with strategic plans for the sustainable development of coastal and marine resources, noting in particular areas which are subject to accelerated environmental changes and development pressures;

(d) Make every effort to achieve substantial progress by the next Global Programme of Action conference in 2006 to protect the marine environment from land-based activities.

33.   Enhance maritime safety and protection of the marine environment from pollution by actions at all levels to:

(a)   Invite States to ratify or accede to and implement the conventions and protocols and other relevant instruments of the International Maritime Organization (IMO) relating to the enhancement of maritime safety and protection of the marine environment from marine pollution and environmental damage caused by ships, including the use of toxic anti-fouling paints and urge IMO to consider stronger mechanisms to secure the implementation of IMO instruments by flag States;

(b)   Accelerate the development of measures to address invasive alien species in ballast water. Urge IMO to finalize the IMO International Convention on the Control and Management of Ships' Ballast Water and Sediments.

33.bis   Governments, taking into account their national circumstances, are encouraged, recalling paragraph 8 of resolution GC (44)/RES/17 of the General Conference of the International Atomic Energy Agency (IAEA) and taking into account the very serious potential for environment and human health impacts of radioactive wastes, to make efforts to examine and further improve measures and internationally agreed regulations regarding safety, while stressing the importance of having effective liability mechanisms in place, relevant to international maritime transportation and other transboundary movement of radioactive material, radioactive waste and spent fuel, including, inter alia, arrangements for prior notification and consultations done in accordance with relevant international instruments.

34.   Improve the scientific understanding and assessment of marine and coastal ecosystems as a fundamental basis for sound decision-making, through actions at all levels to:

(a)   Increase scientific and technical collaboration, including integrated assessment at the global and regional levels, including the appropriate transfer of marine science and marine technologies and techniques for the conservation and management of living and non-living marine resources and expanding ocean-observing capabilities for the timely prediction and assessment of the state of marine environment;

(b)   Establish by 2004 a regular process under the United Nations for global reporting and assessment of the state of the marine environment, including socio-economic aspects, both current and foreseeable, building on existing regional assessments;

(c)   Build capacity in marine science, information and management, through, inter alia, promoting the use of environmental impact assessments and environmental evaluation and reporting techniques, for projects or activities that are potentially harmful to the coastal and marine environments and their living and non-living resources;

(d) Strengthen the ability of the Intergovernmental Oceanographic Commission of the United Nations Educational, Scientific and Cultural Organization, FAO and other relevant international and regional and subregional organizations to build national and local capacity in marine science and the sustainable management of oceans and their resources.

*   *   *

35.   An integrated, multi-hazard, inclusive approach to address vulnerability, risk assessment and disaster management, including prevention, mitigation, preparedness, response and recovery, is an essential element of a safer world in the twenty-first century. Actions are required at all levels to:

(a) Strengthen the role of the International Strategy for Disaster Reduction and encourage the international community to provide the necessary financial resources to its Trust Fund;

(b) Support the establishment of effective regional, subregional and national strategies and scientific and technical institutional support for disaster management;

(c) Strengthen the institutional capacities of countries and promote international joint observation and research, through improved surface-based monitoring and increased use of satellite data, dissemination of technical and scientific knowledge, and the provision of assistance to vulnerable countries;

(d) Reduce the risks of flooding and drought in vulnerable countries by, inter alia, promoting wetland and watershed protection and restoration, improved land-use planning, improving and applying more widely techniques and methodologies for assessing the potential adverse effects of climate change on wetlands and, as appropriate, assisting countries that are particularly vulnerable to those effects;

(e) Improve techniques and methodologies for assessing the effects of climate change, and encourage the continuing assessment of those adverse effects by the Intergovernmental Panel on Climate Change;

(f) Encourage the dissemination and use of traditional and indigenous knowledge to mitigate the impact of disasters, and promote community-based disaster management planning by local authorities, including through training activities and raising public awareness;

(g) Support the ongoing voluntary contribution of, as appropriate, nongovernmental organizations, the scientific community and other partners in the management of natural disasters according to agreed, relevant guidelines;

(h) Develop and strengthen early warning systems and information networks in disaster management, consistent with the International Strategy for Disaster Reduction;

(i) Develop and strengthen capacity at all levels to collect and disseminate scientific and technical information, including the improvement of early warning systems for predicting extreme weather events, especially El Niño/La Niña, through the provision of assistance to institutions devoted to addressing such events, including the International Centre for the Study of the El Niño phenomenon;

(j) Promote cooperation for the prevention and mitigation of, preparedness for, response to and recovery from major technological and other disasters with an adverse impact on the environment in order to enhance the capabilities of affected countries to cope with such situations.

*   *   *

36. Change in the Earth's climate and its adverse effects are a common concern of humankind. We remain deeply concerned that all countries, particularly developing countries including the least developed countries and small island developing States, face increased risks of negative impacts of climate change and recognize that, in this context, the problems of poverty, land degradation, access to water and food and human health remain at the centre of global attention. The United Nations Framework Convention on Climate Change is the key instrument for addressing climate change, a global concern, and we reaffirm our commitment to achieving its ultimate objective of stabilization of greenhouse gas concentrations in the atmosphere at a level that would prevent dangerous anthropogenic interference with the climate system, within a time frame sufficient to allow ecosystems to adapt naturally to climate change, to ensure that food production is not threatened and to enable economic development to proceed in a sustainable manner, in accordance with our common but differentiated responsibilities and respective capabilities. Recalling the United Nations Millennium Declaration, in which heads of State and Government resolved to make every effort to ensure the entry into force of the Kyoto Protocol to the United Nations Framework Convention on Climate Change, preferably by the tenth anniversary of the United Nations Conference on Environment and Development in 2002, and to embark on the required reduction of emissions of greenhouse gases, States that have ratified the Kyoto Protocol strongly urge States that have not already done so to ratify the Kyoto Protocol in a timely manner. Actions at all levels are required to:

(a) Meet all the commitments and obligations under the UNFCCC;

(b) Work cooperatively towards achieving the objectives of the UNFCCC;

(c) Provide technical and financial assistance and capacity-building to developing countries and countries with economies in transition in accordance with commitments under the UNFCCC, including the Marrakech accords;

(d) Build and enhance scientific and technological capabilities, inter alia through continuing support to the IPCC for the exchange of scientific data and information especially in developing countries;

(e) Develop and transfer technological solutions;

(f) Develop and disseminate innovative technologies in respect of key sectors of development, particularly energy, and of investment in this regard, including through private sector involvement, market-oriented approaches, as well as supportive public policies and international cooperation;

(g) Promote the systematic observation of the Earth's atmosphere, land and oceans by improving monitoring stations, increasing the use of satellites, and appropriate integration of these observations to produce high-quality data that could be disseminated for the use of all countries, in particular developing countries;

(h) Enhance the implementation of national, regional and international strategies to monitor the Earth's atmosphere, land and oceans including, as appropriate, strategies for integrated global observations, inter alia with the cooperation of relevant international organizations, especially the United Nations specialized agencies in cooperation with the UNFCCC;

(i) Support initiatives to assess the consequences of climate change, such as the Arctic Council initiative, including the environmental, economic and social impacts on local and indigenous communities.

37.   Enhance cooperation at the international, regional and national levels to reduce air pollution, including transboundary air pollution, acid deposition and ozone depletion bearing in mind the Rio principles, including, inter alia, the principle that, in view of the different contributions to global environmental degradation, States have common but differentiated responsibilities, with actions at all levels to:

(a) Strengthen capacities of developing countries and countries with economies in transition to measure, reduce and assess the impacts of air pollution, including health impacts, and provide financial and technical support for these activities;

(b) Facilitate implementation of the Montreal Protocol on Substances that Deplete the Ozone Layer by ensuring adequate replenishment of its fund by 2003/2005;

(c) Further support the effective regime for the protection of the ozone layer established in the Vienna Convention for the Protection of the Ozone Layer and the Montreal Protocol, including its compliance mechanism;

(d) Improve access by developing countries to affordable, accessible, cost-effective, safe and environmentally sound alternatives to ozone-depleting substances by 2010, and assist them in complying with the phase-out schedule under the Montreal Protocol, bearing in mind that ozone depletion and climate change are scientifically and technically interrelated;

(e) Take measures to address illegal traffic in ozone-depleting substances.

*   *   *

38. Agriculture plays a crucial role in addressing the needs of a growing global population, and is inextricably linked to poverty eradication, especially in developing countries. Enhancing the role of women at all levels and in all aspects of rural development, agriculture, nutrition and food security is imperative. Sustainable agriculture and rural development are essential to the implementation of an integrated approach to increasing food production and enhancing food security and food safety in an environmentally sustainable way. This would include actions at all levels to:

(a) Achieve the Millennium Declaration target to halve by the year 2015 the proportion of the world's people who suffer from hunger and realize the right to a standard of living adequate for the health and well-being of themselves and their families, including food, including by promoting food security and fighting hunger in combination with measures which address poverty, consistent with the outcome of the World Food Summit and, for States Parties, with their obligations under article 11 of the International Covenant on Economic, Social and Cultural Rights;

(b) Develop and implement integrated land management and water-use plans that are based on sustainable use of renewable resources and on integrated assessments of socio-economic and environmental potentials, and strengthen the capacity of Governments, local authorities and communities to monitor and manage the quantity and quality of land and water resources;

(c) Increase understanding of the sustainable use, protection and management of water resources to advance long-term sustainability of freshwater, coastal and marine environments;

(d) Promote programmes to enhance in a sustainable manner the productivity of land and the efficient use of water resources in agriculture, forestry, wetlands, artisanal fisheries and aquaculture, especially through indigenous and local community-based approaches;

(e) Support the efforts of developing countries to protect oases from silt, land degradation and increasing salinity by providing appropriate technical and financial assistance;

(f) Enhance the participation of women in all aspects and at all levels relating to sustainable agriculture and food security;

(g) Integrate existing information systems on land-use practices by strengthening national research and extension services and farmer organizations to trigger farmer-to-farmer exchange on good practices, such as those related to environmentally sound, low-cost technologies, with the assistance of relevant international organizations;

(h) Enact, as appropriate, measures that protect indigenous resource management systems and support the contribution of all appropriate stakeholders, men and women alike, in rural planning and development;

(i) Adopt policies and implement laws that guarantee well defined and enforceable land and water use rights, and promote legal security of tenure, recognizing the existence of different national laws and/or systems of land access and tenure, and provide technical and financial assistance to developing countries as well as countries with economies in transition that are undertaking land tenure reform in order to enhance sustainable livelihoods;

(j) Reverse the declining trend in public sector finance for sustainable agriculture, provide appropriate technical and financial assistance, and promote private sector investment and support efforts in developing countries and countries with economies in transition to strengthen agricultural research and natural resource management capacity and dissemination of research results to the farming communities;

(k) Employ market-based incentives for agricultural enterprises and farmers to monitor and manage water use and quality, inter alia, by applying such methods as small-scale irrigation and wastewater recycling and reuse;

(l) Enhance access to existing markets and develop new markets for value-added agricultural products;

(m) Increase brown-field redevelopment in developed countries and countries with economies in transition, with appropriate technical assistance where contamination is a serious problem;

(n) Enhance international cooperation to combat the illicit cultivation of narcotic plants, taking into account their negative social, economic and environmental impacts;

(o) Promote programmes for the environmentally sound, effective and efficient use of soil fertility improvement practices and agricultural pest control;

(p) Strengthen and improve coordination of existing initiatives to enhance sustainable agricultural production and food security;

(q) Invite countries that have not done so to ratify the International Treaty on Plant Genetic Resources for Food and Agriculture;

(r) Promote the conservation, and sustainable use and management of traditional and indigenous agricultural systems and strengthen indigenous models of agricultural production.

*   *   *

39. Strengthen the implementation of the United Nations Convention to Combat Desertification in Those Countries Experiencing Serious Drought and/or Desertification, particularly in Africa, to address causes of desertification and land degradation in order to maintain and restore land, and to address poverty resulting from land degradation. This would include actions at all levels to:

(a) Mobilize adequate and predictable financial resources, transfer of technologies and capacity-building at all levels;

(b) Formulate national action programmes to ensure timely and effective implementation of the Convention and its related projects, with the support of the international community, including through decentralized projects at the local level;

(c) Encourage the United Nations Framework Convention on Climate Change, the Convention on Biological Diversity and the Convention to Combat Desertification to continue exploring and enhancing synergies, with due regard to their respective mandates, in the elaboration and implementation of plans and strategies under the respective Conventions;

(d) Integrate measures to prevent and combat desertification as well as to mitigate the effects of drought through relevant policies and programmes, such as land, water and forest management, agriculture, rural development, early warning systems, environment, energy, natural resources, health and education, and poverty eradication and sustainable development strategies;

(e) Provide affordable local access to information to improve monitoring and early warning related to desertification and drought;

(f)   Call on the Second Assembly of the Global Environment Facility (GEF) to take action on the recommendations of the GEF Council concerning the designation of land degradation (desertification and deforestation) as a focal area of GEF as a means of GEF support for the successful implementation of the Convention to Combat Desertification; and consequently, consider making GEF a financial mechanism of the Convention, taking into account the prerogatives and decisions of the Conference of the Parties to the Convention, while recognizing the complementary roles of GEF and the Global Mechanism of the Convention in providing and mobilizing resources for the elaboration and implementation of action programmes;

(g)   Improve the sustainability of grassland resources through strengthening management and law enforcement and providing financial and technical support by the international community to developing countries.

*   *   *

40.   Mountain ecosystems support particular livelihoods, and include significant watershed resources, biological diversity and unique flora and fauna. Many are particularly fragile and vulnerable to the adverse effects of climate change and need specific protection. Actions at all levels are required to:

(a)   Develop and promote programmes, policies and approaches that integrate environmental, economic and social components of sustainable mountain development and strengthen international cooperation for its positive impacts on poverty eradication programmes, especially in developing countries;

(b)   Implement programmes to address, where appropriate, deforestation, erosion, land degradation, loss of biodiversity, disruption of water flows and retreat of glaciers;

(c)   Develop and implement, where appropriate, gender-sensitive policies and programmes, including public and private investments that help eliminate inequities facing mountain communities;

(d)   Implement programmes to promote diversification and traditional mountain economies, sustainable livelihoods and small-scale production systems, including specific training programmes and better access to national and international markets, communications and transport planning, taking into account the particular sensitivity of mountains;

(e)   Promote full participation and involvement of mountain communities in decisions that affect them and integrate indigenous knowledge, heritage and values in all development initiatives;

(f) Mobilize national and international support for applied research and capacity-building, provide financial and technical assistance for the effective implementation of sustainable development of mountain ecosystems in developing countries and countries with economies in transition, and address the poverty among people living in mountains through concrete plans, projects and programmes, with sufficient support from all stakeholders, taking into account the spirit of the International Year of Mountains, 2002.

*   *   *

41.   Promote sustainable tourism development, including non-consumptive and eco-tourism, taking into account the spirit of the International Year of Eco-tourism 2002, the United Nations Year for Cultural Heritage in 2002, the World Eco-tourism Summit 2002 and its Quebec Declaration, and the Global Code of Ethics for Tourism as adopted by the World Tourism Organization in order to increase the benefits from tourism resources for the population in host communities while maintaining the cultural and environmental integrity of the host communities and enhancing the protection of ecologically sensitive areas and natural heritages. Promote sustainable tourism development and capacity-building in order to contribute to the strengthening of rural and local communities. This would include actions at all levels to:

(a) Enhance international cooperation, foreign direct investment and partnerships with both private and public sectors, at all levels;

(b) Develop programmes, including education and training programmes, that encourage people to participate in eco-tourism, enable indigenous and local communities to develop and benefit from eco-tourism, and enhance stakeholder cooperation in tourism development and heritage preservation, in order to improve the protection of the environment, natural resources and cultural heritage;

(c) Provide technical assistance to developing countries and countries with economies in transition to support sustainable tourism business development and investment and tourism awareness programmes, to improve domestic tourism, and to stimulate entrepreneurial development;

(d) Assist host communities in managing visits to their tourism attractions for their maximum benefit, while ensuring the least negative impacts on and risks for their traditions, culture and environment, with the support of the World Tourism Organization and other relevant organizations;

(e) Promote the diversification of economic activities, including through the facilitation of access to markets and commercial information, and participation of emerging local enterprises, especially small and medium-sized enterprises.

*   *   *

42.   Biodiversity, which plays a critical role in overall sustainable development and poverty eradication, is essential to our planet, human well-being and to the livelihood and cultural integrity of people. However, biodiversity is currently being lost at unprecedented rates due to human activities; this trend can only be reversed if the local people benefit from the conservation and sustainable use of biological diversity, in particular in countries of origin of genetic resources, in accordance with article 15 of the Convention on Biological Diversity. The Convention is the key instrument for the conservation and sustainable use of biological diversity and the fair and equitable sharing of benefits arising from use of genetic resources. A more efficient and coherent implementation of the three objectives of the Convention and the achievement by 2010 of a significant reduction in the current rate of loss of biological diversity will require the provision of new and additional financial and technical resources to developing countries, and includes actions at all levels to:

(a)   Integrate the objectives of the Convention into global, regional and national sectoral and cross-sectoral programmes and policies, in particular in the programmes and policies of the economic sectors of countries and international financial institutions;

(b)   Promote the ongoing work under the Convention on the sustainable use on biological diversity, including on sustainable tourism, as a cross-cutting issue relevant to different ecosystems, sectors and thematic areas;

(c)   Encourage effective synergies between the Convention and other multilateral environmental agreements, inter alia, through the development of joint plans and programmes, with due regard to their respective mandates, regarding common responsibilities and concerns;

(d)   Implement the Convention and its provisions, including active follow-up of its work programmes and decisions through national, regional and global action programmes, in particular the national biodiversity strategies and action plans, and strengthen their integration into relevant cross-sectoral strategies, programmes and policies, including those related to sustainable development and poverty eradication, including initiatives which promote community-based sustainable use of biological diversity;

(e)   Promote the wide implementation and further development of the ecosystem approach, as being elaborated in the ongoing work of the Convention;

(f)   Promote concrete international support and partnership for the conservation and sustainable use of biodiversity, including in ecosystems, at World Heritage sites and for the protection of endangered species, in particular through the appropriate channelling of financial resources and technology to developing countries and countries with economies in transition;

(g)   To effectively conserve and sustainably use biodiversity, promote and support initiatives for hot spot areas and other areas essential for biodiversity and promote the development of national and regional ecological networks and corridors;

(h)   Provide financial and technical support to developing countries, including capacity-building, in order to enhance indigenous and community-based biodiversity conservation efforts;

(i)   Strengthen national, regional and international efforts to control invasive alien species, which are one of the main causes of biodiversity loss, and encourage the development of effective work programme on invasive alien species at all levels;

(j)   Subject to national legislation, recognize the rights of local and indigenous communities who are holders of traditional knowledge, innovations and practices, and, with the approval and involvement of the holders of such knowledge, innovations and practices, develop and implement benefit-sharing mechanisms on mutually agreed terms for the use of such knowledge, innovations and practices;

(k)   Encourage and enable all stakeholders to contribute to the implementation of the objectives of the Convention, and in particular recognize the specific role of youth, women and indigenous and local communities in conserving and using biodiversity in a sustainable way;

(l)   Promote the effective participation of indigenous and local communities in decision and policy-making concerning the use of their traditional knowledge;

(m)   Encourage technical and financial support to developing countries and countries with economies in transition in their efforts to develop and implement, as appropriate, inter alia, national sui generis systems and traditional systems according to national priorities and legislation, with a view to conserving and the sustainable use of biodiversity;

(n)   Promote the wide implementation of and continued work on the Bonn Guidelines on Access to Genetic Resources and Fair and Equitable Sharing of Benefits arising out of their Utilization of the Convention, as an input to assist Parties to the Convention when developing and drafting legislative, administrative or policy measures on access and benefit-sharing, and contract and other arrangements under mutually agreed terms for access and benefit-sharing;

(o) Negotiate within the framework of the Convention on Biological Diversity, bearing in mind the Bonn Guidelines, an international regime to promote and safeguard the fair and equitable sharing of benefits arising out of the utilization of genetic resources;

(p) Encourage successful conclusion of existing processes under the World Intellectual Property Organization Intergovernmental Committee on Intellectual Property and Genetic Resources, Traditional Knowledge and Folklore, and in the ad hoc open-ended working group on article 8 (j) and related provisions of the Convention;

(q) Promote practicable measures for access to the results and benefits arising from biotechnologies based upon genetic resources, in accordance with articles 15 and 19 of the Convention, including through enhanced scientific and technical cooperation on biotechnology and biosafety, including the exchange of experts, training human resources and developing research-oriented institutional capacities;

(r) With a view to enhancing synergy and mutual supportiveness, taking into account the decisions under the relevant agreements, promote the discussions, without prejudging their outcome, with regard to the relationships between the Convention and agreements related to international trade and intellectual property rights, as outlined in the Doha Ministerial Declaration;

(s) Promote the implementation of the programme of work of the Global Taxonomy Initiative;

(t) Invite all States which have not already done so to ratify the Convention, the Cartagena Protocol on Biosafety and other biodiversity-related agreements, and invite those that have done so, to promote their effective implementation at the national, regional and international levels and to support developing countries and countries with economies in transition technically and financially in this regard.

*   *   *

43.   Forests and trees cover nearly one third of the Earth's surface. Sustainable forest management of both natural and planted forests and for timber and non-timber products is essential to achieving sustainable development and is a critical means to eradicate poverty, significantly reduce deforestation and halt the loss of forest biodiversity and land and resource degradation, and improve food security and access to safe drinking water and affordable energy; highlights the multiple benefits of both natural and planted forests and trees; and contributes to the well-being of the planet and humanity. Achievement of sustainable forest management, nationally and globally, including through partnerships among interested Governments and stakeholders, including the private sector, indigenous and local communities and non-governmental

organizations, is an essential goal of sustainable development. This would include actions at all levels to:

(a) Enhance political commitment to achieve sustainable forest management by endorsing it as a priority on the international political agenda, taking full account of the linkages between the forest sector and other sectors through integrated approaches;

(b) Support the United Nations Forum on Forests, with the assistance of the Collaborative Partnership on Forests, as key intergovernmental mechanisms to facilitate and coordinate the implementation of sustainable forest management at the national, regional and global levels, thus contributing, inter alia, to the conservation and sustainable use of forest biodiversity;

(c) Take immediate action on domestic forest law enforcement and illegal international trade in forest products, including in forest biological resources, with the support of the international community, and provide human and institutional capacity-building related to the enforcement of national legislation in those areas;

(d) Take immediate action at the national and international levels to promote and facilitate the means to achieve sustainable timber harvesting, and to facilitate the provision of financial resources and the transfer and development of environmentally sound technologies, and thereby address unsustainable timber-harvesting practices;

(e) Develop and implement initiatives to address the needs of those parts of the world that currently suffer from poverty and the highest rates of deforestation and where international cooperation would be welcomed by affected Governments;

(f) Create and strengthen partnerships and international cooperation to facilitate the provision of increased financial resources, the transfer of environmentally sound technologies, trade, capacity-building, forest law enforcement and governance at all levels, and integrated land and resource management to implement sustainable forest management, including the Intergovernmental Panel on Forests (IPF)/Intergovernmental Forum on Forests (IFF) proposals for action;

(g) Accelerate implementation of the IPF/IFF proposals for action by countries and by the Collaborative Partnership on Forests, and intensify efforts on reporting to the United Nations Forum on Forests to contribute to an assessment of progress in 2005;

(h) Recognize and support indigenous and community-based forest management systems to ensure their full and effective participation in sustainable forest management;

(i) Implement the Convention on Biological Diversity's expanded action-oriented work programme on all types of forest biological diversity, in close cooperation with the Forum, Partnership members and other forest-related processes and conventions, with the involvement of all relevant stakeholders.

* * *

44.   Mining, minerals and metals are important to the economic and social development of many countries. Minerals are essential for modern living. Enhancing the contribution of mining, minerals and metals to sustainable development includes actions at all levels to:

(a)   Support efforts to address the environmental, economic, health and social impacts and benefits of mining, minerals and metals throughout their life cycle, including workers' health and safety, and use a range of partnerships, furthering existing activities at the national and international levels, among interested Governments, intergovernmental organizations, mining companies and workers, and other stakeholders, to promote transparency and accountability for sustainable mining and minerals development;

(b)   Enhance the participation of stakeholders, including local and indigenous communities and women, to play an active role in minerals, metals and mining development throughout the life cycles of mining operations, including after closure for rehabilitation purposes, in accordance with national regulations and taking into account significant transboundary impacts;

(c)   Foster sustainable mining practices through the provision of financial, technical and capacity-building support to developing countries and countries with economies in transition for the mining and processing of minerals, including small-scale mining, and, where possible and appropriate, improve value-added processing, upgrade scientific and technological information, and reclaim and rehabilitate degraded sites.

V. SUSTAINABLE DEVELOPMENT IN A GLOBALIZING WORLD*

45.   Globalization offers opportunities and challenges for sustainable development. We recognize that globalization and interdependence are offering new opportunities to trade, investment and capital flows and advances in technology, including information technology, for the growth of the world economy, development and the improvement of living standards around the world. At the same time, there remain serious challenges, including serious financial crises, insecurity, poverty, exclusion and inequality within and among societies. The developing countries and countries with economies in transition face special difficulties in responding to those challenges and opportunities. Globalization should be fully inclusive and equitable, and there is a strong need for policies and measures at the national and international levels, formulated and implemented with the full and effective participation of developing countries and countries with economies in transition, to help

them to respond effectively to those challenges and opportunities. This will require urgent action at all levels to:

(a) Continue to promote open, equitable, rules-based, predictable and non-discriminatory multilateral trading and financial systems that benefit all countries in the pursuit of sustainable development. Support the successful completion of the work programme contained in the Doha Ministerial Declaration and the implementation of the Monterrey Consensus. Welcome the decision contained in the Doha Ministerial Declaration to place the needs and interests of developing countries at the heart of the work programme of the Declaration, including through enhanced market access for products of interest to developing countries;

(b) Encourage ongoing efforts by international financial and trade institutions to ensure that decision-making processes and institutional structures are open and transparent;

(c) Enhance the capacities of developing countries, including the least developed countries, landlocked developing countries and small island developing States, to benefit from liberalized trade opportunities, through international cooperation and measures aimed at improving productivity, commodity diversification and competitiveness, community-based entrepreneurial capacity, and transportation and communication infrastructure development;

(d) Support the International Labour Organization and encourage its ongoing work on the social dimension of globalization, as stated in paragraph 64 of the Monterrey Consensus;

(e) Enhance the delivery of coordinated, effective and targeted trade-related technical assistance and capacity-building programmes, including to take advantage of existing and future market access opportunities, and to examine the relationship between trade, environment and development.

45.bis   Implement the outcomes of the Doha Ministerial Conference by WTO members, further strengthen trade-related technical assistance and capacity-building, and ensure the meaningful, effective and full participation of developing countries in multilateral trade negotiations by placing their needs and interests at the heart of the WTO work programme.

45.ter   Actively promote corporate responsibility and accountability, based on the Rio Principles, including through the full development and effective implementation of intergovernmental agreements and measures, international initiatives and public–private partnerships, and appropriate national regulations, and support continuous improvement in corporate practices in all countries.

45.quater   Strengthen the capacities of developing countries to encourage public–private initiatives that enhance the ease of access, accuracy, timeliness and coverage of information on countries and financial markets. Multilateral and regional financial institutions could provide further assistance for these purposes.

45.quinquies   Strengthen regional trade and cooperation agreements, consistent with the multilateral trading system, among developed and developing countries and countries with economies in transition, as well as among developing countries, with the support of international finance institutions and regional development banks, as appropriate, with a view to achieving the objectives of sustainable development.

45.sexties   Assist developing countries and countries with economies in transition in narrowing the digital divide, creating digital opportunities and harnessing the potential of information and communication technologies for development, through technology transfer on mutually agreed terms and the provision of financial and technical support, and in this context support the World Summit on the Information Society.

VI. HEALTH AND SUSTAINABLE DEVELOPMENT

46.   The Rio Declaration on Environment and Development states that human beings are at the centre of concerns for sustainable development, and that they are entitled to a healthy and productive life, in harmony with nature. The goals of sustainable development can only be achieved in the absence of a high prevalence of debilitating diseases, while obtaining health gains for the whole population requires poverty eradication. There is an urgent need to address the causes of ill health, including environmental causes, and their impact on development, with particular emphasis on women and children, as well as vulnerable groups of society, such as people with disabilities, elderly persons and indigenous people.

47.   Strengthen the capacity of health-care systems to deliver basic health services to all, in an efficient, accessible and affordable manner aimed at preventing, controlling and treating diseases, and to reduce environmental health threats, in conformity with human rights and fundamental freedoms and consistent with national laws and cultural and religious values, taking into account the reports of relevant United Nations conferences and summits and of special sessions of the General Assembly. This would include actions at all levels to:

(a)   Integrate the health concerns, including those of the most vulnerable populations, into strategies, policies and programmes for poverty eradication and sustainable development;

(b)   Promote equitable and improved access to affordable and efficient health-care services, including prevention, at all levels of the health system, essential and safe drugs at affordable prices, immunization services and safe vaccines, and medical technology;

(c) Provide technical and financial assistance to developing countries and countries with economies in transition to implement the Health for All Strategy, including health information systems and integrated databases on development hazards;

(d) Improve the development and management of human resources in health-care services;

(e) Promote and develop partnerships to enhance health education with the objective of achieving improved health literacy on a global basis by 2010, with the involvement of United Nations agencies, as appropriate;

(f) Develop programmes and initiatives to reduce, by the year 2015, mortality rates for infants and children under 5 by two thirds, and maternal mortality rates by three quarters, of the prevailing rate in 2000, and reduce disparities between and within developed and developing countries as quickly as possible, with particular attention to eliminating the pattern of disproportionate and preventable mortality among girl infants and children;

(g) Target research efforts and apply research results to priority public health issues, in particular those affecting susceptible and vulnerable populations, through the development of new vaccines, reducing exposures to health risks, building on equal access to health-care services, education, training and medical treatment and technology, and addressing the secondary effects of poor health;

(h) Promote the preservation, development and use of effective traditional medicine knowledge and practices, where appropriate, in combination with modern medicine, recognizing indigenous and local communities as custodians of traditional knowledge and practices, while promoting effective protection of traditional knowledge, as appropriate, consistent with international law;

(i) Ensure equal access of women to health-care services, giving particular attention to maternal and emergency obstetric care;

(j) Address effectively, for all individuals of appropriate age, the promotion of their healthy lives, including their reproductive and sexual health, consistent with the commitments and outcomes of recent United Nations conferences and summits, including the World Summit for Children, the United Nations Conference on Environment and Development, the International Conference of Population and Development, the World Summit for Social Development and the Fourth World Conference on Women, and their respective reviews and reports;

(k) Launch international capacity-building initiatives, as appropriate, that assess health and environment linkages and use the knowledge gained to create more effective national and regional policy responses to environmental threats to human health;

(l) Transfer and disseminate, on mutually agreed terms, including through public–private multisector partnerships, technologies for safe water, sanitation and waste management for rural and urban areas in developing countries and countries with economies in transition, with international financial support, taking into account country-specific conditions and gender equality including specific technology needs of women;

(m) Strengthen and promote ILO and World Health Organization (WHO) programmes to reduce occupational deaths, injuries and illnesses, and link occupational health with public health promotion as a means of promoting public health and education;

(n) Improve availability and access for all to sufficient, safe, culturally acceptable and nutritionally adequate food, increase consumer health protection, address issues of micronutrient deficiency, and implement existing internationally agreed commitments and relevant standards and guidelines;

(o) Develop or strengthen, where applicable, preventive, promotive and curative programmes to address non-communicable diseases and conditions, such as cardiovascular diseases, cancer, diabetes, chronic respiratory diseases, injuries, violence and mental health disorders and associated risk factors, including alcohol, tobacco, unhealthy diets and lack of physical activity.

48.   Implement, within the agreed time frames, all commitments agreed in the Declaration of Commitment on HIV/AIDS adopted by the General Assembly at its twenty-sixth special session, emphasizing in particular the reduction of HIV prevalence among young men and women aged 15–24 by 25 per cent in the most affected countries by 2005 and globally by 2010, as well as combat malaria, tuberculosis and other diseases by, inter alia:

(a) Implementing national preventive and treatment strategies, regional and international cooperation measures, and the development of international initiatives to provide special assistance to children orphaned by HIV/AIDS;

(b) Fulfilling commitments for the provision of sufficient resources to support the Global Fund to Fight AIDS, Tuberculosis and Malaria, while promoting access to the Fund by countries most in need;

(c) Protecting the health of workers and promoting occupational safety, by, inter alia, taking into account, as appropriate the voluntary ILO code of practice on HIV/AIDS and the world of work, to improve conditions of the workplace;

(d) Mobilizing adequate public and encouraging private financial resources for research and development on diseases of the poor, such as HIV/AIDS, malaria, tuberculosis, directed at biomedical and health research, as well as new vaccine and drug development.

49.   Reduce respiratory diseases and other health impacts resulting from air pollution, with particular attention to women and children, by:

(a) Strengthening regional and national programmes, including through public–private partnerships, with technical and financial assistance to developing countries;

(b) Supporting the phasing out of lead in gasoline;

(c) Strengthening and supporting efforts for the reduction of emissions, through the use of cleaner fuels and modern pollution control techniques;

(d) Assisting developing countries in providing affordable energy to rural communities, particularly to reduce dependence on traditional fuel sources for cooking and heating, which affect the health of women and children.

50.   Phase out lead in lead-based paints and other sources of human exposure, work to prevent, in particular, children's exposure to lead, and strengthen monitoring and surveillance efforts and the treatment of lead poisoning.

[Paragraph 51 is deleted]

VII. SUSTAINABLE DEVELOPMENT OF SMALL ISLAND DEVELOPING STATES

52.   Small island developing States are a special case both for environment and development. Although they continue to take the lead in the path towards sustainable development in their countries, they are increasingly constrained by the interplay of adverse factors clearly underlined in Agenda 21, the Programme of Action for the Sustainable Development of Small Island Developing States and the decisions adopted at the twenty-second special session of the General Assembly. This would include actions at all levels to:

(a) Accelerate national and regional implementation of the Programme of Action, with adequate financial resources, including through GEF focal areas, transfer of environmentally sound technologies and assistance for capacity-building from the international community;

(b) Further implement sustainable fisheries management and improve financial returns from fisheries by supporting and strengthening relevant regional fisheries management organizations, as appropriate, such as the recently established Caribbean Regional Fisheries Mechanism and such agreements as the Convention on the Conservation and Management of Highly Migratory Fish Stocks in the Western and Central Pacific Ocean;

(c) Assist small island developing States, including through the elaboration of specific initiatives, in delimiting and managing in a sustainable manner their coastal areas and exclusive economic zones and the continental shelf (including, where appropriate, the continental shelf areas beyond 200 miles from coastal baselines), as well as relevant regional management initiatives within the context of the United Nations Convention on the Law of the Sea and the UNEP regional seas programmes;

(d) Provide support, including for capacity-building, for the development and further implementation of:

    (i) Small island developing States-specific components within programmes of work on marine and coastal biological diversity;

    (ii) Freshwater programmes for small island developing States, including through the GEF focal areas;

(e) Effectively reduce, prevent and control waste and pollution and their health-related impacts by undertaking by 2004 initiatives aimed at implementing the Global Programme of Action for the Protection of the Marine Environment from Land-based Activities in small island developing States;

(f) Work to ensure that, in the ongoing negotiations and elaboration of the WTO work programme on trade in small economies, due account is taken of small island developing States, which have severe structural handicaps in integrating into the global economy, within the context of the Doha development agenda;

(g) Develop community-based initiatives on sustainable tourism by 2004, and build the capacities necessary to diversify tourism products, while protecting culture and traditions, and effectively conserving and managing natural resources;

(h) Extend assistance to small island developing States in support of local communities and appropriate national and regional organizations of small island developing States for comprehensive hazard and risk management, disaster prevention, mitigation and preparedness, and help relieve the consequences of disasters, extreme weather events and other emergencies;

(i)   Support the finalization and subsequent early operationalization, on agreed terms, of economic, social and environmental vulnerability indices and related indicators as tools for the achievement of the sustainable development of the small island developing States;

(j)   Assist small island developing States in mobilizing adequate resources and partnerships for their adaptation needs relating to the adverse effects of climate change, sea level rise and climate variability, consistent with commitments under the United Nations Framework Convention on Climate Changes, where applicable;

(k)   Support efforts by small island developing States to build capacities and institutional arrangements to implement intellectual property regimes.

53.   Support the availability of adequate, affordable and environmentally sound energy services for the sustainable development of small island developing States by, inter alia:

(a)   Strengthening ongoing and supporting new efforts on energy supply and services, by 2004, including through the United Nations system and partnership initiatives;

(b)   Developing and promoting efficient use of sources of energy, including indigenous sources and renewable energy, and building the capacities of small island developing States for training, technical know-how and strengthening national institutions in the area of energy management.

54.   Provide support to SIDS to develop capacity and strengthen:

(a)   Health-care services for promoting equitable access to health care;

(b)   Health systems for making available necessary drugs and technology in a sustainable and affordable manner to fight and control communicable and non-communicable diseases, in particular HIV/AIDS, tuberculosis, diabetes, malaria and dengue fever;

(c)   Efforts to reduce and manage waste and pollution and building capacity for maintaining and managing systems to deliver water and sanitation services, in both rural and urban areas;

(d)   Efforts to implement initiatives aimed at poverty eradication, which have been outlined in section II of the present document.

55.   Undertake a full and comprehensive review of the implementation of the Barbados Programme of Action for the Sustainable Development of Small Island Developing States in 2004, in accordance with the provisions set forth in General Assembly resolution S-22/2, and in this context requests the General

Assembly at its fifty-seventh session to consider convening an international meeting for the sustainable development of small island developing States.

VIII. SUSTAINABLE DEVELOPMENT FOR AFRICA

56. Since the United Nations Conference on Environment and Development, sustainable development has remained elusive for many African countries. Poverty remains a major challenge and most countries on the continent have not benefited fully from the opportunities of globalization, further exacerbating the continent's marginalization. Africa's efforts to achieve sustainable development have been hindered by conflicts, insufficient investment, limited market access opportunities and supply side constraints, unsustainable debt burdens, historically declining ODA levels and the impact of HIV/AIDS. The World Summit on Sustainable Development should reinvigorate the commitment of the international community to address these special challenges and give effect to a new vision based on concrete actions for the implementation of Agenda 21 in Africa. The New Partnership for Africa's Development (NEPAD) is a commitment by African leaders to the people of Africa. It recognizes that partnerships among African countries themselves and between them and with the international community are key elements of a shared and common vision to eradicate poverty, and furthermore it aims to place their countries, both individually and collectively, on a path of sustained economic growth and sustainable development, while participating actively in the world economy and body politic. It provides a framework for sustainable development on the continent to be shared by all Africa's people. The international community welcomes NEPAD and pledges its support to the implementation of this vision, including through utilization of the benefits of South–South cooperation supported, inter alia, by the Tokyo International Conference on African Development. It also pledges support for other existing development frameworks that are owned and driven nationally by African countries and that embody poverty reduction strategies, including poverty reduction strategy papers. Achieving sustainable development includes actions at all levels to:

(a) Create an enabling environment at the regional, subregional, national and local levels in order to achieve sustained economic growth and sustainable development and support African efforts for peace, stability and security, the resolution and prevention of conflicts, democracy, good governance, respect for human rights and fundamental freedoms, including the right to development and gender equality;

(b) Support the implementation of the vision of NEPAD and other established regional and subregional efforts, including through financing, technical cooperation and institutional cooperation, and human and institutional capacity-building at the regional, subregional and national levels, consistent with national policies, programmes and nationally owned and led strategies for poverty reduction and sustainable development, such as, where applicable, poverty reduction strategy papers;

(c) Promote technology development, transfer and diffusion to Africa and further develop technology and knowledge available in African centres of excellence;

(d) Support African countries to develop effective science and technology institutions and research activities capable of developing and adapting to world class technologies;

(e) Support the development of national programmes and strategies to promote education within the context of nationally owned and led strategies for poverty reduction, and strengthen research institutions in education in order to increase the capacity to fully support the achievement of internationally agreed development goals related to education, including those contained in the Millennium Declaration on ensuring that, by 2015, children everywhere, boys and girls alike, will be able to complete a full course of primary schooling, and that girls and boys will have equal access to all levels of education relevant to national needs;

(f) Enhance the industrial productivity, diversity and competitiveness of African countries through a combination of financial and technological support for the development of key infrastructure, access to technology, networking of research centres, adding value to export products, skills development and enhancing market access in support of sustainable development;

(g) Enhance the contribution of the industrial sector, in particular mining, minerals and metals, to the sustainable development of Africa by supporting the development of effective and transparent regulatory and management frameworks and value addition, broad-based partic-ipation, social and environmental responsibility and increased market access in order to create an attractive and conducive environment for investment;

(h) Provide financial and technical support to strengthen the capacity of African countries to undertake environmental legislative policy and institutional reform for sustainable development and to undertake environmental impact assessments and, as appropriate, to negotiate and implement multilateral environment agreements;

(i) Develop projects, programmes and partnerships with relevant stake-holders and mobilize resources for the effective implementation of the outcome of the African Process for the Protection and Development of the Marine and Coastal Environment;

(j) Deal effectively with energy problems in Africa, including through initiatives to:

   (i) Establish and promote programmes, partnerships and initiatives to support Africa's efforts to implement NEPAD objectives on energy, which seek to secure access for at least 35 per cent of the African population within 20 years, especially in rural areas;

(ii) Provide support to implement other initiatives on energy, including the promotion of cleaner and more efficient use of natural gas and increased use of renewable energy, and to improve energy efficiency and access to advanced energy technologies, including cleaner fossil fuel technologies, particularly in rural and peri-urban areas;

(k) Assist African countries in mobilizing adequate resources for their adaptation needs relating to the adverse effects of climate change, extreme weather events, sea level rise and climate variability, and assist in developing national climate change strategies and mitigation programmes, and continue to take actions to mitigate the adverse effects on climate change in Africa, consistent with the United Nations Framework Convention on Climate Change;

(l) Support African efforts to develop affordable transport systems and infrastructure that promote sustainable development and connectivity in Africa;

(m) Further to paragraph 40 above, address the poverty affecting mountain communities in Africa;

(n) Provide financial and technical support for afforestation and reforestation in Africa and to build capacity for sustainable forest management, including combating deforestation and measures to improve the policy and legal framework of the forest sector.

57.   Provide financial and technical support for Africa's efforts to implement the Convention to Combat Desertification at the national level and integrate indigenous knowledge systems into land and natural resources management practices, as appropriate, and improve extension services to rural communities and promote better land and watershed management practices, including through improved agricultural practices that address land degradation, in order to develop capacity for the implementation of national programmes.

58.   Mobilize financial and other support to develop and strengthen health systems that aim at:

(a) Promoting equitable access to health-care services;

(b) Making available necessary drugs and technology in a sustainable and affordable manner to fight and control communicable diseases, including HIV/AIDS, malaria and tuberculosis, and trypanosomiasis, as well as non-communicable diseases, including those caused by poverty;

(c) Building capacity of medical and paramedical personnel;

(d) Promoting indigenous medical knowledge, as appropriate, including traditional medicine;

(e) Researching and controlling the Ebola disease.

59.   Deal effectively with natural disasters and conflicts, including their humanitarian and environmental impacts, recognizing that conflicts in Africa have hindered and in many cases obliterated both the gains and efforts aimed at sustainable development, with the most vulnerable members of society, particularly women and children, being the most impacted victims, through efforts and initiatives, at all levels, to:

(a) Provide financial and technical assistance to strengthen the capacities of African countries, including institutional and human capacity, including at the local level, for effective disaster management, including observation and early warning systems, assessments, prevention, preparedness, response and recovery;

(b) Provide support to African countries to enable them to better deal with the displacement of people as a result of natural disasters and conflicts, and put in place rapid response mechanisms;

(c) Support Africa's efforts for the prevention and resolution, management and mitigation of conflicts and its early response to emerging conflict situations to avert tragic humanitarian consequences;

(d) Provide support to refugee host countries in rehabilitating infrastructure and environment, including ecosystems and habitats, that were damaged in the process of receiving and settling refugees.

60.   Promote integrated water resources development and optimize the upstream and downstream benefits therefrom, the development and effective management of water resources across all uses and the protection of water quality and aquatic ecosystems, including through initiatives at all levels, to:

(a) Provide access to potable domestic water, hygiene education and improved sanitation and waste management at the household level through initiatives to encourage public and private investment in water supply and sanitation that give priority to the needs of the poor, within stable and transparent national regulatory frameworks provided by Governments, while respecting local conditions involving all concerned stakeholders and monitoring the performance and improving the accountability of public institutions and private companies; and develop critical water supply, reticulation and treatment infrastructure, and build capacity to maintain and manage systems to deliver water and sanitation services, in both rural and urban areas;

(b) Develop and implement integrated river basin and watershed management strategies and plans for all major water bodies, consistent with paragraph 25 above;

(c) Strengthen regional, subregional and national capacities for data collection and processing, and for planning, research, monitoring, assessment and enforcement, as well as arrangements for water resource management;

(d) Protect water resources, including groundwater and wetland ecosystems, against pollution, as well as, in cases of most acute water scarcity, support efforts for developing non-conventional water resources, including the energy-efficient, cost-effective and sustainable desalination of seawater, rainwater harvesting and recycling of water.

61.   Achieve significantly improved sustainable agricultural productivity and food security in furtherance of the agreed millennium development goals, including those contained in the Millennium Declaration, in particular to halve by 2015 the proportion of people who suffer from hunger, including through initiatives at all levels to:

(a) Support the development and implementation of national policies and programmes, including research programmes and development plans of African countries to regenerate their agricultural sector and sustainably develop their fisheries, and increase investment in infrastructure, technology and extension services, according to country needs. African countries should be in the process of developing and implementing food security strategies, within the context of national poverty eradication programmes, by 2005;

(b) Promote and support efforts and initiatives to secure equitable access to land tenure and clarify resource rights and responsibilities, through land and tenure reform processes which respect the rule of law and are enshrined in national law, and to provide access to credit to all, especially to women, and that enable economic and social empowerment and poverty eradication as well as efficient and ecologically sound utilization of land, and enable women producers to become decision makers and owners in the sector, including the right to inherit land;

(c) Improve market access for goods, including goods originating from African countries, in particular least developed countries, within the framework of the Doha Ministerial Declaration, without prejudging the outcome of the WTO negotiations and also within the framework of preferential agreements;

(d) Provide support for African countries to improve regional trade and economic integration between African countries. Attract and increase investment in regional market infrastructure;

(e) Support livestock development programmes aimed at progressive and effective control of animal diseases.

62.   Achieve sound management of chemicals, with particular focus on hazardous chemicals and wastes, inter alia, through initiatives to assist African countries in elaborating national chemical profiles, and regional and national frameworks and strategies for chemical management and establishing chemical focal points.

63.   Bridge the digital divide and create digital opportunity in terms of access infrastructure and technology transfer and application, through integrated initiatives for Africa. Create an enabling environment to attract investments, accelerate existing and new programmes and projects to connect essential institutions, and stimulate the adoption of information communication technologies in government and commerce programmes and other aspects of national economic and social life.

64.   Support Africa's efforts to attain sustainable tourism that contributes to social, economic and infrastructure development through the following measures:

   (a)   Implementing projects at the local, national and subregional levels, with specific emphasis on marketing African tourism products, such as adventure tourism, eco-tourism and cultural tourism;

   (b)   Establishing and supporting national and cross-border conservation areas to promote ecosystem conservation according to the ecosystem approach, and to promote sustainable tourism;

   (c)   Respecting local traditions and cultures and promoting the use of indigenous knowledge in natural resource management and eco-tourism;

   (d)   Assisting host communities in managing their tourism projects for maximum benefit, while limiting negative impact on their traditions, culture and environment;

   (e)   Support the conservation of Africa's biological diversity, the sustainable use of its components and the fair and equitable sharing of the benefits arising out of the utilization of genetic resources, in accordance with commitments that countries have under biodiversity-related agreements to which they are parties, including such agreements as the Convention on Biological Diversity and the Convention on International Trade in Endangered Species of Wild Fauna and Flora, as well as regional biodiversity agreements.

65.   Support African countries in their efforts to implement the Habitat Agenda and the Istanbul Declaration through initiatives to strengthen national and local institutional capacities in the areas of sustainable urbanization and human settlements, provide support for adequate shelter and basic services and the development of efficient and effective governance

systems in cities and other human settlements, and strengthen, inter alia, the United Nations Human Settlements Programme/UNEP managing water for African cities programme.

VIII.BIS OTHER REGIONAL INITIATIVES

66.   Important initiatives have been developed within other United Nations regions and regional, subregional and transregional forums to promote sustainable development. The international community welcomes these efforts and the results already achieved, and calls for actions at all levels for their further development, while encouraging interregional, intraregional and international cooperation in this respect, and expresses its support for their further development and implementation by the countries of the regions.

Sustainable Development in Latin America and the Caribbean

67.   The Initiative of Latin America and the Caribbean on Sustainable Development is an undertaking by the leaders of that region that, building on the Platform for Action on the Road to Johannesburg 2002, which was approved in Rio de Janeiro in October 2001, recognizes the importance of regional actions towards sustainable development and takes into account the region's singularities, shared visions and cultural diversity. It is targeted towards the adoption of concrete actions in different areas of sustainable development, such as biodiversity, water resources, vulnerabilities and sustainable cities, social aspects (including health and poverty), economic aspects (including energy) and institutional arrangements (including capacity-building, indicators and participation of civil society), taking into account ethics for sustainable development.

68.   The Initiative envisages the development of actions among countries in the region that may foster South–South cooperation and may count with the support of groups of countries, as well as multilateral and regional organizations, including financial institutions. Being a framework for cooperation, the Initiative is open to partnerships with governments and all major groups.

Sustainable Development in Asia and the Pacific

69.   Bearing in mind the target of halving the number of people who live in poverty by the year 2015, as provided in the Millennium Declaration, the Phnom Penh Regional Platform on Sustainable Development for Asia and the Pacific recognized that the region contains over half of the world's population and the largest number of the world's people living in poverty. Hence, sustainable development in the region is critical to achieving sustainable development at the global level.

70.   The Regional Platform identified seven initiatives for follow-up action: capacity-building for sustainable development; poverty reduction for sustainable development; cleaner production and sustainable energy; land management and biodiversity conservation; protection and management of

and access to freshwater resources; oceans, coastal and marine resources and sustainable development of small island developing States; and action on atmosphere and climate change. Follow-up actions of these initiatives will be taken through national strategies and relevant regional and subregional initiatives, such as the Regional Action Programme for Environmentally Sound and Sustainable Development and the Kitakyushu Initiative for a Clean Environment, adopted at the Fourth Ministerial Conference on Environment and Development in Asia and the Pacific organized by the Economic and Social Commission for Asia and the Pacific.

Sustainable Development in the West Asia region

71.   The West Asia region is known for its scarce water and limited fertile land resources. The region has made progress to a more knowledge-based production of higher value-added commodities.

72.   The regional preparatory meeting endorsed the following priorities: poverty alleviation, relief of debt burden; and sustainable management of natural resources, including, inter alia, integrated water resources management, implementation of programmes to combat desertification, integrated coastal zone management, and land and water pollution control.

Sustainable Development in the Economic Commission for Europe Region

73.   The Economic Commission for Europe (ECE) regional ministerial meeting for the World Summit on Sustainable Development recognized that the region has a major role to play and responsibilities in global efforts to achieve sustainable development by concrete actions. The region recognized that different levels of economic development in countries of the region may require the application of different approaches and mechanisms to implement Agenda 21. In order to address the three pillars of sustainable development in a mutually reinforcing way, the region identified its priority actions for the ECE region for sustainable development in paragraphs 32–46 of a ministerial statement.

74.   In furtherance of the region's commitment to sustainable development, there are ongoing efforts at the regional, subregional and transregional levels, including, inter alia, the Environment for Europe process; the fifth ECE ministerial conference, to be held in Kiev in May 2003; the development of an environmental strategy for the 12 countries of Eastern Europe; the Caucasus and Central Asia; the Central Asian Agenda 21; OECD work on sustainable development, the EU sustainable development strategy; and regional and subregional conventions and processes relevant to sustainable development, including, inter alia, the Aarhus Convention, the Alpine Convention, the North American Commission on Environmental Cooperation, the Boundary Waters Treaty, the Iqaluit Declaration of the Arctic Council, the Baltic Agenda 21 and the Mediterranean Agenda 21.

IX. MEANS OF IMPLEMENTATION*

75.   The implementation of Agenda 21 and the achievement of the internationally agreed development goals, including those contained in the Millennium Declaration as well as in the present plan of action, require a substantially increased effort, both by countries themselves and by the rest of the international community, based on the recognition that each country has primary responsibility for its own development and that the role of national policies and development strategies cannot be overemphasized, taking fully into account the Rio principles, including, in particular, the principle of common but differentiated responsibilities, which states:

> States shall cooperate in a spirit of global partnership to conserve, protect and restore the health and integrity of the Earth's ecosystem. In view of the different contributions to global environmental degradation, States have common but differentiated responsibilities. The developed countries acknowledge the responsibility that they bear in the international pursuit of sustainable development in view of the pressures their societies place on the global environment and of the technologies and financial resources they command.

The internationally agreed development goals, including those contained in the Millennium Declaration and Agenda 21, as well as in the present plan of action, will require significant increases in the flow of financial resources as elaborated in the Monterrey Consensus, including through new and additional financial resources, in particular to developing countries, to support the implementation of national policies and programmes developed by them, improved trade opportunities, access to and transfer of environmentally sound technologies on a concessional or preferential basis, as mutually agreed, education and awareness-raising, capacity-building, and information for decision-making and scientific capabilities within the agreed time frame required to meet these goals and initiatives. Progress to this end will require that the international community implement the outcomes of major United Nations conferences, such as the programmes of action adopted at the Third United Nations Conference on the Least Developed Countries, and the Global Conference on the Sustainable Development of Small Island Developing States, and relevant international agreements since 1992, particularly those of the International Conference on Financing for Development and the Fourth WTO Ministerial Conference, including building on them as part of a process of achieving sustainable development.

76.   Mobilizing and increasing the effective use of financial resources and achieving the national and international economic conditions needed to fulfil internationally agreed development goals, including those contained in the Millennium Declaration, to eliminate poverty, improve social conditions and raise living standards and protect our environment, will be our first step to ensuring that the twenty-first century becomes the century of sustainable development for all.

77.   In our common pursuit of growth, poverty eradication and sustainable development, a critical challenge is to ensure the necessary internal conditions for mobilizing domestic savings, both public and private, sustaining adequate levels of productive investment and increasing human capacity. A crucial task is to enhance the efficacy, coherence and consistency of macroeconomic policies. An enabling domestic environment is vital for mobilizing domestic resources, increasing productivity, reducing capital flight, encouraging the private sector, and attracting and making effective use of international investment and assistance. Efforts to create such an environment should be supported by the international community.

78.   Facilitate greater flows of foreign direct investment so as to support the sustainable development activities, including the development of infrastructure, of developing countries, and enhance the benefits that developing countries can draw from foreign direct investment, with particular actions to:

(a)   Create the necessary domestic and international conditions to facilitate significant increases in the flow of FDI to developing countries, in particular the least developed countries, which is critical to sustainable development, particularly FDI flows for infrastructure development and other priority areas in developing countries to supplement the domestic resources mobilized by them;

(b)   Encourage foreign direct investment in developing countries and countries with economies in transition through export credits that could be instrumental to sustainable development.

79.   Recognize that a substantial increase in ODA and other resources will be required if developing countries are to achieve the internationally agreed development goals and objectives, including those contained in the Millennium Declaration. To build support for ODA, we will cooperate to further improve policies and development strategies, both nationally and internationally, to enhance aid effectiveness, with actions to:

(a)   Make available the increased ODA commitments announced by several developed countries at the International Conference on Financing for Development. Urge the developed countries that have not done so to make concrete efforts towards the target of 0.7 per cent of GNP as ODA to developing countries, and effectively implement their commitment on ODA to the least developed countries as contained in paragraph 83 of the Programme of Action for the Least Developed Countries for the Decade 2001–2010. We also encourage developing countries to build on progress achieved in ensuring that ODA is used effectively to help achieve development goals and targets in accordance with the outcome of the International Conference on Financing for Development. We acknowledge the efforts of all donors, commend those donors whose ODA contributions exceed, reach or are increasing towards the targets, and underline the importance of undertaking to examine the means and time frames for achieving the targets and goals;

(b) Encourage recipient and donor countries, as well as international institutions, to make ODA more efficient and effective for poverty eradication, sustained economic growth and sustainable development. In this regard, intensify efforts by the multilateral and bilateral financial and development institutions, in accordance with paragraph 43 of the Monterrey Consensus, in particular to harmonize their operational procedures at the highest standards, so as to reduce transaction costs and make ODA disbursement and delivery more flexible and more responsive to the needs of developing countries, taking into account national development needs and objectives under the ownership of recipient countries, and to use development frameworks that are owned and driven by developing countries and that embody poverty reduction strategies, including poverty reduction strategy papers, as vehicles for aid delivery, upon request.

80.   Make full and effective use of existing financial mechanisms and institutions, including through actions at all levels to:

(a) Strengthen ongoing efforts to reform the existing international financial architecture, to foster a transparent, equitable and inclusive system that is able to provide for the effective participation of developing countries in the international economic decision-making processes and institutions, as well as for their effective and equitable participation in the formulation of financial standards and codes;

(b) Promote, inter alia, measures in source and destination countries to improve transparency and information about financial flows to contribute to stability in the international financial environment. Measures that mitigate the impact of excessive volatility of short-term capital flows are important and must be considered;

(c) Work to ensure that the funds are made available on a timely, more assured and predictable basis to international organizations and agencies, where appropriate, for their sustainable development activities, programmes and projects;

(d) Encourage the private sector, including transnational corporations, private foundations and civil society institutions, to provide financial and technical assistance to developing countries;

(e) Support new and existing public/private sector financing mechanisms for developing countries and countries with economies in transition, to benefit in particular small entrepreneurs and small, medium-sized and community-based enterprises and to improve their infrastructure, while ensuring the transparency and accountability of such mechanisms.

81.   Welcome the successful and substantial third replenishment of the GEF, which will enable it to address the funding requirements of new focal areas and existing ones and continue to be responsive to the needs and concerns

of its recipient countries, in particular developing countries, and further encourage GEF to leverage additional funds from key public and private organizations, improve the management of funds through more speedy and streamlined procedures and simplify its project cycle.

82.   Explore ways of generating new public and private innovative sources of finance for development purposes, provided that those sources do not unduly burden developing countries, noting the proposal to use special drawing rights allocations for development purposes, as set forth in paragraph 44 of the Monterrey Consensus.

83.   Reduce unsustainable debt burden through such actions as debt relief and, as appropriate, debt cancellation and other innovative mechanisms geared to comprehensively address the debt problems of developing countries, in particular the poorest and most heavily indebted ones. Therefore, debt relief measures should, where appropriate, be pursued vigorously and expeditiously, including within the Paris and London Clubs and other relevant forums, in order to contribute to debt sustainability and facilitate sustainable development, while recognizing that debtors and creditors must share responsibility for preventing and resolving unsustainable debt situations, and that external debt relief can play a key role in liberating resources that can then be directed towards activities consistent with attaining sustainable growth and development. Therefore, we support paragraphs 47 through 51 of the Monterrey Consensus dealing with external debt. Debt relief arrangements should seek to avoid imposing any unfair burdens on other developing countries. There should be an increase in the use of grants for the poorest, debt-vulnerable countries. Countries are encouraged to develop national comprehensive strategies to monitor and manage external liabilities as a key element in reducing national vulnerabilities. In this regard, actions are required to:

(a) Implement speedily, effectively and fully the enhanced heavily indebted poor countries (HIPC) initiative, which should be fully financed through additional resources, taking into consideration, as appropriate, measures to address any fundamental changes in the economic circumstances of those developing countries with unsustainable debt burden caused by natural catastrophes, severe terms-of-trade shocks or affected by conflict, taking into account initiatives which have been undertaken to reduce outstanding indebtedness;

(b) Encourage participation in the HIPC initiative of all creditors that have not yet done so;

(c) Bring international debtors and creditors together in relevant international forums to restructure unsustainable debt in a timely and efficient manner, taking into account the need to involve the private sector in the resolution of crises due to indebtedness, where appropriate;

(d) Acknowledge the problems of the debt sustainability of some non-HIPC low-income countries, in particular those facing exceptional circumstances;

(e) Encourage exploring innovative mechanisms to comprehensively address the debt problems of developing countries, including middle-income countries and countries with economies in transition. Such mechanisms may include debt-for-sustainable-development swaps;

(f) Encourage donor countries to take steps to ensure that resources provided for debt relief do not detract from ODA resources intended to be available for developing countries.

84.   Recognizing the major role that trade can play in achieving sustainable development and in eradicating poverty, we encourage WTO members to pursue the work programme agreed at the Fourth WTO Ministerial Conference. In order for developing countries, especially the least developed among them, to secure their share in the growth of world trade commensurate with the needs of their economic development, we urge WTO members to take the following actions:

(a) Facilitate the accession of all developing countries, particularly the least developed countries, as well as countries with economies in transition, that apply for membership of WTO, in accordance with the Monterrey Consensus;

(b) Support the Doha work programme as an important commitment on the part of developed and developing countries to mainstream appropriate trade policies in their respective development policies and programmes;

(c) Implement substantial trade-related technical assistance and capacity-building measures and support the Doha Development Agenda Global Trust Fund established after the Fourth WTO Ministerial Conference as an important step forward in ensuring a sound and predictable basis for WTO-related technical assistance and capacity-building;

(d) Implement the New Strategy for WTO Technical Cooperation for Capacity-Building, Growth and Integration;

(e) Fully support the implementation of the Integrated Framework for Trade-Related Technical Assistance to Least Developed Countries, and urge development partners to significantly increase contributions to the Trust Fund of the Framework, in accordance with the Doha Ministerial Declaration.

85.   In accordance with the Doha Declaration as well as with relevant decisions taken at Doha, we are determined to take concrete action to address issues and concerns raised by developing countries regarding the implemen-

tation of some WTO agreements and decisions, including the difficulties and resource constraints faced by them in fulfilling those agreements.

86.   Call upon WTO members to fulfil the commitments made in the Doha Ministerial Declaration, notably in terms of market access, in particular for products of export interest to developing countries, especially least developed countries, by implementing the following actions, taking into account paragraph 45 of the Doha Ministerial Declaration:

(a)   Review all special and differential treatment provisions with a view to strengthening them and making them more precise, effective and operational, in accordance with paragraph 44 of the Doha Ministerial Declaration;

(b)   Aim to reduce or, as appropriate, eliminate tariffs on non-agricultural products, including the reduction or elimination of tariff peaks, high tariffs and tariff escalation, as well as non-tariff barriers, in particular on products of export interest to developing countries. Product coverage should be comprehensive and without a priori exclusions. The negotiations shall take fully into account the special needs and interests of developing and least developed countries, including through less than full reciprocity in reduction commitments, in accordance with the Doha Ministerial Declaration;

(c)   Fulfil, without prejudging the outcome of the negotiations, the commitment for comprehensive negotiations initiated under article 20 of the Agreement on Agriculture as referred to in paragraphs 13 and 14 of the Doha Ministerial Declaration, aiming at substantial improvements in market access, reductions of with a view to phasing out all forms of export subsidies, and substantial reductions in trade-distorting domestic support, while agreeing that the provisions for special and differential treatment for developing countries shall be an integral part of all elements of the negotiations and shall be embodied in the schedules of concession and commitments and, as appropriate, in the rules and disciplines to be negotiated, so as to be operationally effective and to enable developing countries to effectively take account of their development needs, including food security and rural development. Take note of the non-trade concerns reflected in the negotiating proposals submitted by WTO members and confirm that non-trade concerns will be taken into account in the negotiations as provided for in the Agreement on Agriculture, in accordance with the Doha Ministerial Declaration.

87.   Call on developed countries that have not already done so to work towards the objective of duty-free and quota-free access for all least developed countries' exports, as envisaged in the Programme of Action for the Least Developed Countries for the Decade 2001–2010, which was adopted in Brussels on 20 May 2001.

88.   Commit to actively pursue the WTO work programme to address the trade-related issues and concerns affecting the fuller integration of small, vulnerable economies into the multilateral trading system in a manner commensurate with their special circumstances and in support of their efforts towards sustainable development, in accordance with paragraph 35 of the Doha Declaration.

89.   Build the capacity of commodity-dependent countries to diversify exports through, inter alia, financial and technical assistance, international assistance for economic diversification and sustainable resource management, and address the instability of commodity prices and declining terms of trade, as well as strengthen the activities covered by the Second Account of the Common Fund for Commodities to support sustainable development.

90.   Enhance the benefits for developing countries, as well as countries with economies in transition, from trade liberalization, including through public–private partnerships, through, inter alia, action at all levels, including through financial support for technical assistance, the development of technology and capacity-building to developing countries to:

(a)   Enhance trade infrastructure and strengthen institutions;

(b)   Increase developing country capacity to diversify and increase exports to cope with the instability of commodity prices and declining terms of trade;

(c)   Increase the value added of developing country exports.

91.   Continue to enhance the mutual supportiveness of trade, environment and development with a view to achieving sustainable development through actions at all levels to:

(a)   Encourage the WTO Committee on Trade and Environment and the WTO Committee on Trade and Development, within their respective mandates, to each act as a forum to identify and debate developmental and environmental aspects of the negotiations, in order to help achieve an outcome which benefits sustainable development in accordance with the commitments made under the Doha Ministerial Declaration;

(b)   Support the completion of the work programme of the Doha Ministerial Declaration on subsidies so as to promote sustainable development and enhance the environment, and encourage reform of subsidies that have considerable negative effects on the environment and are incompatible with sustainable development;

(c)   Encourage efforts to promote cooperation on trade, environment and development, including in the field of providing technical assistance to developing countries, between the secretariats of WTO, UNCTAD,

UNDP, UNEP and other relevant international environmental and development and regional organizations;

(d) Encourage the voluntary use of environmental impact assessments as an important national-level tool to better identify trade, environment and development interlinkages. Further encourage countries and international organizations with experience in this field to provide technical assistance to developing countries for these purposes.

92.   Promote mutual supportiveness between the multilateral trading system and the multilateral environmental agreements, consistent with sustainable development goals, in support of the work programme agreed through WTO, while recognizing the importance of maintaining the integrity of both sets of instruments.

93.   Complement and support the Doha Ministerial Declaration and the Monterrey Consensus by undertaking further action at the national, regional and international levels, including through public/private partnerships, to enhance the benefits, in particular for developing countries as well as for countries with economies in transition, of trade liberalization, through, inter alia, actions at all levels to:

(a) Establish and strengthen existing trade and cooperation agreements, consistent with the multilateral trading system, with a view to achieving sustainable development;

(b) Support voluntary WTO compatible market-based initiatives for the creation and expansion of domestic and international markets for environmentally friendly goods and services, including organic products, which maximize environmental and developmental benefits through, inter alia, capacity-building and technical assistance to developing countries;

(c) Support measures to simplify and make more transparent domestic regulations and procedures that affect trade so as to assist exporters, particularly those from developing countries.

94.   Address the public health problems affecting many developing and least developed countries, especially those resulting from HIV/AIDS, tuberculosis, malaria and other epidemics, while noting the importance of the Doha Declaration on the TRIPS Agreement and Public Health, in which it has been agreed that the TRIPS Agreement does not and should not prevent WTO members from taking measures to protect public health. Accordingly, while reiterating our commitment to the TRIPS Agreement, we reaffirm that the Agreement can and should be interpreted and implemented in a manner supportive of WTO members' right to protect public health and in particular to promote access to medicines for all.

95.   States should cooperate to promote a supportive and open international economic system that would lead to economic growth and sustainable development in all countries to better address the problems of environmental degradation. Trade policy measures for environmental purposes should not constitute a means of arbitrary or unjustifiable discrimination or a disguised restriction on international trade. Unilateral actions to deal with environmental challenges outside the jurisdiction of the importing country should be avoided. Environmental measures addressing transboundary or global environmental problems should, as far as possible, be based on an international consensus.

96.   Take steps with a view to the avoidance of and refrain from any unilateral measure not in accordance with international law and the Charter of the United Nations that impedes the full achievement of economic and social development by the population of the affected countries, in particular women and children, that hinders their well-being and that creates obstacles to the full enjoyment of their human rights, including the right of everyone to a standard of living adequate for their health and well-being and their right to food, medical care and the necessary social services. Ensure that food and medicine are not used as tools for political pressure.

97.   Take further effective measures to remove obstacles to the realization of the right of peoples to self-determination, in particular peoples living under colonial and foreign occupation, which continue to adversely affect their economic and social development and are incompatible with the dignity and worth of the human person and must be combated and eliminated. People under foreign occupation must be protected in accordance with the provisions of international humanitarian law.

98.   In accordance with the Declaration on Principles of International Law concerning Friendly Relations and Cooperation among States in accordance with the Charter of the United Nations, this shall not be construed as authorizing or encouraging any action which would dismember or impair, totally or in part, the territorial integrity or political unity of sovereign and independent States conducting themselves in compliance with the principle of equal rights and self-determination of peoples and thus possessed of a Government representing the whole people belonging to the territory without distinction of any kind.

*   *   *

99.   Promote, facilitate and finance, as appropriate, access to and the development, transfer and diffusion of environmentally sound technologies and corresponding know-how, in particular to developing countries and countries with economies in transition on favourable terms, including on concessional and preferential terms, as mutually agreed, as set out in chapter 34 of Agenda 21, including through urgent actions at all levels to:

(a)   Provide information more effectively;

(b) Enhance existing national institutional capacity in developing countries to improve access to and the development, transfer and diffusion of environmentally sound technologies and corresponding know-how;

(c) Facilitate country-driven technology needs assessments;

(d) Establish legal and regulatory frameworks in both supplier and recipient countries that expedite the transfer of environmentally sound technologies in a cost-effective manner by both public and private sectors and support their implementation;

(e) Promote the access and transfer of technology related to early warning systems and to mitigation programmes to developing countries affected by natural disasters.

100.   Improve the transfer of technologies to developing countries, in particular at the bilateral and regional levels, including through urgent actions at all levels to:

(a) Improve interaction and collaboration, stakeholder relationships and networks between and among universities, research institutions, government agencies and the private sector;

(b) Develop and strengthen networking of related institutional support structures, such as technology and productivity centres, research, training and development institutions, and national and regional cleaner production centres;

(c) Create partnerships conducive to investment and technology transfer, development and diffusion, to assist developing countries, as well as countries with economies in transition, in sharing best practices and promoting programmes of assistance, and encourage collaboration between corporations and research institutes to enhance industrial efficiency, agricultural productivity, environmental management and competitiveness;

(d) Provide assistance to developing countries, as well as countries with economies in transition, in accessing environmentally sound technologies that are publicly owned or in the public domain, as well as available knowledge in the public domain on science and technology, and in accessing the know-how and expertise required in order for them to make independent use of this knowledge in pursuing their development goals;

(e) Support existing mechanisms and, where appropriate, establish new mechanisms for the development, transfer and diffusion of environmentally sound technologies to developing countries and economies in transition.

*   *   *

101.   Assist developing countries in building capacity to access a larger share of multilateral and global research and development programmes. In this regard, strengthen and, where appropriate, create centres for sustainable development in developing countries.

102.   Build greater capacity in science and technology for sustainable development, with action to improve collaboration and partnerships on research and development and their widespread application among research institutions, universities, the private sector, governments, NGOs and networks, as well as between and among scientists and academics of developing and developed countries, and in this regard encourage networking with and between centres of scientific excellence in developing countries.

103.   Improve policy and decision-making at all levels through, inter alia, improved collaboration between natural and social scientists, and between scientists and policy makers, including through urgent actions at all levels to:

(a)   Increase the use of scientific knowledge and technology, and increase the beneficial use of local and indigenous knowledge in a manner respectful of the holders of that knowledge and consistent with national law;

(b)   Make greater use of integrated scientific assessments, risk assessments and interdisciplinary and intersectoral approaches;

(c)   Continue to support and collaborate with international scientific assessments supporting decision-making, including the Intergovernmental Panel on Climate Change, with the broad participation of developing country experts;

(d)   Assist developing countries in developing and implementing science and technology policies;

(e)   Establish partnerships between scientific, public and private institutions, and by integrating scientists' advice into decision-making bodies in order to ensure a greater role for science, technology development and engineering sectors;

(f)   Promote and improve science-based decision-making and reaffirm the precautionary approach as set out in principle 15 of the Rio Declaration on Environment and Development, which states:

In order to protect the environment, the precautionary approach shall be widely applied by States according to their capabilities. Where there are threats of serious or irreversible damage, lack of full scientific certainty shall not be used as a reason for postponing cost-effective measures to prevent environmental degradation.

104.   Assist developing countries, through international cooperation, in enhancing their capacity in their efforts to address issues pertaining to envi-

ronmental protection including in their formulation and implementation of policies for environmental management and protection, including through urgent actions at all levels to:

(a) Improve their use of science and technology for environmental monitoring, assessment models, accurate databases and integrated information systems;

(b) Promote and, where appropriate, improve their use of satellite technologies for quality data collection, verification and updating, and further improvement of aerial and ground-based observations, in support of their efforts to collect quality, accurate, long-term, consistent and reliable data;

(c) Set up and, where appropriate, further develop national statistical services capable of providing sound data on science education and research and development activities that are necessary for effective science and technology policy-making.

105.   Establish regular channels between policy makers and the scientific community for requesting and receiving science and technology advice for the implementation of Agenda 21, and create and strengthen networks for science and education for sustainable development, at all levels, with the aim of sharing knowledge, experience and best practices and building scientific capacities, particularly in developing countries.

106.   Use information and communication technologies, where appropriate, as tools to increase the frequency of communication and the sharing of experience and knowledge, and to improve the quality of and access to information and communications technology in all countries, building on the work facilitated by the United Nations Information and Communications Technology Task Force and the efforts of other relevant international and regional forums.

107.   Support publicly funded research and development entities to engage in strategic alliances for the purpose of enhancing research and development to achieve cleaner production and product technologies, through, inter alia, the mobilization from all sources of adequate financial and technical resources, including new and additional resources, and encourage the transfer and diffusion of those technologies, in particular to developing countries.

108.   Examine issues of global public interest through open, transparent and inclusive workshops to promote a better public understanding of such questions.

108.bis   Further resolve to take concerted action against international terrorism, which causes serious obstacles to sustainable development.

*   *   *

109.   Education is critical for promoting sustainable development. It is therefore essential to mobilize necessary resources, including financial resources at all levels, by bilateral and multilateral donors, including the World Bank and the regional development banks, by civil society and by foundations, to complement the efforts by national governments to pursue the following goals and actions:

  (a) Meet the development goal contained in the Millennium Declaration of achieving universal primary education, ensuring that, by 2015, children everywhere, boys and girls alike, will be able to complete a full course of primary schooling;

  (b) Provide all children, particularly those living in rural areas and those living in poverty, especially girls, with the access and opportunity to complete a full course of primary education.

110.   Provide financial assistance and support to education, research, public awareness programmes and developmental institutions in developing countries and countries with economies in transition in order to:

  (a) Sustain their educational infrastructures and programmes, including those related to environment and public health education;

  (b) Consider means of avoiding the frequent, serious financial constraints faced by many institutions of higher learning, including universities around the world, particularly in developing countries and countries in transition.

111.   Address the impact of HIV/AIDS on the educational system in those countries seriously affected by the pandemic.

112.   Allocate national and international resources for basic education as proposed by the Dakar Framework for Action on Education for All and for improved integration of sustainable development into education and in bilateral and multilateral development programmes, and improve integration between publicly funded research and development and development programmes.

113.   Eliminate gender disparity in primary and secondary education by 2005, as provided in the Dakar Framework for Action on Education for All, and at all levels of education no later than 2015, to meet the development goals contained in the Millennium Declaration, with action to ensure, inter alia, equal access to all levels and forms of education, training and capacity-building by gender mainstreaming, and by creating a gender-sensitive educational system.

114.   Integrate sustainable development into education systems at all levels of education in order to promote education as a key agent for change.

115.   Develop, implement, monitor and review education action plans and programmes at the national, subnational and local levels, as appropriate, that reflect the Dakar Framework for Action on Education for All and that are relevant to local conditions and needs leading to the achievement of community development, and make education for sustainable development a part of those plans.

116.   Provide all community members with a wide range of formal and non-formal continuing educational opportunities, including volunteer community service programmes, in order to end illiteracy and emphasize the importance of lifelong learning and promote sustainable development.

117.   Support the use of education to promote sustainable development, including through urgent actions at all levels to:

(a)   Integrate information and communications technology in school curriculum development to ensure its access by both rural and urban communities, and provide assistance particularly to developing countries, inter alia, for the establishment of an appropriate enabling environment required for such technology;

(b)   Promote, as appropriate, affordable and increased access to programmes for students, researchers and engineers from developing countries in the universities and research institutions of developed countries in order to promote the exchange of experience and capacity that will benefit all partners;

(c)   Continue to implement the work programme of the Commission on Sustainable Development on education for sustainable development;

(d)   Recommend to the United Nations General Assembly that it consider adopting a decade of education for sustainable development, starting in 2005.

*   *   *

118.   Enhance and accelerate human, institutional and infrastructure capacity-building initiatives, and promote partnerships in that regard that respond to the specific needs of developing countries in the context of sustainable development.

119.   Support local, national, subregional and regional initiatives, with action to develop, use and adapt knowledge and techniques and to enhance local, national, subregional and regional centres of excellence for education, research and training in order to strengthen the knowledge capacity of developing countries and countries with economies in transition through, inter alia, the mobilization from all sources of adequate financial and other resources, including new and additional resources.

119.bis   Provide technical and financial assistance to developing countries, including through the strengthening of capacity-building efforts, such as the United Nations Development Programme Capacity 21 programme, to:

(a) Assess their own capacity development needs and opportunities at the individual, institutional and societal levels;

(b) Design programmes for capacity-building and support for local, national and community-level programmes that focus on meeting the challenges of globalization more effectively and attaining the internationally agreed development goals, including those contained in the Millennium Declaration;

(c) Develop the capacity of civil society, including youth, to participate, as appropriate, in designing, implementing and reviewing sustainable development policies and strategies at all levels;

(d) Build and, where appropriate, strengthen national capacities for carrying out effective implementation of Agenda 21.

*   *   *

119.ter   Ensure access, at the national level, to environmental information and judicial and administrative proceedings in environmental matters, as well as public participation in decision-making, so as to further principle 10 of the Rio Declaration on Environment and Development, taking into full account principles 5, 7 and 11 of the Declaration.

119.quater   Strengthen national and regional information and statistical and analytical services relevant to sustainable development policies and programmes, including data disaggregated by sex, age and other factors, and encourage donors to provide financial and technical support to developing countries to enhance their capacity to formulate policies and implement programmes for sustainable development.

119.quinquies   Encourage further work on indicators for sustainable development by countries at the national level, including integration of gender aspects, on a voluntary basis, in line with national conditions and priorities.

119.sexties   Promote further work on indicators, in conformity with paragraph 3 of decision 9/4 of the Commission on Sustainable Development.

119.septies   Promote the development and wider use of earth observation technologies, including satellite remote sensing, global mapping and geographic information systems, to collect quality data on environmental impacts, land use and land-use changes, including through urgent actions at all levels to:

(a) Strengthen cooperation and coordination among global observing systems and research programmes for integrated global observations, taking into account the need for building capacity and sharing of data from ground-based observations, satellite remote sensing and other sources among all countries;

(b) Develop information systems that make the sharing of valuable data possible, including the active exchange of Earth observation data;

(c) Encourage initiatives and partnerships for global mapping.

119.octies   Support countries, particularly developing countries, in their national efforts to:

(a) Collect data that are accurate, long-term, consistent and reliable;

(b) Use satellite and remote-sensing technologies for data collection and further improvement of ground-based observations;

(c) Access, explore and use geographic information by utilizing the technologies of satellite remote sensing, satellite global positioning, mapping and geographic information systems.

119.noviens   Support efforts to prevent and mitigate the impacts of natural disasters, including through urgent actions at all levels to:

(a) Provide affordable access to disaster-related information for early warning purposes;

(b) Translate available data, particularly from global meteorological observation systems, into timely and useful products.

119.deciens   Develop and promote the wider application of environmental impact assessments, inter alia, as a national instrument, as appropriate, to provide essential decision-support information on projects that could cause significant adverse effects to the environment.

119.undeciens   Promote and further develop methodologies at policy, strategy and project levels for sustainable development decision-making at the local and national levels, and where relevant at the regional level. In this regard, emphasize that the choice of the appropriate methodology to be used in countries should be adequate to their country-specific conditions and circumstances, should be on a voluntary basis and should conform to their development priority needs.

X. INSTITUTIONAL FRAMEWORK FOR SUSTAINABLE DEVELOPMENT

120.   An effective institutional framework for sustainable development at all levels is key to the full implementation of Agenda 21, the follow-up to

the outcomes of the World Summit on Sustainable Development and meeting emerging sustainable development challenges. Measures aimed at strengthening such a framework should build on the provisions of Agenda 21 as well as the 1997 Programme for its further implementation and the principles of the Rio Declaration on Environment and Development and should promote the achievement of the internationally agreed development goals, including those contained in the Millennium Declaration, taking into account the Monterrey Consensus and relevant outcomes of other major United Nations conferences and international agreements since 1992. It should be responsive to the needs of all countries, taking into account the specific needs of developing countries including the means of implementation. It should lead to the strengthening of international bodies and organizations dealing with sustainable development, while respecting their existing mandates, as well as to the strengthening of relevant regional, national and local institutions.

120.bis   Good governance is essential for sustainable development. Sound economic policies, solid democratic institutions responsive to the needs of the people and improved infrastructure are the basis for sustained economic growth, poverty eradication, and employment creation. Freedom, peace and security, domestic stability, respect for human rights, including the right to development, and the rule of law, gender equality, market-oriented policies, and an overall commitment to just and democratic societies are also essential and mutually reinforcing.

Objectives

121.   Measures to strengthen sustainable development institutional arrangements at all levels should be taken within the framework of Agenda 21[1] and should build on developments since UNCED, and should lead to the achievement of, inter alia, the following objectives:

(a) Strengthening commitments to sustainable development;

(b) Integration of the economic, social and environmental dimensions of sustainable development in a balanced manner;

(c) Strengthening of the implementation of Agenda 21, including through the mobilization of financial and technological resources, as well as capacity-building programmes, particularly for developing countries;

(d) Strengthening coherence, coordination and monitoring;

(e) Promoting the rule of law and strengthening of governmental institutions;

(f) Increasing effectiveness and efficiency through limiting overlap and duplication of activities of international organizations, within and outside the United Nations system, based on their mandates and comparative advantages;

(g) Enhancing participation and effective involvement of civil society and other relevant stakeholders in the implementation of Agenda 21, as well as promoting transparency and broad public participation;

(h) Strengthening capacities for sustainable development at all levels, including the local level, in particular those of developing countries;

(i) Strengthening international cooperation aimed at reinforcing the implementation of Agenda 21 and the outcomes of the Summit.

Strengthening the Institutional Framework for Sustainable Development at the International Level

122.   The international community should:

(a) Enhance the integration of sustainable development goals as reflected in Agenda 21 and support for implementation of Agenda 21 and the outcomes of the Summit into the policies, work programmes and operational guidelines of relevant United Nations agencies, programmes and funds, GEF and international financial and trade institutions within their mandates, while stressing that their activities should take full account of national programmes and priorities, particularly those of developing countries, as well as, where appropriate, countries with economies in transition, to achieve sustainable development;

(b) Strengthen collaboration within and between the United Nations system, international financial institutions, the Global Environment Facility and WTO, utilizing the United Nations Chief Executives Board for Coordination (CEB), the United Nations Development Group, the Environment Management Group and other inter-agency coordinating bodies. Strengthened inter-agency collaboration should be pursued in all relevant contexts, with special emphasis on the operational level and involving partnership arrangements on specific issues to support, in particular, developing countries' efforts in implementing Agenda 21;

(c) Strengthen and better integrate the three dimensions of sustainable development policies and programmes, and promote the full integration of sustainable development objectives into programmes and policies of bodies that have a primary focus on social issues. In particular, the social dimension of sustainable development should be strengthened, inter alia, by emphasizing follow-up to the outcomes of the World Summit for Social Development and its five-year review, and taking into account their reports, and by support to social protection systems;

(d) Fully implement the outcomes of decision I on international environmental governance adopted by the UNEP Governing Council at its seventh special session, and invite the General Assembly at its fifty-seventh session to consider the important but complex issue of establishing universal membership for the Governing Council/Global Ministerial Environment Forum;

(e)   Engage actively and constructively in ensuring the timely completion of the negotiations on a comprehensive United Nations convention against corruption, including the question of repatriation of funds illicitly acquired to countries of origin;

(f)   Promote corporate responsibility and accountability and the exchange of best practices in the context of sustainable development, including, as appropriate, through multi-stakeholder dialogue, such as through the Commission on Sustainable Development, and other initiatives;

(g)   Take concrete action to implement the Monterrey Consensus at all levels.

123.   Good governance at the international level is fundamental for achieving sustainable development. In order to ensure a dynamic and enabling international economic environment, it is important to promote global economic governance through addressing the international finance, trade, technology and investment patterns that have an impact on the development prospects of developing countries. To this effect, the international community should take all necessary and appropriate measures, including ensuring support for structural and macroeconomic reform, a comprehensive solution to the external debt problem and increasing market access for developing countries. Efforts to reform the international financial architecture need to be sustained with greater transparency and the effective participation of developing countries in decision-making processes. A universal, rule-based, open, non-discriminatory and equitable multilateral trading system, as well as meaningful trade liberalization, can substantially stimulate development worldwide, benefiting countries at all stages of development.

124.   A vibrant and effective United Nations system is fundamental to the promotion of international cooperation for sustainable development and to a global economic system that works for all. To this effect, a firm commitment to the ideals of the United Nations and to the principles of international law and those enshrined in the Charter of the United Nations, and to strengthening the United Nations system and other multilateral institutions and promoting the improvement of their operations, is essential. States should also fulfil their commitment to negotiate and finalize as soon as possible a United Nations convention against corruption in all its aspects, including the question of repatriation of funds illicitly acquired to countries of origin and also to promoting stronger cooperation to eliminate money-laundering.

Role of the General Assembly
125.   The General Assembly of the United Nations should adopt sustainable development as a key element of the overarching framework for United Nations activities, particularly for achieving the internationally agreed devel-

opment goals, including those contained in the Millennium Declaration, and should give overall political direction to the implementation of Agenda 21 and its review.

Role of the Economic and Social Council

126.   Pursuant to the relevant provisions of the Charter of the United Nations and Agenda 21 provisions regarding the Economic and Social Council and General Assembly resolutions 48/162 and 50/227, which reaffirmed the Council as the central mechanism for the coordination of the United Nations system and its specialized agencies and supervision of subsidiary bodies, in particular its functional commissions, and to promote the implementation of Agenda 21 by strengthening system-wide coordination, the Council should:

(a)   Increase its role in overseeing system-wide coordination and the balanced integration of economic, social and environmental aspects of United Nations policies and programmes aimed at promoting sustainable development;

(b)   Organize periodic consideration of sustainable development themes in regard to the implementation of Agenda 21, including the means of implementation. Recommendations in regard to such themes could be made by the Commission on Sustainable Development;

(c)   Make full use of its high-level, coordination, operational activities and the general segments to effectively take into account all relevant aspects of the work of the United Nations on sustainable development. In this context, the Council should encourage the active participation of major groups in its high-level segment and the work of its relevant functional commissions, in accordance with the respective rules of procedure;

(d)   Promote greater coordination, complementarity, effectiveness and efficiency of activities of its functional commissions and other subsidiary bodies that are relevant to the implementation of Agenda 21;

(e)   Terminate the work of the Committee on Energy and Natural Resources for Development and transfer its work to the Commission on Sustainable Development;

(f)   Ensure that there is a close link between the role of the Council in the follow-up to the Summit and its role in the follow-up to the Monterrey Consensus, in a sustained and coordinated manner. To that end, the Council should explore ways to develop arrangements relating to its meetings with the Bretton Woods institutions and WTO, as set out in the Monterrey Consensus;

(g)   Intensify its efforts to ensure that gender mainstreaming is an integral part of its activities concerning the coordinated implementation of Agenda 21.

Role and Function of the Commission on Sustainable Development

127.   The Commission on Sustainable Development should continue to be the high-level commission on sustainable development within the United Nations system and serve as a forum for consideration of issues related to integration of the three dimensions of sustainable development. Although the role, functions and mandate of the Commission as set out in relevant parts of Agenda 21 and adopted in General Assembly resolution 47/191 continue to be relevant, the Commission needs to be strengthened, taking into account the role of relevant institutions and organizations. An enhanced role of the Commission should include reviewing and monitoring progress in the implementation of Agenda 21 and fostering coherence of implementation, initiatives and partnerships.

128.   Within that context, the Commission should give more emphasis on actions that enable implementation at all levels, including promoting and facilitating partnerships involving Governments, international organizations and relevant stakeholders for the implementation of Agenda 21.

129.   The Commission should:

(a) Review and evaluate progress and promote further implementation of Agenda 21;

(b) Focus on the cross-sectoral aspects of specific sectoral issues and provide a forum for better integration of policies, including through interaction among Ministers dealing with the various dimensions and sectors of sustainable development through the high-level segments;

(c) Address new challenges and opportunities related to the implementation of Agenda 21;

(d) Focus on actions related to implementation of Agenda 21, limiting negotiations in the sessions of the Commission to every two years;

(e) Limit the number of themes addressed in each session.

130.   In relation to its role in facilitating implementation, the Commission should emphasize the following:

(a) Review progress and promote the further implementation of Agenda 21. In this context, the Commission should identify constraints on implementation and make recommendations to overcome those constraints;

(b) Serve as a focal point for the discussion of partnerships that promote sustainable development, including sharing lessons learned, progress made and best practices;

(c) Review issues related to financial assistance and transfer of technology for sustainable development, as well as capacity-building, while making full use of existing information. In this regard, the Commission on Sustainable Development could give consideration to more effective use of national reports and regional experience and to this end make appropriate recommendations;

(d) Provide a forum for analysis and exchange of experience on measures that assist sustainable development planning, decision-making and the implementation of sustainable development strategies. In this regard, the Commission could give consideration to more effective use of national and regional reports;

(e) Take into account significant legal developments in the field of sustainable development, with due regard to the role of relevant intergovernmental bodies in promoting the implementation of Agenda 21 relating to international legal instruments and mechanisms.

131.   With regard to the practical modalities and programme of work of the Commission, specific decisions on those issues should be taken by the Commission at its next session, when the Commission's thematic work programme will be elaborated. In particular, the following issues should be considered:

(a) Giving a balanced consideration to implementation of all of the mandates of the Commission contained in General Assembly resolution 47/191;

(b) Continuing to provide for more direct and substantive involvement of international organizations and major groups in the work of the Commission;

(c) Give greater consideration to the scientific contributions to sustainable development through, for example, drawing on the scientific community and encouraging national, regional and international scientific networks to be involved in the Commission;

(d) Furthering the contribution of educators to sustainable development, including, where appropriate, in the activities of the Commission;

(e) The scheduling and duration of intersessional meetings.

132.   Undertake further measures to promote best practices and lessons learned in sustainable development, and in addition promote the use of contemporary methods of data collection and dissemination, including broader use of information technologies.

Role of International Institutions

133.   Stress the need for international institutions both within and outside the United Nations system, including international financial institutions, WTO and GEF, to enhance, within their mandates, their cooperative efforts to:

   (a) Promote effective and collective support to the implementation of Agenda 21 at all levels;

   (b) Enhance the effectiveness and coordination of international institutions to implement Agenda 21, the outcomes of the World Summit on Sustainable Development, relevant sustainable development aspects of the Millennium Declaration, the Monterrey Consensus and the outcomes of the fourth WTO ministerial meeting, held in Doha in November 2001.

134.   Request the Secretary-General of the United Nations, utilizing the United Nations System Chief Executives Board for Coordination, including through informal collaborative efforts, to further promote system-wide inter-agency cooperation and coordination on sustainable development, to take appropriate measures to facilitate exchange of information, and to continue to keep the Economic and Social Council and the Commission informed of actions being taken to implement Agenda 21.

135.   Significantly strengthen support for UNDP capacity-building programmes for sustainable development, building on the experience gained from Capacity 21, as important mechanisms for supporting local and national development capacity-building efforts, in particular in developing countries.

136.   Strengthen cooperation among UNEP and other United Nations bodies and specialized agencies, the Bretton Woods institutions and WTO, within their mandates.

137.   UNEP, UN-Habitat, UNDP and UNCTAD, within their mandates, should strengthen their contribution to sustainable development programmes and the implementation of Agenda 21 at all levels, particularly in the area of promoting capacity-building.

138.   To promote effective implementation of Agenda 21 at the international level, the following should also be undertaken:

   (a) Streamline the international sustainable development meeting calendar and, as appropriate, reduce the number of meetings, the length of meetings and the amount of time spent on negotiated outcomes in favour of more time spent on practical matters related to implementation;

   (b) Encourage partnership initiatives for implementation by all relevant actors to support the outcome of the World Summit on Sustainable

Development. In this context, further development of partnerships and partnership follow-up should take note of the preparatory work for the Summit;

(c) Make full use of developments in the field of information and communication technologies.

[Paragraph 139 is deleted]

140.   Strengthening of the international institutional framework for sustainable development is an evolutionary process. It is necessary to keep under review relevant arrangements; identify gaps; eliminate duplication of functions; and continue to strive for greater integration, efficiency and coordination of the economic, social and environmental dimensions of sustainable development aiming at the implementation of Agenda 21.

Strengthening Institutional Arrangements for Sustainable Development at the Regional Level

141.   Implementation of Agenda 21 and the outcomes of the Summit should be effectively pursued at the regional and subregional levels, through the regional commissions and other regional and subregional institutions and bodies.

142.   Intraregional coordination and cooperation on sustainable development should be improved among the regional commissions, United Nations Funds, programmes and agencies, regional development banks, and other regional and subregional institutions and bodies. This should include, as appropriate, support for development, enhancement and implementation of agreed regional sustainable development strategies and action plans, reflecting national and regional priorities.

143.   In particular and taking into account relevant provisions of Agenda 21, the regional commissions, in collaboration with other regional and subregional bodies, should:

(a) Promote the integration of the three dimensions of sustainable development into their work in a balanced way, including through implementation of Agenda 21. To this end, the regional commissions should enhance their capacity through internal action and be provided, as appropriate, with external support;

(b) Facilitate and promote a balanced integration of the economic, social and environmental dimensions of sustainable development into the work of regional, subregional and other bodies, for example by facilitating and strengthening the exchange of experiences, including national experience, best practices, case studies and partnership experience related to the implementation of Agenda 21;

(c) Assist in the mobilization of technical and financial assistance, and facilitate the provision of adequate financing for the implementation of regionally and subregionally agreed sustainable development programmes and projects, including addressing the objective of poverty eradication;

(d) Continue to promote multi-stakeholder participation and encourage partnerships to support the implementation of Agenda 21 at the regional and subregional levels.

144.   Regionally and subregionally agreed sustainable development initiatives and programmes, such as the New Partnership for Africa's Development (NEPAD) and the interregional aspects of the globally agreed Programme of Action for the Sustainable Development of Small Island Developing States, should be supported.

Strengthening Institutional Frameworks for Sustainable Development at the National Level

145.   States should:

(a) Continue to promote coherent and coordinated approaches to institutional frameworks for sustainable development at all national levels, including through, as appropriate, the establishment or strengthening of existing authorities and mechanisms necessary for policy-making, coordination and implementation and enforcement of laws;

(b) Take immediate steps to make progress in the formulation and elaboration of national strategies for sustainable development and begin their implementation by 2005. To this end, as appropriate, strategies should be supported through international cooperation, taking into account the special needs of developing countries, in particular the least developed countries. Such strategies, which, where applicable, could be formulated as poverty reduction strategies that integrate economic, social and environmental aspects of sustainable development, should be pursued in accordance with each country's national priorities.

146.   Each country has the primary responsibility for its own sustainable development, and the role of national policies and development strategies cannot be overemphasized. All countries should promote sustainable development at the national level by, inter alia, enacting and enforcing clear and effective laws that support sustainable development. All countries should strengthen governmental institutions, including by providing necessary infrastructure and by promoting transparency, accountability and fair administrative and judicial institutions.

146.bis   All countries should also promote public participation, including through measures that provide access to information regarding legislation, regulations, activities, policies and programmes. They should also foster full public participation in sustainable development policy formulation and implementation. Women should be able to participate fully and equally in policy formulation and decision-making.

147.   Further promote the establishment or enhancement of sustainable development councils and/or coordination structures at the national level, including at the local level, in order to provide a high-level focus on sustainable development policies. In that context, multi-stakeholder participation should be promoted.

148.   Support efforts by all countries, particularly developing countries, as well as countries with economies in transition, to enhance national institutional arrangements for sustainable development, including at the local level. That could include promoting cross-sectoral approaches in the formulation of strategies and plans for sustainable development, such as, where applicable, poverty reduction strategies, aid coordination, encouraging participatory approaches and enhancing policy analysis, management capacity and implementation capacity, including mainstreaming a gender perspective in all those activities.

149.   Enhance the role and capacity of local authorities as well as stakeholders in implementing Agenda 21 and the outcomes of the Summit and in strengthening the continuing support for local Agenda 21 programmes and associated initiatives and partnerships, and encourage, in particular, partnerships among and between local authorities and other levels of government and stakeholders to advance sustainable development as called for in, inter alia, the Habitat Agenda.

Participation of Major Groups

150.   Enhance partnerships between governmental and non-governmental actors, including all major groups, as well as volunteer groups, on programmes and activities for the achievement of sustainable development at all levels.

[Paragraph 151 is deleted]

152.   Acknowledge the consideration being given to the possible relationship between environment and human rights, including the right to development, with full and transparent participation of Member States of the United Nations and observer States.

153.   Promote and support youth participation in programmes and activities relating to sustainable development through, for example, supporting local youth councils or their equivalent, and by encouraging their establishment where they do not exist.

Notes

INTRODUCTION

1. Achcar, 2002.
2. Middleton and O'Keefe, 1998, 2001.
3. Achcar, 2002, 64.

CHAPTER 1

1. The Permanent Conference was succeeded by the Organisation for Security and Cooperation in Europe (OSCE) which now has fifty-five member states. CSCE now stands for Commission on Security and Cooperation in Europe and is a department of the US Government; its purpose is to 'encourage' pursuit of the Helsinki Declaration.
2. WCED, 1987, ix–xv.
3. WCED, 1987, x.
4. Middleton, O'Keefe and Moyo, 1993.
5. See Middleton, O'Keefe and Moyo, 1993 and Middleton and O'Keefe, 2001. Perhaps J.K. Galbraith's gloss on Bismarck should be borne in mind: 'Politics is not the art of the possible. It consists in choosing between the disastrous and the unpalatable (letter to J.F. Kennedy).'
6. See Sitarz, 1994 for a useful abridged version of Agenda 21.
7. See Klaus Töpfer and Jeb Brugman in Dodds and Middleton, 2001.
8. Sitarz, 1994, 308.
9. See, Naomi Klein in Panitch and Leys, 2001.
10. For a much fuller account of the outcome, and of its failures, see Dodds and Middleton, 2001.
11. Worldwatch Institute, 2002, 42.
12. WWF was formerly the abbreviation for Worldwide Fund for Nature, but it has recently changed its name to World Wildlife Fund.
13. WWF web site www.panda.org.
14. Worldwatch Institute, 2002, 127–32.
15. Malthus, 1798/1970, 71.
16. Malthus, 1830/1970, 227.
17. Malthus, 1798/1970, 98–100.
18. UNEP, 2002.
19. Global Scenario Group, 1997 and 1998.
20. UNEP, 2002, 329, 334, 339, 344.
21. Global Scenario Group, 1997, 2.
22. Global Scenario Group, 1997, 11.
23. Global Scenario Group, 1997, 12.
24. Global Scenario Group, 1997, 38.
25. Global Scenario Group, 1998, 6.
26. See www.undp.org.
27. FAO, 1996.

28. OECD, 2001.
29. Global Scenario Group, 1998, 12.
30. Global Scenario Group, 1998, 14.
31. Global Scenario Group, 1998, 29.
32. Global Scenario Group, 2002.
33. Chevron, one of the largest oil corporations, has named one of its super-tankers Condoleezza; it is not without significance that Ms Condoleezza Rice, prior to her appointment to the US administration, was a senior executive in that corporation.
34. Michael Byers, 'The World According to Cheney, Rice and Rumsfeld' in *London Review of Books*, 21 February, 2002.
35. www.opcw.org.
36. A letter from Brian Eno, Robbie Williams *et al.*, the *Guardian*, 20 April 2002.
37. Julian Borger, the *Guardian*, 20 April 2002.
38. Oliver Burkeman, the *Guardian*, 31 July 2002.
39. It is pointless to list, yet again, the violent interventions by the US in other countries, ranging from minor terrorist attacks to full-scale wars. Of particular interest in this connection is the innovative work by Lindqvist, 2001. The reader is also referred to, *inter alia*, Blum, 2002.
40. 'Fatal Attraction', *Guardian On Line*, 4 July 2002

CHAPTER 2

1. See appendices A and B.
2. The regions were Africa, Asia and the Pacific, Europe and North America, Latin America and the Caribbean and West Africa.
3. Ed Vulliamy, Paul Webster and Nick Paton-Walsh in the *Observer*, 6 October 2002.
4. *Declaration on Sustainable Development*, paragraphs 11, 12, 14 and 15, www.johannesburgsummit.org.
5. Sen, 1981.
6. *Declaration*, paragraph 17.
7. *Declaration*, paragraphs 18–20.
8. Middleton, O'Keefe and Visser, 2001.
9. www.johannesburgsummit.org.
10. One of the best accounts of contract farming is to be found in Bernstein, Crow, Mackintosh and Martin, 1990.
11. 'Rio Declaration on Environment and Development: Application and Implementation, Report of the Secretary General.' Posted by the United Nations Department of Economic and Social Affairs (DESA), www.un.org.
12. For a succinct account of those events go to the website of the American University's Mandala Projects, www.american.edu/TED/. The present authors also told the story in Middleton, O'Keefe and Moyo, 1993.
13. All the cases American University cited here may be found on the American University's website.
14. www.aei.org. Lomborg, a statistician by trade, briefly became famous for his Pollyanna version of the world's environmental predicament (Lomborg, 2001).

15. The other seven states are: Cambodia, Eritrea, Guinea, India, Jordan, Malawi and Sudan.
16. www.un.org/esa/sustdev/uncpf.htm and un.org/esa/sustdev/forests respectively.
17. UNEP 2002, 92.
18. Worldwatch Institute 2002, 166.
19. Worldwatch Institute 2002, 164–6.
20. Simon, 1997.
21. For a fuller account of these instruments go to Friends of the Earth International website: www.foei.org.
22. Infant mortality per 1,000 live births: 1970 – 148, 2000 – 98. Under-five mortality per 1,000 live births: 1970 – 240, 2000 – 155. UNDP, 2002, Human Development Indicators, table 8.
23. Small Island Developing States Network, www.sidsnet.org.
24. 'What Is Nepad?' The 37th Summit of the OAU in July 2001, is the Summit to which this passage refers, www.nepad.org.

CHAPTER 3

1. UNEP, 2002, 150.
2. UNEP, 2002, 151.
3. Regional and national food security reports, www.fao.org.
4. 'West Asia' is the term, increasingly used by the UN, to cover Bahrain, Jordan, Kuwait, Lebanon, the Occupied Palestinian Territories, Oman, Qatar, Saudi Arabia, Syria, the United Arab Emirates and Yemen.
5. UNEP, 2002, 173–5.
6. Figure compiled from UNDP, 2000 and UNDP, 2001.
7. Mercedes González de la Rocha, and Alejandro Grinspun, 'Private Adjustments: Household Responses to the Erosion of Work' in Middleton, O'Keefe and Visser, 2001.
8. Figure compiled from UNDP, 2000 and UNDP, 2001. Note that, in 1999, the total population of developing countries was just over 4.6 billion, the total population in countries for which these statistics are not available is 0.7 billion.
9. Global Scenario Group, 1998, 61.
10. Global Scenario Group, 1998, 63.
11. *Jordan Times*, 9 August 2000.
12. Sacco, 2003, 171.
13. Chairperson's summary of the partnership plenary discussion on water and sanitation, energy, health, agriculture and biodiversity, 31 August 2002. www.johannesburgsummit.org.
14. www.johannesburgsummit.org.
15. www.johannesburgsummit.org.
16. www.johannesburgsummit.org.
17. Bond, 2002, 36.
18. Bond, 2002, 212–13.
19. www.dfid.gov.uk.

20. Sources for this paragraph: Andrew Clark, the *Guardian*, 25 August 2000; David Gow, the *Guardian*, 5 November 2001; Geoff Gibbs, the *Guardian*, 29 November 2001; Rob Evans and Jeevan Vasagar, the *Guardian*, 5 October 2001; Damien Crystal, the *Observer*, 28 July 2002 and 15 September 2002; www.awg.org.
21. Hobsbawm, 1962, 110.
22. Hobsbawm, 1962, 110.
23. Hobsbawm, 1995.
24. Perry Anderson, 'Confronting Defeat' in *London Review of Books*, 24/20, 17 October 2002.
25. Foster, 2002.

CHAPTER 4

1. Foster, 2002.
2. World Bank, 2000/2001. UNDP, 2002.
3. Foster, 2002, 20–1.
4. www.uscib.org.
5. Others included the Clean Air Act of 1970, the Endangered Species Act of 1973 and the Clean Water Act of 1977, www.epa.gov.
6. Ed Vulliamy, the *Observer*, 8 December 2002.
7. Suzanne Goldenberg, the *Guardian*, 29 November 2002, Christopher Doering, Reuters News Service, 29 November 2002.
8. www.valdezscience.com.
9. *Plan of Implementation*, paragraph 19.t.
10. Roy, 1999.
11. The survey is derived from the World Energy Council's *Survey of Energy Resources* which is available on their web site. www.worldenergy.org.
12. The Ixtoc 1 explosion was also the second largest oil spill ever recorded; the largest was the deliberate leaking of oil during the Gulf War.
13. Global Scenario Group, 1998, 52–6.
14. A joule is an SI (*Système International d'Unités*) measurement of a unit of work or energy; exa (its symbol is E) is the expression of a factor of 10 to the power of 18.
15. www.globalclimate.org.
16. Middleton and O'Keefe, 2001.
17. Global Scenario Group, 1998, A-9.
18. www.worldenergy.org.
19. *Survey of Energy Resources*.
20. Global Scenario Group, 1998, A-14.
21. Press release from the United Nations Department of Economic and Social Affairs, Division for Sustainable Development, 24 September 2002.

CHAPTER 5

1. *The Penguin Dictionary of Economics* gives a useful and simple definition of externalities: 'Consequences for welfare or opportunity costs not fully

accounted for in the price and market system.' It goes on to describe them as 'external diseconomies'.

2. UNEP, 2002, 241.
3. GATT Secretariat, 1994, 365–403.
4. Larry Elliot and Charlotte Denny, the *Guardian*, 21 December 2002.
5. www.fao.org.
6. Burma (Myanmar), Cambodia, Canada, Eritrea, Ghana, Guinea, India, Jordan, Malawi, Nicaragua, Sierra Leone and Sudan.
7. Middleton, O'Keefe and Moyo, 1993.
8. In Africa the ratifying states are: Botswana, Djibouti, Kenya, Lesotho, Liberia, Mali, Mauritius, Uganda; in Asia/Pacific: Bhutan, Fiji, Maldives, Nauru, Niue, Samoa; in Central and Eastern Europe: Belarus, Bulgaria, Croatia, the Czech Republic; in Latin America/Caribbean: Barbados, Bolivia, Cuba, Mexico, Nicaragua, Panama, Saint Kitts and Nevis, Trinidad and Tobago, Venezuela; in the Western Europe and others group: Austria, Denmark, the European Community, Luxembourg, The Netherlands, Norway, Spain, Sweden, Switzerland. States about to confirm their ratification are Cameroon, Colombia, India and Slovenia.

CHAPTER 6

1. An example of the genre may be seen in Middleton, O'Keefe and Visser, 2001.
2. The Marshall plan was the popular name for the European Recovery Programme which ran from 1948–51. It had been so named after its originator, the US General George Marshall. US$12 billion was provided for the economic recovery of Europe following the Second World War. It, too, consisted of a mix of loans and grants and, like so many later agreements, this generosity carried a price tag: all US subsidiaries of European businesses were sequestered and turned over to US control. The present authors do not know if the rate of profit to the US from the Marshall plan has actually been calculated.
3. Hayter, 1971.
4. One example of a humanly induced 'natural' disaster may be seen in the landslide which, in October 1966, smothered a school in Aberfan, South Wales, and killed so many children; the land that slid was a gigantic spoil heap created by generations of coalmining. It is probable that the devastating droughts of the late twentieth and early twenty-first centuries are, at least, exacerbated by climate change consequent on global warming – a phenomenon to which the industrialised world has resolutely contributed.
5. Middleton and O'Keefe, 1998, 67.
6. Stephen Sedley, 'No More Victor's Justice?' in *London Review of Books*, 2 January 2003.
7. Global Scenario Group, 1998, xi.
8. Global Scenario Group, 2002, 7.
9. Global Scenario Group, 2002, 8.
10. Middleton and O'Keefe, 2001, 101–3.

11. Global Scenario Group, 2002, 24.
12. *CNS (Capitalism Nature Socialism)*, Vol. 13 (4), Issue 52, December, 2002.
13. Global Scenario Group, 2002, 25–7.
14. Global Scenario Group, 2002, 26.
15. Global Scenario Group, 2002, 27.
16. Agamben, 1998, 1.
17. Agamben, 1998, 8.
18. Agamben, 1998, 9–10.
19. Agamben, 1998, 8.
20. Agamben, 1998, 26.
21. 'Travellers' is the name given, particularly in Ireland, to people who are culturally nomadic, but are neither Roma nor pastoralists. Irish constitutional law has recognised them as a distinct ethnic group.
22. Achcar, 2002, 13–26. Blum, 2002, 125–66.
23. Agamben, 1998, 179.
24. Middleton and O'Keefe, 1998.
25. Agamben, 1998, 133.
26. Agamben, 1998, 180.

References

Achcar, Gilbert, 2002, *The Clash of Barbarisms: September 11 and the Making of the New World Disorder*, New York: Monthly Review Press.

Agamben, Giorgio, 1998, *Homo Sacer: Sovereign Power and Bare Life*, Stanford: Stanford University Press.

Bernstein, Henry, Crow, Ben, Mackintosh, Maureen and Martin, Charlotte, 1990, *The Food Question: Profits Versus People?*, London: Earthscan Publications.

Blum, William, 2002 (2nd edition), *Rogue State: a Guide to the World's Only Superpower*, London: Zed Books.

Bond, Patrick, 2002, *Unsustainable South Africa: Environment, Development and Social Protest*, London: Merlin Press, Scottsville: University of Natal Press.

Capitalism, Nature Socialism: a Journal of Socialist Ecology (CNS), tri-monthly.

Carson, Rachel, 1992, *The Silent Spring*, Harmondsworth: Penguin Books.

Dodds, Felix and Middleton, Toby, 2001, *Earth Summit 2002: a New Deal*, London: Earthscan Publications.

FAO, 1996, *Sixth World Food Survey*, Rome: Food and Agricultural Organisation.

Foster, John Bellamy, 2002, *Ecology Against Capitalism*, New York: Monthly Review Press.

GATT Secretariat, 1994, *The Results of the Uruguay Round of Multilateral Trade Negotiations: the Legal Texts*, Geneva: GATT Secretariat.

Global Scenario Group (Gilberto Gallopin, Al Hammond, Paul Raskin and Bob Swart), 1997, *Branch Points: Global Scenarios and Human Choice*, Stockholm: Stockholm Environment Institute, www.sei.se.

— (Paul Raskin, Gilberto Gallopin, Pablo Gutman, Al Hammond and Bob Swart), 1998, *Bending the Curve: Toward Global Sustainability*, Stockholm: Stockholm Environment Institute, www.sei.se.

— Paul Raskin, Tariq Banuri, Gilberto Gallopin, Pablo Gutman, Al Hammond, Robert Kates and Bob Swart), 2002, *Great Transition: the Promise and Allure of the Times Ahead*, Stockholm: Stockholm Environment Institute, www.sei.se.

Hayter, Teresa, 1971, *Aid as Imperialism*, Harmondsworth: Penguin Books.

Hobsbawm, Eric, 1962, *The Age of Revolution: Europe 1789–1848*, London: Weidenfeld and Nicolson.

— 1995, *Age of Extremes: the Short Twentieth Century 1914–1991*, London: Abacus.

Lindqvist, Sven, 2001, *A History of Bombing*, London: Granta Books.

Lomborg, Bjørn, 2001, *The Skeptical Environmentalist: Measuring the Real State of the World*, Cambridge: Cambridge University Press.

Malthus, Thomas, 1798/1830 (edition consulted, 1970), *An Essay on the Principle of Population* and *A Summary View of the Principle of Population*, London: Penguin Books.

Middleton, Neil and O'Keefe, Phil, 1998, *Disaster and Development*, London: Pluto Press.

— 2001, *Redefining Sustainable Development*, London: Pluto Press.

— with Moyo, Sam, 1993, *Tears of the Crocodile: from Rio to Reality in the Developing World*, London: Pluto Press.

— with Visser, Rob (eds), 2001, *Negotiating Poverty: New Directions, Renewed Debate*, London: Pluto Press.

OECD, 2001, *The DAC Guidelines: Poverty Reduction*, Paris: OECD.

Panitch, Leo and Leys, Colin (eds), 2001, *A World Of Contradictions: Socialist Register 2002*, London: Merlin Press.

Roy, Arundhati, 1999, *The Cost of Living*, London: Flamingo.

Sacco, Joe, 2003, *Palestine*, London: Jonathan Cape.

Sen, Amartya, 1981, *Poverty and Famines: an Essay on Entitlement and Deprivation*, Oxford: Oxford University Press.

Simon, Joel, 1997, *Endangered Mexico, an Environment on the Edge*, London: Latin America Bureau.

Sitarz, Daniel (ed.), 1994, *Agenda 21: the Earth Summit Strategy to Save Our Planet*, Boulder, Co.: Earthpress.

UNDP, annual, *Human Development Report*, Oxford: Oxford University Press.

UNEP, 2002, *Global Environment Outlook 3*, London: Earthscan Publications.

WCED, 1987, *Our Common Future*, Oxford: Oxford University Press.

World Bank, annual, *World Development Report*, Oxford: Oxford University Press.

Worldwatch Institute, annual, *State of the World*, New York: W.W. Norton and Co.

WWF, 2002, *The Living Planet Report, 2002*, Gland: WWF International, www.panda.org.

Index

Except for the WSSD, all UN summits, organisations and conferences are given under the entry for United Nations. Because the entries are so extensive, the WSSD is given separately.